ANDREW STEVENSON was born in Canada and brought up in Hong Kong, India, Kenya, Scotland, Singapore and Malaysia before attending university in Canada and France. He has worked in Canada, Tanzania and Norway as an investment banker, United Nations economist, safari operator and adventure company owner and manager. When he isn't travelling, he can be found in Bermuda. He is the author of several books, including *Annapurna Circuit* and *Nepalese Journey*, a pictorial work. (Andrew's photography can be seen at www.awstevenson.com, his website.) His *Kiwi Tracks: A New Zealand Journey* is published by Lonely Planet.

SUMMER LIGHT
A Walk across Norway

Andrew Stevenson

LONELY PLANET PUBLICATIONS
Melbourne • Oakland • London • Paris

Summer Light: A Walk across Norway

Published by Lonely Planet Publications
Head Office: 90 Maribyrnong Street, Footscray, Vic 3011, Australia
Locked Bag 1, Footscray, Vic 3011, Australia
Branches: 150 Linden Street, Oakland CA 94607, USA
10a Spring Place, London NW5 3BH,UK
1 rue Dahomey, 75011, Paris, France

Published 2002
Printed by The Bookmaker International Ltd
Printed in China

Edited by Meaghan Amor
Maps by Natasha Velleley
Designed by Simon Bracken

National Library of Australia Cataloguing-in-Publication entry

Stevenson, Andrew.
Summer Light: a walk across Norway.

ISBN 1 86450 347 5.

1. Stevenson, Andrew – Journeys – Norway. 2. Norway –
Description and travel. I. Title. (Series: Lonely Planet
journeys).

914.81049

Text © Andrew Stevenson 2002
Maps © Lonely Planet 2002

Contents

For Bonso

Acknowledgements

Many thanks are due to Kirsten for her enduring friendship, generosity, thoughtfulness and meticulous reading of my manuscript, and to my friends Lars and Martha Louise Ness, Stephan and Miann Rowe, and Jostein and Marian Hatteborg for their hospitality. Thanks to Meaghan Amor for her detailed editing, and to Belinda Carter, Elisabeth Heyerdahl-Jensen, Mona Kjos, Ingrid Nernas, Siri Giil, Lars Åge Hilde, Sue Mills, Carina Palomba, Rosemary Rayfuse, Ine Skørten, Caroline Stockdale, Hege Stroemme and Nina Sønsteng for their editorial suggestions to the original draft. A very special note of thanks to Ulf Prytz who facilitated the last-minute decision to visit Spitsbergen, and to Carl-Erik Anfindsen and Vidar Fosslien for storing my belongings for so many years in office attics and chicken barns. Thanks to my godchildren Endre and Tuva, and to all the Norwegians who welcomed me into their magnificent country and became my friends.

Thanks most of all to Annabel, for her affection, patience, humour and moral support, and for being my best buddy. Just wish my knees were in as good shape . . .

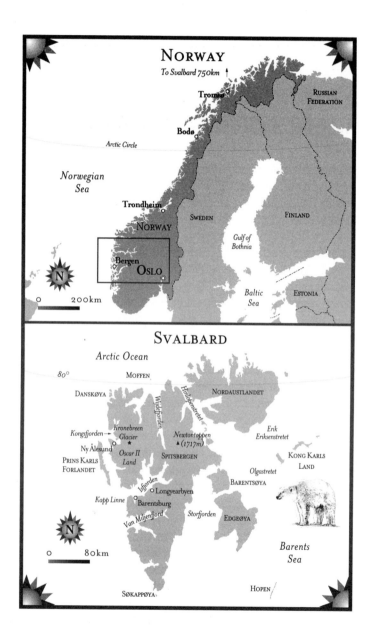

NORWAY

To Svalbard 750km

Tromsø

RUSSIAN FEDERATION

Bodø

Arctic Circle

Norwegian
Sea

Trondheim

NORWAY

SWEDEN

FINLAND

Gulf of
Bothnia

Bergen

OSLO

Baltic
Sea

ESTONIA

N

200km

SVALBARD

Arctic Ocean

80°

MOFFEN

DANSKØYA

Wijdefjorden

Hinlopenstretet

NORDAUSTLANDET

Kongsfjorden

Kronebreen
Glacier

Newtontoppen
▲ (1717m)

Erik
Eriksenstretet

Ny Ålesund

Oscar II
Land

SPITSBERGEN

KONG KARLS
LAND

PRINS KARLS
FORLANDET

Olgastretet

BARENTSØYA

Isfjorden

Kapp Linne

Longyearbyen

Barentsburg

Storfjorden

EDGEØYA

Van Miljenfjord

N

80km

SØKAPPØYA

HOPEN

Barents
Sea

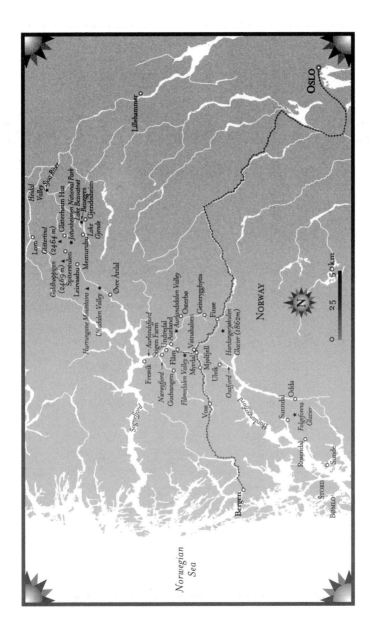

Norwegian Sea

Bergen

OSLO

Lillehammer

Heidal Valley
Lom
Glittertind
Sjoa River
Guldhøppigen (2469 m)
Glitterheim Hut (2464 m)
Spiterstulen
Johunheimen National Park
Leirvassbu
Lake Bessvatnet
Memurubu
Besseggen
Lake Gjendesheim
Gjende
Øvre Årdal

Hurrungane Mountains
Utladalen Valley

Fresvik
Aurlandsfjord
Stigen Farm
Nærøyfjord
Gudvangen
Undredal
Flåm
Aurland
Aurlandsdalen Valley
Østerbo
Flåmsdalen Valley
Myrdal
Vatnahalsen
Geiterygghytta
Finse
Sognefjord
Mjølfjell
Hardangerjøkulen Glacier (1862m)
Voss
Uvik
Ødfjord

NORWAY

Hardangerfjord
Sunndal
Odda
Folgefonna Glacier
Rosendal
Sunde
STORD
BØMLO

N

25   50 km

xi

Prologue

A midsummer night and the sunset is a fiery ball ricocheting off the North Sea. Annabel goes down to our cabin. Alone on deck, I lean against the rail, watching gannets glide silently over the burnished sea; there is no swell, not even a ripple, as the ship slices into the water towards an incandescent horizon. Spectacular beneath dark clouds, the shimmering sunset draws us northwards as a bruised sky swallows our silvery wake; the surge of the bow waves is as soothing as surf rolling on a beach. The ship vibrates with the thrust of the engines ferrying us towards that bright sweep of northern light. It feels good to be coming back.

Harildstad Farm, Heidal Valley

'Did you sleep well?' I ask Annabel in the morning, while staring at the smouldering embers in the open soapstone fireplace in the corner of our log-walled bedroom. Except for the white sound of the Sjoa River rushing through the bottom of the valley, it is so quiet.

'Mmmm,' she murmurs, head buried in a soft pillow. 'Did you sleep well?' She reaches out a hand.

'Like a log.' I feel so much at peace. It must be the fresh air, the stillness of the mountains, the cosiness of this sixteenth-century log farmhouse.

'Despite the bruises from rafting yesterday?'

'Despite the bruises.' I turn to look at her. 'How's your neck?'

She rotates her head from side to side. 'Still stiff.'

We dress quickly in the cold air and I open the heavy wrought-iron lock in the carved door leading outside to the grass courtyard. Enclosed by three log farmhouses typical of Norwegian farms, normally with one farmhouse for each of three generations of the family, the fourth side of the yard is framed by a log granary mounted on carved wooden legs and topped with a wooden belfry. The farmyard scene could be from a mid-nineteenth century painting, or just as easily out of an illustrated Norwegian fairy tale.

Puffy clouds cast benign dancing shadows down the lower stretches of the Heidal Valley, while boiling black storm clouds congeal over the Jotunheimen Mountains at the upper end. Although it is the end of June, it looks as if it is snowing heavily up there. I lean against the corner of the main farmhouse where the windblown branches of a birch tree have scraped a wide swathe against the sun-darkened logs; a graphic reminder of how harsh the winters can be.

This summer has lasted only two weeks – the first fortnight in May. The fact that it has rained every day since, and we are now in the last week of June, accounts for the lushness of the fields and the iridescent green leaves of the birch trees. Swifts feed their fledglings in holes they have made in the overhanging edges of the turf roofs. On clear nights here in past summers, I'd sleep outside rather than indoors and watch the adult birds train their young for their long flight south, circling endlessly above the turf roofs as if racing on an invisible track. It's a lasting and enchanting image.

Each of the five summers I spent here is indelibly etched in my mind. I've walked the mountains on either side of the valley so many times they have become an essential part of me. I let all this into my heart willingly some years ago, and now I've come back to confront these memories.

Liv-Marie Harildstad, the owner of the farm and a direct descendent of the Harild who first settled here, calls us in to the main farmhouse to a table loaded with condiments and several burning candles. 'We have to make *nistepakker*, lunch packs, today. You use those specially made sheets of wax paper in that little box to keep the sandwiches apart,' I tell Annabel.

Annabel picks up the box and reads from the package depicting a stack of sandwiches. '"*Mellom–leggs–papir*"?'

I demonstrate, taking a piece of bread, buttering it, placing a piece of ham and a slice of cheese on it, topping it with sliced pickles, then placing the wax paper on top. 'See?'

'Where's the other slice of bread?'

'What other slice of bread?'

Annabel isn't usually as obtuse as this; far from it.

'The top part of the sandwich. You've put the wax paper *inside* the sandwich.'

'Norwegians don't make double-sided sandwiches. Just one slice of bread covered in *pålegg*, which translates literally to "lay on top".' Although there are only two of us, the table is decked with plates of smoked salmon, scrambled eggs, ham, cheese, tomatoes, pickles, salami, liver pâté and jam. 'Lay what you want on the slice of bread and seal it with a piece of wax paper to separate it from the sandwich stacked above,' I explain as I reach for a small, clear plastic bag and slide the stacked sandwiches neatly into it.

'If they made their sandwiches with a slice of bread on top, then they wouldn't have to use the . . . ' Annabel picks up the box and reads aloud, '*mellom–leggs–papir.*'

I shrug. 'One of those things in life.' I cut more slices of the crusty Norwegian bread. Why can't they make crunchy bread everywhere? Full of grains and lumps and bits and pieces – you can happily eat Norwegian bread alone with butter, it tastes so good.

Annabel looks out the window, assessing the weather. Depending on the window she chooses to look out of, it is either gloriously fine or bloody awful out there. 'What's the plan?' she asks.

Originally this trip had been planned for a year ago – just before I started dating Annabel. The intention had been to walk across Norway last summer, but in April my brother died, suddenly and unexpectedly. There are no words that can express the depth of sorrow and grief his death caused. Six weeks later I broke my back in an accident and spent the summer in hospital, and then at home lying in bed with two back braces. The plans to walk across Norway were effectively scotched. Within five months of going out with Annabel, I had my accident and was suddenly totally dependent on her. It wasn't an arrangement I found easy to accept. A sports medicine and orthopaedic physician, Annabel spends the majority of her time rehabilitating patients with spinal problems. Were she not willing to take full responsibility for me, I wouldn't have been released from hospital as soon as I had been. My sister took care of me during the day, and Annabel took over in the evenings and on weekends.

I unfold the Cappelen's map of 'South Norway – north'. Our entire trip fits conveniently onto the one map occupying the widest part of Norway between Oslo and Bergen – we'll cover the Jotunheimen Mountains and the two largest fjords – Sognefjord and Hardangerfjord. 'From here, we'll walk through the Jotunheimen Mountains . . . ' I show Annabel where we are on the map. 'Jotunheimen translates as "Home of the Giants". It's Norway's best-known national park. We'll walk over Besseggen, a knife-like mountain ridge above Lake Gjende, later today. Tomorrow we'll climb Glittertind, Norway's second-highest mountain, followed by Norway's highest mountain, Galdhøpiggen, the day after. We'll continue through Jotunheimen and descend through the Hurrungane Mountains down to Sognefjord, before climbing back into the mountains up the Aurland Valley to Finse. From there, we'll cycle on the old railway supply track over Hardangervidda Plateau, the Roof of Norway, down to Flåm and then take the Flåm train back up and walk over the mountains to Hardangerfjord.' My finger traces easily enough the route we will take, although the reality will be a series of long climbs and knee-crunching descents. 'From Ulvik we'll cycle to Odda and then hike over the top of the Folgefonna Glacier to Rosendal on the sea, at the mouth of Hardangerfjord.'

'You're sure we don't need tents or stoves?'

'There are huts every few hours and they are equipped with everything we need, including pots and pans, cutlery, crockery.'

'And food?'

'Yes, whether it's a self-service hut or a serviced one.' Den Norske Turistforening, DNT, or the Norwegian Mountain Touring Association has over 300 huts of varying descriptions, spread a few hours apart all over the country and connected by 20,000 kilometres of tracks. Every Norwegian I have met seems to be a member of DNT, although that might be a biased survey.

Liv-Marie offers to drive us up the valley to Gjendesheim. Like many Norwegians, her surname is derived from the place her family came from, although originally the farm was named after Harild. 'Stad' means 'place', so 'Harildstad' means 'the place of Harild'. The surname Fosslien, on the other hand, comes from 'foss' which means 'falls' and 'lien' which means 'hill'.

Norwegians have more varied surnames than anywhere else. Sometimes their surnames derive from the place, and sometimes the place is named after the family who lived there.

The spectacular journey up the remainder of the Heidal Valley compensates for leaving Harildstad. Strangely enough, given the lushness of the valley, water is pumped up from the river to irrigate the fields. The log houses are well preserved because there is little rainfall here; the valley is surrounded by mountain ranges, which collect most of the rain. Less rainfall occurs here than in the Sahara, someone once told me. Even in this valley, which is comparatively wide and where the sixteenth-century log farmhouses and farms are larger than the national average, the sloping fields are only isolated patches of ground set amidst pine forests.

In the lower section of the valley, the log farms are roofed in overlapping trimmed slate resembling the symmetrical scales of a snake. The barns are often roofed in huge, irregular slabs of uncut slate, each of which must have taken several men to lift into place.

Higher up, away from the slate quarries, farm buildings like Harildstad were, and still are, roofed in grass turf, layered over silver birch bark. The heavy turf doesn't provide insulation, in the winter it would be like having a block of ice up there, but rather weighs down the log walls, compressing them together so they don't warp and let in drafts. The silver birch bark on the roof provides a degree of waterproofing. Any chinks left between logs in the walls were traditionally insulated with moss.

Norway, even after millennia of human habitation, is only colonised in the more accessible valleys with a scattering of small farms carved out of forests, quaint fishing villages gripping the coast, or huts lodged between mountains or perched around lakes. And despite the rags to riches story of the national economy in the six decades since World War II, the farms remain by and large smallholdings. Only 3 per cent of Norway is cultivated. While in other parts of Europe the rolling farm landscape may be interspersed with the occasional clump of trees, here it is the reverse; the cleared patches of farmland are the exception to a landscape dominated by forested hills, mountains and glaciers comprising almost 90 per cent of Norway. With urban areas negligible at less than half a per cent, there is a sense of equilibrium to this nature. The craggy mountains and glaciers, and the winter climate have enforced a balance in favour of the wilderness over farmland and cities.

Moving to Norway almost a decade ago, I couldn't speak Norwegian and I couldn't get a job related to my training as an international economist. Instead, I started up two companies: Askeladdens Eventyrreiser AS and Villmarken Kaller AS. Both limited companies catered to activity-oriented tourists visiting Norway. I named Askeladden Eventyrreiser after my favourite archetypal Norwegian folk hero, Askeladden. Literally translated as the Ash Lad, Askeladden is named for his tendency to sit by the fire gazing at the burning embers and dreaming about adventures in far off places. He is the lesser-known male version of Cinderella, or Askepott. The youngest of three brothers, a dreamer, kind and honest, Askeladden is a lateral thinker who invariably wins the hand of the princess and half the kingdom, despite his humble beginnings and even humbler disposition. The word 'Eventyrreiser' was a play on the word '*eventyr*', which means both 'adventure' and 'fairy tales'.

Askeladdens Eventyrreiser eventually offered several cycling, hiking, mountain bike and glacier-walking tours; one of these was a ten-day hiking trip based at Liv-Marie's farm in Heidal for three days. Surrounded by the more glamourous national parks, the ridges on either side of the Heidal Valley, despite their beauty and spectacular views, were used only occasionally by locals and then usually only on weekends. This seclusion amidst so much natural beauty lent a sense of exclusivity to the experience despite the humble seventeenth-century accommodation.

Together with three partners I also set up a rafting company based on the Sjoa River, reputedly the best and most exciting rafting in Europe. Villmarken Kaller, Call of the Wild – a name my younger partners suggested – was geared specifically at rafting on this river coursing through the Heidal Valley. Both these companies catered to tourists coming to Norway to do the kinds of trips I could imagine doing myself.

As we head up the valley I show Annabel where the 'Guts' are, the stretch of water in the depths of a canyon that we didn't raft yesterday because the water was too high.

While helping to run the rafting business during the frenetic two-month season, I lived at another seventeenth-century farmhouse further up the valley. Sør Stein belonged to Astrid Steine, a widow of some years and a delightful spirit who loved company. Astrid didn't come from the Heidal Valley. She came from the adjacent Murudal Valley some fifty years ago and told me she was still considered a 'foreigner' by the close-knit Heidal community. Despite her youthful attitude, work as a farmer's wife had taken its toll and Astrid had hip problems. During the summers I rented the empty log farmhouse in the courtyard immediately adjacent to hers, Astrid's door was always open and, at the end of a long day running a rafting business, she was inevitably sitting in the kitchen waiting for me to come in for a cup of coffee and a piece of pie.

A deer suddenly crosses the road in front of us. I have often seen elk here too and there are reputedly bears down some of the less-frequented side valleys. As we reach the top of a rise, I point out Astrid's farmhouse on our right with its spectacular view down both the Heidal and Murudal valleys.

Astrid's farmhouses are more basic than Liv-Marie's and not suitable for international clients, but I liked them. One log building was so higgledy-piggledy the door and window frames were trapezoids rather than squares or rectangles. In the middle of the night, I'd listen to the roar of the river in the valley and absorb the incredible stillness and magic of the mountains.

When the daily buzz of running the rafting business was over, often late in the evening but still with plenty of mid-summer light, Astrid and I would drive to her hut in the mountains nestled beside a small lake. The highlight of those rafting summers were those occasional evenings, and early mornings, Astrid and I spent together laying out and pulling in fishnets full of trout on the lake by her summer farm. Traditionally, the farm's cows would be taken there during the summers to feed, leaving the grass in the pastures around the main farm to be cut, dried, and stored in the barn for the winter. Because Astrid could no longer get into or out of the small rowboat herself, I would have to help her, but she proudly displayed her independence by insisting she rowed as I lay out the nets.

In Norway, you cannot have a motorised boat on a lake that is smaller than two square kilometres, even if you live beside that lake. Whether or not you have rights, you are entitled to canoe, kayak, row or sail on any lake. Prohibiting engines on these lakes seems to me a marvellous, civilised rule. Those long, sunlit evenings laying out the nets with Astrid were always so peaceful, disturbed only by the creaking sound of the oarlocks as the oars dipped silently into the water.

Jotunheimen Mountains

Liv-Marie drops us off at Gjendesheim at the tip of Lake Gjende and wishes us, '*Go' tur.*'

Walking to the wooden dock projecting out into the turquoise lake, Annabel grabs me from behind. 'What's "Go tour" mean?'

'"*God tur*" means "Have a good trip".'

We dump our backpacks on a pile of others and take only what we need for the day: lunch packs, water bottles, warm clothes and wet-weather gear.

Explaining what's going to happen to the packs, I point out the mountain on the right rising some hundreds of metres perpendicularly above the lake. It is so precipitous it looks like a mountain cut vertically in half. 'We're going to climb up that ridge to the top of the mountain there. A boat takes the packs, and passengers, to the hut we're staying at tonight while we'll climb and follow the top of the ridge to the cut you can just see way over there, about halfway down Lake Gjende. The boat saves us carrying the heavy packs, it only costs a couple of dollars for the service, and it'll give us a chance to get settled into hiking mode again.'

Annabel studies the large mound of expensive packs, no doubt containing costly equipment within. 'Must be the last place in the world where you can leave your pack unattended for half a day and still expect to see it again.'

As part of a recent survey of European countries, researchers deliberately left wallets, containing cash and the address of the owner, unattended in public places. Norway was the only country where all five wallets were returned. Bottom of the list was Italy.

I scavenge two discarded walking sticks made from birch branches and we start the climb up Besseggen. The top of the infamous ridge is hidden within dark, bulging snow clouds. It is already past midday and we are the only ones ascending. Annabel waits for me. She points at the red 'T's painted on the rocks and on cairns.

'Markers put up by the DNT. Most of the paths are marked like this. It's good because it makes it easy to follow the route, but it also encourages hikers to come into these mountains without maps or compass,' I explain.

Past a drift of snow we stop to admire the view down the length of the glacier-gauged turquoise lake. It reminds me of a more spectacular English Lake District. Given this snowy, cold weather in the middle of summer, it's hardly surprising disgruntled Vikings took themselves off and settled in England's Lake District in the tenth century. Evidence of them being there is obvious in the local Lake District vocabulary: '*fjell*' became 'fell', '*dal*' became 'dale', '*bekk*' became 'brook', '*tjern*' became 'tarn', '*vik*' became 'wick' and of course all those towns with 'by' on the end of their names came from the Viking word '*by*', meaning 'town'. I'm constantly discovering English words that have come from the Viking invasions. '*Strand*' is another, meaning 'beach'.

I look behind to see Annabel busily putting on her Helly-Hansen mountain jacket. Helly Hansen is one of many Norwegian products sold on the international market. A fisherman understandably fed up with being cold and wet, Helly Hansen originally designed his waterproofs from canvas soaked in linseed oil and dried in front of a fire. The company, headquartered outside Oslo, progressed from those humble beginnings 125 years ago to being one of the best-known suppliers of outdoor weather gear.

The top of Besseggen is so cold we are clad in most of the mountain gear we have brought with us, including heavy gloves. At the top of the rise we collect a stone each and add it to a huge cairn, then we sit down to eat our sandwiches. Hikers stagger out of the mist as large, wet snowflakes float down, coating whatever they touch. Visibility is down to a few metres and within minutes the quietly descending flakes turn into a miniature snowstorm, covering our packs, jackets and the hoods over our heads with a layer of wet, white snow.

I have been here many times when the sun has been shining and the lake is a turquoise-coloured milky body of water bordered by steep mountains and brilliant white glaciers. I have even been here in the late fall when the mountain heather has turned rusty brown and the sun has shone so intensely it was warm enough to walk in a T-shirt. But it isn't always like that in these mountains, and right now we're having a spate of some of the worst summer weather ever recorded.

Soon after lunch we catch up to three strapping Norwegians carrying backpacks the size of coffins as they descend towards a perfect example of a hanging valley. One glacier has carved out the smaller upper valley filled by Lake Bessvatnet, and later, another bigger glacier gouged spectacular Lake Gjende far below. The contrast in colour in the two lakes is dramatic. The hanging, rain-fed Lake Bessvatnet has a narrow tongue of rock holding its dark, blue-black waters suspended almost vertically above turquoise-hued Lake Gjende.

A Danish family ascends the famous Besseggen ridge, the father crawling on all fours, gripping the rocks as if his life depended on it. He manoeuvres in a way I could easily imagine myself imitating if I allowed that spectre of vertigo into my thoughts. True to the stereotypical image Norwegians have of many Danes in Norway, the Dane wears shorts, running shoes and a T-shirt and little else. His wife and children, equally scantily dressed, watch from an adjacent rock, encouraging him to keep going. There is a drop of hundreds of metres on either side of the crest and to look down is to invite dizziness.

'It's easier climbing up here rather than going down; at least you don't have to look at how far down you could fall,' Annabel says, paraphrasing the DNT guidebook, which, as usual, understates in typical Norwegian fashion: 'the route is narrow and can seem exposed' and 'those who think they suffer from vertigo should make the trip in the opposite direction'.

'This is the most famous hiking route in Norway, where Ibsen's Peer Gynt rode on the back of a reindeer,' I shout to Annabel, but she's already too far below me to hear. I step to the left and am faced with a sheer drop almost straight down to Lake Gjende. It's amazing that, with hundreds of thousands of hikers climbing down this narrow ridge since Jotunheimen became a national park in 1980, no-one has been killed.

Descending and ascending a couple of times, we stop for a second lunch break to finish off our *nistepakker* before the final drop into the Memuru Valley. This is supposed to have been a six-hour walk, but with foul weather, snowdrifts and icy rocks, it's taken us almost eight hours and three medium-sized chocolate bars, assiduously shared between the two of us, to get here.

Walking into the clearing that is Memurubu, I notice the original main building is no longer there; the foundations remain but nothing else.

Memurubu has changed dramatically since I was here for the first time almost thirteen years ago. It had been a mountain *seter*, or summer farm, for farmers from Lom. Then it became a tourist destination in the mid-1800s when wealthy British adventurers 'discovered' Lake Gjende. It was subsequently immortalised in the classic travelogue, *Three in Norway by Two of Them.* Paintings on the walls and fireplace of the main hut here were based on etchings in the original book. I would like to think the hut has been transported somehow to Lom, for historical reasons. We walk down to the dock where we find our packs tucked under a tarpaulin. Lugging them back up to the main lodge building we remove our boots just as it begins to rain heavily.

'I expected a . . . hut!' Annabel exclaims as she enters. 'This is a lodge!'

We walk to the reception desk and I recognise the owner. He has been a farmer most of his life, his hands betray that, and he wears an old, worn Norwegian sweater. I ask him, in Norwegian, if he recognises me. I can see that he does, but then he looks at Annabel. He looks a couple of times from Annabel to me, back to Annabel. He shakes his head, but I think he is just too polite to say anything.

'What happened to your old main house?'

He looks as if I have slapped him across the face. He turns away. 'It burnt down,' he replies simply.

Thirteen years ago I had a scholarship to take a two-month post-graduate summer course in economics of developing countries at the University of Oslo. I met a Norwegian woman, Kirsten, one weekend while hiking here at Memurubu. A year later, after being with each other for three months in Canada, we were married at this same spot in a civil ceremony in the old main building. Kirsten emigrated from Norway to live with me in Ottawa. It seems so long ago now.

'When did it burn down?' I ask. Had I thought about it, I wouldn't have been so blunt – the charred timbers should have been a clue.

'August 1998.'

'What happened?'

'Someone drying their socks...' His face is sad and my question is a rude reminder of the disaster.

'I'm so sorry,' I tell him. It's as if a door in my life that was almost closed has now slammed firmly shut.

He puts on a brave front. 'At least no-one was hurt.'

We go to our room. Annabel can't believe the luxury of it. 'It's more like a hotel room than a hiker's hut.' Since I told her we were staying in huts, she associated them with the basic structure and facilities of a typical New Zealand hut. Instead we have the luxury of a double bed with our own bathroom.

'Don't worry, they're not all like this.'

There's not much time before dinner is served, so we shower and stagger stiff-legged to the large but simple dining room. Annabel and I order two light beers and I raise my glass.

'Old Viking custom,' I declare, her private oracle of information on Norway. 'When Norwegians toast each other, they look into each other's eyes, lift their glasses, toast and clink glasses, and keep looking into each other's eyes as they drink. It's probably a habit from when the Vikings used to thump goblets together to deliberately spill the contents into each other's mug, so that if one mug were poisoned, the other would have poison spilled into it too; then they watched each other to make sure they were both drinking.'

The waitress serves us a huge poltroon of soup with flat bread, all of which disappears with frightening efficiency. A platter heaped high with *kjøttkaker* – Norwegian meatballs – peeled potatoes and assorted vegetables follows. Groups of Japanese travellers sit at three adjacent tables and although many of them are relatively young, they don't appear to be hikers. They look too fresh, with neatly pressed clothes. Their Norwegian guide, however, not only looks like a rugged hiker, he looks as if he fell down Besseggen. He is about sixty-five – he must be retired – with white, short-cropped hair. Wearing a DNT fleece jacket, he is as crumpled as his clothes, but most noticeably he has a bloody bandage wrapped around his head, covering one temple where blood has congealed and dried. Although his eye is black and swollen, he looks happy enough swigging a beer and conversing sporadically in English with his Japanese clients.

Excusing ourselves from the table we limp into the adjacent living room. Outside it pours with rain. 'It's amazing to be in the middle of nowhere, or at least the middle of these mountains, and still have hot meals and showers,' Annabel comments.

We slouch into armchairs, bodies stretched out, and watch through the pane-glass windows at the falling sheets of rain as more hikers arrive looking cold and miserable. 'Annabel?'

'Yes,' she replies warily, taking note of the pleading tone of my voice.

'Can you get me a glass of water, I'm really badly dehydrated.'

'What?' she replies, laughing.

'Get me a glass of water?' I ask again, the beseeching pitch more obvious.

'You must be kidding?'

'If you knew how much it hurts…'

She reaches for the back of her neck and massages it. 'My C5–6 and my C6–7 still hurt from coming out of the raft yesterday,' she says with professional aplomb.

'Well . . . my . . . H₂O hurts,' I reply, casting about for impressive specifics.

'Your what?'

'H₂O.'

'H₂O is water.'

'Yeah, and my body is 70 per cent water and my H₂O hurts.'

She doesn't say anything but gets up and fetches us both a glass of water.

The Norwegian guide with the black eye sits on the sofa behind me with another DNT tour leader accompanying American clients. I lie back and listen to their banter. It transpires that the DNT guide for the Japanese group had too much to drink the night before and while on the way to bed he tripped outside, landing on his head, which accounts for the bloody bandages. Not nearly as dramatic as falling off Besseggen.

'What's that noise?'

'Rain.'

'Rain?'

Annabel gets up and opens the curtains. 'Sheets of rain pounding the roof, and we've got to hike in that!' The Norwegian flag is blown horizontal by the wind. 'It's like a tropical-monsoon deluge in freezing temperatures!'

On the notice board in the reception area I check the weather forecast. 'Couple of degrees above freezing and the prediction is for more rain and snow over the next three days,' I translate, very quietly.

From the breakfast buffet table packed with varieties of raw herring, cheese, hams and salami, boiled eggs, jam and marmalade, I help myself to heaped spoonfuls of raw herring marinated in pickled onion for breakfast, then pile the cheese and ham on bread for the *nistepakke*.

Annabel slices brown goat's cheese, lays it on a piece of bread, and tops it with strawberry jam. 'Tastes like peanut butter and jam,' she says when she sees me staring, putting a slice of bread on the top and then a *mellomleggspapir* over that as extra security to make sure the jam doesn't leak out.

The Japanese guests are outfitted with Tyrolean hats and white gloves, towels around the neck and heavy waterproofs, as they head down to the dock to catch the boat to Gjendesheim. I wonder if they have hiked here at all, or whether they took the boat in and out, and that will be the sum extent of their mountain experience.

I have a waterproof cover for my external-frame pack but Annabel hasn't brought one along. Everything is wrapped in individual plastic bags within our packs. We find a large plastic shopping bag and pull that down as far as it will go over the outside of her pack, then step out into the rain in boots that are still soaking wet from yesterday.

With the hood of the jacket over my head, I keep burping up breakfast: pickled herring and onion. Water pours down the eroded path as if we were climbing a waterfall. Not far above us, the mountains are buried in thick cloud. I don't blame the Japanese tourists for opting to take the boat; there'd be no point climbing Besseggen today when there's the alternative of a boat ride back to Gjendesheim. We branch off from the trail we had taken yesterday and head towards Russvatnet, a long Scottish-like loch complete with appropriately mysterious mist and drizzle. Somewhere to our left, buried in cloud, should be a glacier.

We've been told by all and sundry that not only is this the coldest summer on record, but one of the heaviest snowfalls ever recorded fell during the previous winter as well. The combination of the two seasons of inclement weather has meant that although it is now almost July, there is snow everywhere in the mountains. As we cross a bridge of snow, I jab my stick firmly in front of me, probing for any weaknesses that might signal the snow bridge is about to collapse under my weight. Clear of the snowdrift, we then face another obstacle – a stream. Under normal circumstances in the middle of summer, the stream would be a trickle, crossed easily over stepping stones. But with the melting snow and the torrential rain, the stream is almost a river, and difficult to traverse. We unfasten our packs and drape them loosely over a shoulder, so that if we slip and fall, they won't weigh us down.

We remove our woollen socks and wring them out, before putting them back into boots that immediately become soaked again as we walk along the lake, through slanting rain that pelts us with the stinging sharpness of hail.

Lost in our thoughts, we almost walk into a herd of reindeer lying on a bank of snow. We both manage to take photographs before they disappear up the side of the mountain.

'Did you see the albino?' Annabel asks.

'Never seen that before.'

It begins to snow heavily. I have given up taking notes. The pages of my notebook, although hidden in my 'water-resistant' jacket, are so wet the pen will no longer write on them.

Despite this inclement weather, the scenery is starkly beautiful and, making it even more special, we haven't seen another person all day. If we were in the Lake District in England during the summer, even with this weather, we'd be tripping over other hikers.

In an effort to console both of us, I say, 'If we were lying on a beach somewhere, we wouldn't recall this day ten years from now, but I'm sure we'll always remember *this* effort.'

'Every minute of it,' Annabel replies with just a hint of irony. 'But I could do with a hot bath and a bed right now.'

We pause to shelter by a boulder, out of the rain and snow, and study the 1:100,000 map of Jotunheimen. We have a final snowy col in front of us to traverse, and then a long descent beside the swollen waters of Hestbekken before we reach the hut.

'How're you feeling?'

'If you really want to know, I'm so tired right now, Andrew, I feel sick,' Annabel says emphatically as we put the map away. We have been walking non-stop for several hours.

We eat another row of Freia chocolate squares, shoulder our packs and continue up to the col. Crossing the saddle we see Glitterheim hut in the distance but we have to divert around a lake to get to it. Slowing down from the fatigue, Annabel waits for me a short distance from the hut.

'When you go into the hut, don't limp,' I order as we continue together, limping. 'Like we're not in any pain. Okay?'

'Okay,' she replies, humouring me.

Entering the building we notice a sign indicating walking times to different huts. Memurubu is advertised as five hours away although the map we have suggests six. Before opening the door to the hut, Annabel looks at her watch and mutters, 'It's taken us ten hours to get here. Do Norwegians underestimate the walking times just to make us feel bad?'

'That's the *walking* time. It doesn't include lunch or other breaks,' I reply as we sit on benches and remove our boots in the outer room.

'We stopped fifteen minutes for lunch and even that was spent standing on our feet.'

'In the rain,' I add.

'Literally, we haven't been off our feet in the last ten hours. This is the first time I've sat down since we left Memurubu.'

'Don't limp,' I remind her as she stands up, opens the inner door and heads inside.

Our soaked woollen socks leave a soppy-wet trail behind us as we splash up to reception.

'Where have you come from?' the manager asks in Norwegian, thinking we are tough, mountain-hiking compatriots. Annabel with her long blonde hair and blue eyes looks Norwegian enough, but if he had an inkling of how much we hurt, he'd know we were fakes, despite our Helly-Hansen outfits and Annabel's Scandinavian appearance.

'Memurubu,' I reply as bravely as I can.

He looks up. 'Oi.'

'We saw two herds of reindeer on the way here and both herds had albinos,' I tell him in English. 'Do you have lots of albino reindeer?'

'More than before,' he replies, switching languages.

'Why is that?'

'The hunters have agreed not to shoot them.'

'Ah, that's nice,' Annabel says, leaning on the counter, happy to hear that hunters have a soft spot.

'They save the albinos,' he replies matter-of-factly, 'because glimpsing albino reindeer is easier against the rocky, brown terrain. Leaving albinos alive makes it easier to find the herd and shoot the others.'

We have arrived so late we don't have time to shower before dinner. They keep the dining room open and a setting for two people with welcoming candles awaits us. 'That was one of the longest days I can ever remember,' Annabel says, and she is not one prone to exaggeration.

This admission makes me feel better for feeling such a wimp and waddling around like a penguin. She's been up to Everest Base Camp for the Everest Marathon twice, did the Annapurna Circuit before I did, so if *she's* feeling tired...

Surkål, sauerkraut, and *kjøttkaker* in heavy gravy with potatoes are served immediately.

'I've never seen so much water in my life,' Annabel complains, looking out the window. 'Whether it was in the form of snow, sleet, hail, or rain, rivers, streams, waterfalls, glaciers, puddles, bogs, lakes – I've never seen so much of it.'

Despite all the water, we are dehydrated and knock back a jug of water between us before we eat the meal, polishing off the tray full of food that is deposited in front of us. After jelly dessert topped with vanilla sauce, for the second night running, Annabel says, 'I'm going to lie down and never, ever get up again.' She looks at me and then giggles at her predicament. 'There isn't a part of my body that doesn't hurt.'

We head back out into the rain to our room for a shower.

'You've washed all your clothes,' Annabel observes astutely several minutes later, as I drip water everywhere in our tiny room. I don't tell her I simply showered with my clothes on, shampooing my hair, washing myself with a bar of soap through the clothes, and then stripping the layers off while rinsing.

I hang my long thermal Helly-Hansen underwear and synthetic T-shirt on a clothesline in a smelly, but satisfyingly hot, drying room, return to our cosy room, and flop heavily on the lower bunk.

Annabel says, 'Want a massage?'

'Sure.'

'But you have to reciprocate.'

'I'll time you. Ten minutes each.'

'I'll time myself.' She starts on my lower back. 'I can still feel where you injured your vertebra.'

'You can?'

'I can even see it.'

That impresses me.

She massages my feet for what seems like ten seconds and then says, 'Dang, that was *twelve and a half minutes*! I forgot to keep time.'

It is past eleven and still light outside despite the overcast sky.

Sitting at the breakfast table, my eyes almost shut, Annabel kicks me under the table with a stockinged foot. 'Why do so many Norwegian men walk around with little knives in leather sheaths hanging from their belts?' She reaches forwards and picks at the sleep in the corners of my eyes.

'It's part of the get-up. Japanese wear white gloves and Tyrolean hats; Kiwis wear shorts and gaiters even when there's no snow or prospect of snow. Norwegians wear little knives in leather sheaths hanging from their belts because they never know when they're going to need them.'

'Against marauding . . . bears?'

'Drunk Finns, except drunk Finns carry *really* long knives.'

As we are paying our bill at the reception desk, Annabel checks with the manager, 'Do you think it's safe to climb Glittertind today?' I don't know why she's asking him, I've already told her it's safe.

He gets up and looks out the window then assesses the two of us. 'If you leave now and give yourself the whole day, I think you'll find enough clear weather to get to the top.' He takes our cash. 'Be careful though. Two weeks ago a Dutchman fell over the edge at the top and dropped 200 metres. He's the first to have survived doing that.'

Annabel studies the numerous postcards in a rack on the counter showing the summit of Glittertind. 'And that's the edge you're talking about?' she asks, pointing at the giant Mr Whippy ice-cream curl listing to the side.

'Yes, it's dangerous if it is snowing or cloudy and you can't see, because it is very easy to walk over the rim.' He stands up and points at a postcard graphically depicting the ice-cream curl cornice at the summit. 'It is easy to walk out too far on this over-hang and it can suddenly collapse under you.' Annabel adds a couple of large Norwegian Freia chocolate bars and several Kvikk Lunsj, the Norwegian version of a Kit Kat, to the bill, 'Purely for security reasons in case of an avalanche,' she says.

Norwegian chocolate is without any doubt, the best-tasting chocolate anywhere. It's thick and creamy and tastes of . . . chocolate. Other chocolate bars taste like brown wax after experiencing the delights of a Freia chocolate bar. My opinion is backed up by some four million Norwegians who eat an average of eight kilos of chocolate annually, most of it while hiking in the mountains.

When Kirsten moved to Ottawa, her girlfriends mailed us Freia chocolate bars but we never benefited from their thoughtfulness. All the evidence we ever saw were the empty wrappers when we came home from work. Kirsten had brought her dog Bonso, a handsome cross between a collie and a Gordon setter, with her, and he missed this little bit of Norway as much as we did. Being home all day, the temptation, once that chocolaty-smelling package was shoved through the letterbox, was far too much for him to ignore.

Before we set out, Annabel studies the map. 'Oh no!' she mutters.

'What?'

'Yesterday's walking time is described as five hours and it took us ten. Today's route over the top of Glittertind to . . . ' she studies the map, 'Spiterstulen is supposed to be seven hours. If

five hours equals ten, then seven hours is likely to take us . . . '
She can't even utter the word fourteen.

'Sixteen kilometres *and* we have to climb to 2,464 metres, and that's just to the top of the rock,' I comment malevolently. 'The real summit depends on how much of an icecap there is. With the heavy snowfall they had this past winter and the cold we're having this summer, it's going to be higher than Galdhøpiggen. Probably add another ten metres.'

'You know, it wouldn't be bad to have a rest day.'

'Annabel, we've just *started* our walk across Norway.'

It begins snowing again but today I am prepared, with my pen and notebook in a plastic bag in my pocket. We come across reindeer droppings melted into deep craters in the snow, and a rabbit sitting almost invisible amongst some rocks. As we near the forbidding cornice leading up to the summit it begins snowing heavily.

'There are no more red "T" markers,' Annabel observes.

'Hard to paint on snow.' I open the map holder and compass I have hanging from my neck. 'We'll have to use a map and a compass.' There's so much snow blowing it's hard to take a bearing on the unidentifiable lumps of snow and ice surrounding us.

We catch up to nine Norwegians who, although they are not climbing together, have bottlenecked on the last bit of rock before the expanse of snow that is the summit of Glittertind. The snow squall swirls around us as the Norwegians collectively study a map. I suggest to Annabel that we wait to see if it stops snowing.

'Wouldn't it be better to follow them and all go together?'

'Over the edge?' I'd climbed up to the summit once before when it was cloudy and I couldn't see exactly where the edge was. I decided to turn around and descend, knowing I was only a few metres from the summit. The next day was clear and as I retraced my footprints at the top I realised I had walked some distance onto the overhanging cornice. It was a lesson I wasn't about to repeat.

The others continue up but don't go much more than thirty metres before one of them suddenly sinks to his waist. He struggles to take his pack off his back before finally throwing it down to the others, then extricates himself, gingerly moving further down the slope of snow, away from the curling drift.

I remove my sunglasses and take a photo of the ascending Norwegians as they disappear into the snowstorm. 'I think it's clearing,' I tell Annabel.

She laughs. 'You always say that when you take a photo. You've just removed your sunglasses; of course everything seems brighter.'

We press on, walking diagonally across the snow-covered glacier until we reach the top where the Norwegians are sitting down comfortably on Styrofoam insulating pads they've sensibly brought with them. Safely ensconced on the summit, they have broken off into their respective couples again, with sufficient personal space around them to provide a bit of privacy, quietly eating their *nistepakker* or boiling water for soup on gas stoves. If they were French or Italian they'd be taking photos of each other, cracking open the champagne, celebrating, having a loud party. The Norwegians are so quiet by contrast that Annabel and I could easily imagine being the only ones up here.

The cloud drifts off the summit and we are afforded a brief view directly down below to the lateral ridges on either side of us. A slippery slide down the glacier in front of us would end in a sheer drop. Ditto if we stepped over the cornice behind us. The view through the banks of mist flowing over us is fleeting, and daunting.

Black, snow-laden clouds start to boil again. We set off down the opposite ridge of the mountain while we can still see its outline. As we descend, the snow changes to sleet and then finally rain. Annabel waits for me at the bottom of the final, steep, rock ridge. My legs feel as sturdy as cooked spaghetti. I take off my pack and jacket to cool down and immediately it begins to hail and sleet again.

When we continue, Annabel slips and jabs her eye with her walking stick. The eye swells up immediately. She walks resolutely ahead of me but I can't keep up. Today I feel as tired as she felt yesterday. By the time I reach Visdalen Valley, I've lost

Annabel. Spiterstulen – the next accommodation, originally a mountain *seter* but now a lodge with several huts – is in sight but it's still some kilometres up the valley and doesn't seem to get any closer, like an optical illusion. My feet are moving in the right direction but the huts seem to remain stuck a distance away. To my right, barely visible beneath the cloud, is the base of Galdhøpiggen, the peak we'll climb tomorrow.

Or rather, the peak we are supposed to climb tomorrow.

Annabel waits further down the path.

'It's not worth it,' I complain after slipping yet again while crossing an icy snow bridge that looks as if it's about to collapse. 'Let's go to Spain. It's dry, there's a heat wave going on there right now, there's no water on the plain as the song goes, and we can lie on the beach and let our kneecaps grow back.'

'You're joking, right?'

I sit leaning my pack against a rock. 'No, I'm not joking.'

'What about our trip?'

'We'll cancel it.'

'What happened to the bit about holidays on the beach being eminently forgettable?'

'That was rubbish.'

She studies me trying to figure out if I am joking or not. *I* don't know if I am joking or not so I don't know how *she* will figure it out. 'Is it always like this in the middle of summer in Norway?'

'I have to admit, this is the worst I've experienced.'

'It *can't* get much worse.'

I slap my hand against my forehead. 'Don't say that!'

'Anyway, the scenery is still spectacular, even in weather like this,' she says, grabbing my hand and pulling me along.

Like Memurubu, Spiterstulen has expanded, recently adding several additional buildings to accommodate the increasing number of hikers taking to the mountains. We take off our boots in the outer room before slopping messily in wet woollen socks to the reception. Annabel studies postcards of the area displayed in a rack on the counter. 'You'd think it never snowed, rained, hailed, sleeted or was even overcast in Norway looking at these postcards of blue skies.' We collect the key for our room and walk down to one of several buildings, each with some twenty rooms. 'They must be making a fortune,' Annabel calculates. 'Multiply what we're paying for the room with the number of rooms in this building, multiplied by the number of buildings . . . '

'*And* they collect money from the campers across the river,' I point at the numerous tents pitched on the other side. 'If we thought *we* had it rough, imagine what it's like for the campers.'

'I thought you were allowed to camp for free anywhere in Norway.'

'You can camp anywhere for two days as long as you don't disturb farmers, or their animals, and are about 150 metres away from any building. It's called *allemannsretten,* but here I think they've made it a one-kilometre exclusion zone. Remember the designated camp site about a kilometre down the road where all the cars with Polish and Czech license plates were?'

When I lived in Norway there was an annual influx of Polish migrant workers during the summer months. Passing themselves off as tourists they sought out odd jobs, painting houses, working in gardens, doing anything to earn hard currency to take home with them. Now, some ten years after the Berlin Wall came down, Eastern bloc nationals, and others, are coming to Norway in droves to holiday, many taking advantage of Norway's pristine wilderness, and also taking full advantage of the fact that as long as you camp and bring your own food, it's all free.

Down the Heidal Valley from Harildstad is another striking farm called Kruke Farm. The owner has spent decades collecting log farmhouses from all over Norway, and repairing and resurrecting them on his farm. Fed up with tourists driving into his courtyard as if his farm were a living museum, he fenced off his property to keep the inquisitive visitors out. In his view, some of the tourists coming into Norway in their camping wagons, trailer-homes and caravans, stuffed to the gunwales with food, beer, sausages and everything they needed for their holiday, were a liability. Many of them camped beside the road or near his farm for free, and left nothing behind but their refuse, he claimed. His suggestion was that as soon as one of these mobile homes entered Norway, they should have the doors locked and sealed by the appropriate authorities, with the seal only permitted to be broken at designated camping grounds. When exiting the camp site, a seal would be re-placed on the lock and the interior sealed off until the vehicle entered another official camping ground. Anyone caught driving with the seal broken would be subject to a hefty fine. *Allemannsretten* worked fine within Norway, but with the increasing number of foreign tourists driving into the country and camping for free, many Norwegians feel their system is open to abuse.

Annabel and I take off our boots outside the new building and enter our room. There's a bunk bed and a third small bed by the window leaving hardly any room to manoeuvre in the remaining floor space. I throw my pack on the floor, collapse on the bed by the window, and rest my feet up against the wall. They throb in time to my heartbeat. I study my watch. 'That was another ten hours today on our feet carrying heavy rucksacks.' The day seems to have gone on forever.

Included in the hefty price for a bunk bed, in a tiny room, in our own sleeping bags, is a metal disc, the size of a coin, to activate the showers in another building.

In the men's showers, still wearing my sweat-soaked thermal underwear, T-shirt and woollen socks, I put the metal disc into the appropriate slot and stand under the showerhead fully dressed, soaping myself through clothes and socks. I peel the layers of clothes off onto the shower floor and knead them with my feet as I shampoo my hair before rinsing. Someone else comes in, undresses and dumps his clothes into a sink, leaving the hot water on while furtively washing himself with a face cloth. I guess he is one of the campers from down the road taking advantage of the hot water in here.

I wander back to our room and with some ingenuity arrange our walking sticks so that they serve as clotheslines more or less above the electric heater. I crank the heat up and leave our clothes to dry.

At dinner, after a waitress brings us our *kjøttkaker* with sauer-kraut, Annabel observes, 'She didn't have a wrinkle in her skin, not a flaw. And the other waitresses are the same.'

'Because they live in these mountains and they've hardly ever seen sunlight.'

'They're so good-looking.' It's a valid comment coming from Annabel.

'By Western standards.'

'Which is the standard all over the world now. Blonde hair, fair skin, high cheekbones, small noses, regular features, smooth skin, tall, athletic.'

'In other societies tribal scars on the face, missing front teeth, big asses, fat bodies would be deemed beautiful instead,' I reply.

'Yes dear.'

When we have finished eating dinner we roll into the large living room with a library and a blazing fire. I discover a cheap novel someone left behind. Annabel looks for an English book too, but can't find one. 'How about we go back to our room and I read it aloud for both of us?' she suggests.

We walk stiffly to our room, which looks like a Chinese laundry with wet clothes dangling from walking sticks, the curtain rail, rungs of the bunk ladder, the doorknob and light fixture. I lie down and Annabel inspects my bad knee mapped with surgical scars. 'There's a constant pain inside,' I tell her. I let the bad knee flop down and raise my good one. 'But my good knee was killing me coming down from Glittertind today.'

'That's because you were overcompensating.'

'It's like a knife going in, right there, under the kneecap, but it only hurts when I go down.'

'Excessive loading of the patella-femoral compartment.'

'How's your blister?' I ask, with less acuity.

'Sore.'

We experiment lying on the single bed head to feet, and knead each other's soles simultaneously. Annabel is good at foot massages so I imitate her, using both hands.

When we finish Annabel climbs into the adjacent lower bunk and reads aloud from the trashy novel, something about creatures with red eyes that vaguely look like men but move like wolves and can keep up with a speeding car.

Bellies more than full from breakfast, we are waddling back to our room, when Annabel uses the 'f' word.

'What's wrong?' I ask. She never uses the 'f' word unless it is serious.

'The blister on my heel is *really* sore.'

'Look, today's an optional day,' I respond, stopping in my tracks.

She pauses and slowly turns around. 'It is?'

'We're spending two nights here so if you don't want to climb Galdhøpiggen, Norway's highest mountain, you don't have to.' I continue walking.

She follows me. 'But *you're* going up?'

'Yup.'

This is the equivalent of waving a red flag at a bull.

'You said what we did yesterday, Glitter-what's-it-called . . . ?'

'-tind.'

' . . . Glittertind was Norway's highest mountain.'

'Well, it sort of is right now because of the icecap on it, but technically, as far as the bare rock is concerned, Galdhøpiggen is acknowledged as being higher. We wouldn't have to carry everything with us today because we'll be coming back down here,' I tempt her. 'Also, there's going to be a special treat at the top . . . '

That does it.

There isn't a long line of people heading up the mountain, but we certainly aren't alone today. A boy, probably no more than twelve, rushes past us as if he were out for a quick jog.

It isn't raining, or snowing, which is good, although the grey clouds hide the summits of the mountains around us. Almost as soon as we have started up Galdhøpiggen we come across the first drifts of snow. Within an hour we are walking through fresh, heavy snow. After the initial snowfields, we climb narrow rock ridges that offer spectacular views, and sheer drops, to Styggebreen Glacier on one side, and then higher up, equally stunning vistas, and sheer drops, down the other side to Svellnosbreen Glacier. On both glaciers far below, like tiny safari ants, we see lines of glacier-walkers roped together, slowly making their way across the white expanse of glacier.

We stop to take a break on a grey rock, and an elderly couple walk past us as we dig into the first half of our *nistepakker.*

'Not far to go,' he tells us in Norwegian.

'From the sublime to the ridiculous,' Annabel comments. 'Kids who aren't even teenagers are running up past us, and now a couple approaching eighty encourages us by telling us it's not far to go? Don't these Norwegians know when to stop? He was wearing *gumboots!*'

Annabel and I study the false summits – ridges with humps that consistently look like the summit, but aren't. We go over these false tops and descend a short distance on the other side before climbing again. Each time we descend, my good knee feels as if there's a knife plunging into it. Fortunately the descents are short, but it's also a sobering indication of the pain I'm going to feel when we have to descend all the way back down this mountain.

Clouds hug the summit of Galdhøpiggen as we approach its peak. Annabel stops and points. 'That's not a hut is it?'

'Told you there was a surprise at the top.'

She studies the stone building, barely recognisable as a hut against the outcrop of identical rocks. 'Sounds impressive saying we've climbed Norway's highest mountain, but we've had a leisurely hike up here accompanied by eighty-year-old Norwegian couples in gumboots and Norwegian pre-teenagers in T-shirts, and now we have a cup of tea waiting for us in a hut at the top. I mean, friends back home would have visions of Alpine peaks, crampons, climbing ropes, isolation and instead . . . '

'Don't tell them, okay?' I reply, feeling a bit of a charlatan for having climbed Norway's highest peak so easily. 'Sort of ruins the impression if they know there is a hut up at the top.'

The hut is cosy and warm. Steam from a dozen bodies mists the windows with condensation. Behind the counter two boys with wicked bed-heads tell us what's on offer. 'There's bouillon, tea bags and flavoured water.' It's definitely not a McDonald's offering hamburgers, hot dogs and milkshakes but still, it's a warm, dry, cosy hut at the top of a mountain.

'It's normally a great view from up here,' I comfort Annabel when we go back outside and climb the remaining metres to the top, 'when it's clear.' I shrug my shoulders helplessly. 'At least it's not snowing or raining; last time I was up here you could see literally right across Norway. I was dressed in shorts and a T-shirt, and I flew a kite.'

'Flew a kite?'

'Wanted to be the first person to fly a kite from the top of Norway's highest mountain.'

'Oh please . . . '

Just the few metres back down to the Galdhøpiggen summit hut are painful. We go inside and Annabel digs out an elastic bandage from her pack, gives me a painkiller and wraps up my good, now bad, knee. 'Were you this busy when you were the doctor for those two Everest Marathons?'

She chuckles. 'No. But I didn't have such a vested interest either.'

We put on our waterproof pants and as soon as we step outside the hut, we slide on our backsides down a long bank of snow. Most of the other climbers have done the same thing and we have several snow chutes to choose from. I let Annabel go first. 'Yeehahh!' Annabel yells as she careens down at exhilarating but alarming speed. It takes a determined effort sticking our boot heels into the snow to stop in a plume of ice, before the inevitable outcropping ridge of exposed boulders. In other sections the slopes aren't so steep and I use my walking stick like an oar to paddle myself with more momentum down the snow chute.

Nearing the bottom, we encounter an exceptionally tall man staggering down through a pathway twisting through a bedlam of boulders. I commiserate in Norwegian as I pass him, 'Hard on the knees coming down, isn't it?'

He looks roughly in my direction. 'No, my knees are fine,' he replies. 'It's my eyesight that is bad.' It's mind-boggling that he'd tackle this mountain on his own with such bad eyesight, even if he is Norwegian and born to this kind of thing.

There is so much snow still lying on Galdhøpiggen we can toboggan most of the way down to the bottom. The dreaded descent of Norway's highest mountain has turned out to be a lark. The DNT guidebook says four hours to the top and two down. It took us three hours to the top and less than two to get back down. With my wobbly knees, I was counting on four or five hours on the descent alone.

'We beat the DNT book's suggested total time for the trip,' I comment.

'We cheated, sliding all the way down like that.'

We get to our room and I realise we haven't been given additional metal discs to activate the showers. When I return from the reception desk I give Annabel a disc and we walk to the shower block. Back in the men's shower again with all my clothes on, I start washing. But this time I've misjudged the timing and just as maximum suds are working into the thermal underwear, T-shirt and woollen socks, hair and face, the water shuts off. I wipe the shampoo out of my eyes, step out of the shower and clear a swipe of soap from around my face with a towel. Then I pull off all the soapy clothes and dump them in the sink. Someone walks into the shower room wearing a little knife in a leather sheath hanging from his belt. He strips in front of the shower stalls, carefully hanging his spotless mountaineering clothes on pegs.

'Ahem,' I cough conspicuously, armpits and groin still lathered, shampoo dripping down my face, stinging my eyes. I don't speak to him in Norwegian; I'd rather he thought I was just another stupid tourist, which I suppose I am. 'I've just soaped myself and the time ran out in the shower. Do you think I could just use the first ten seconds of your shower time to rinse the soap off me?'

He looks at me, trying to determine if I'm a camper free-loading hot water from Spiterstulen and now about to con him. He thinks about the request before replying, 'That would be fine.'

He puts in the coin, and I rinse myself for half a minute before coming out. 'Thank you very much,' I tell him as he slips by me into the shower. I finish rinsing my clothes in the sink and then wander back to our room.

When I open the unlocked door of our room I discover a very tall man standing in the cramped space amidst the drying cotton underwear. He turns around to look at me, his pack still on his back. I vaguely recognise him.

'This is *my* room,' he says, surprised that I must have dumped all my things in *his* room.

I automatically assume, this being Norway, that we have to share our room with this hiker, although I would have thought with the price we paid it should have allowed Annabel and I more privacy. 'Sorry, I'll tidy up,' I say quickly in Norwegian, and shuffle about disassembling the Chinese laundry and removing odds and ends off the third bed. Why didn't they tell us at reception that we might have to share with someone else?

As I'm tidying, he ducks back out the doorframe and with his nose almost pressed to the wooden door, says in Norwegian, '*Herregud*, this is 114 not 104.'

It's the semi-blind guy we'd met on the way down.

'Sorry . . . ' he apologises before stumbling down the corridor.

To celebrate climbing Norway's two highest mountains one day after another, we blow our budget and order a glass of wine each at dinner.

When we head down to our room, it's still broad daylight outside and I don't know if it's wishful thinking, but the overcast sky seems to be clearing, and it's not because I've just removed my sunglasses to take a photo.

Annabel reads aloud again from the trashy novel, continuing from where she left off.

I've rarely felt happier.

Damp mist floats in through the open window.

Annabel asks me how much I can recall of what she read last night. Apparently it's not much more than I can remember from the night before, and she was reading for an hour. I don't know where she gets the extra reserves of energy. Sometimes at home, even after a hard day at work, she'll start playing the piano late at night. She never plays if anyone is listening, and it took her some time to play with me in the house. Even now I have to be in another room. I've never met anyone with as many diverse talents as Annabel.

No matter how much I stuff myself at breakfast, and no matter how big I make my *nistepakke*, I never seem to have enough goodies in my lunch package after a few hours hiking.

'I've never hiked this stretch to Leirvassbu before,' I admit.

'Good.' Before we knew each other we had both somehow contrived to walk some of the classic hiking routes in the world. An inveterate traveller, Annabel's also travelled around Europe in a Kombi with two girlfriends, and over most of Asia.

We walk up Visdalen Valley, with Visbreen Glacier dominating the head of the valley on the left. This day's walk is described in the DNT book as only a five-hour stroll from Spiterstulen to Leirvassbu, most of it contouring easily enough up the valley. As we go over a col, Annabel observes aloud, 'According to the map, we've crossed the watershed separating water heading east down through Oslo and water flowing west to the fjords.'

The other side of the col could be Siberia. The lake is frozen and covered in ice. On either side of us are steep mountains; Kyrkja, named the Church, for obvious reasons, looms to the left, with Tverrbotntindane on the right, their ragged, bleak peaks protruding like needles through their glaciers.

'It looks like the middle of winter,' Annabel says. 'There's more ice and snow and glacier around us than there is rock.

We walk most of the day without meeting another soul except for three young Poles who ask if this is the route to Spiterstulen.

Leirvassbu doesn't look particularly attractive, especially when we notice a dozen cars parked outside. It seems strange walking through this desolate landscape only to come to a hut at the end of a road. To further confuse matters, a dozen pairs of cross-country skis are stuck in a snow bank beside the front door. Despite the functional outer appearance of the hut, inside it is cosy, with exposed wooden beams and ceiling, and candles burning. Although it has been overcast, with clouds hanging low over us, it hasn't rained beyond drizzling, and in Norway that almost doesn't count as rain.

Later, at the dinner table, I ask the waitress for another bowl of meaty wild mushroom soup. I speak to her in Norwegian but cannot understand her when she replies. I ask her where she is from.

Annabel waits until the waitress heads back into the kitchen before asking, 'You didn't understand her?'

'She's from Tromsø in the north of Norway and she speaks a dialect almost impossible for me to comprehend. To make it more difficult, there are two official languages in Norway: Bokmål, or Book Norwegian, and Nynorsk, New Norwegian. It's all a bit confusing because New Norwegian is more like Gammelnorsk or Old Norwegian.'

Norway's two languages are a legacy from when Norway and Denmark were in a union from the fourteenth century to 1814 when the Danes backed the wrong side during the Napoleonic Wars and in the settling of accounts, lost Norway to Sweden. Norway's valleys and fjords were so effectively cut off from each other that the local dialects were almost incomprehensible from one valley or fjord to the next. Compiled by Danish colonial administrators to forge a comprehensive language that everyone could understand, Bokmål became the official language of Norway.

After the union with Denmark ended in 1814, many Norwegians denounced Bokmål as a reminder of Norway's inferior position during the union. One of them, a gifted Norwegian linguist called Ivar Åsen, went around to those valleys where the local dialect was most like the original Norwegian, and came up with the written 'New Norwegian' based on how Norwegian was spoken in the districts. Old Norwegian is actually more like modern Icelandic.

Despite the linguistic backlash against the Danes, when Norway separated from Sweden in 1905, the Norwegian people chose a Danish prince, married to Princess Maud, daughter of the British king, to be their Norwegian monarch. He changed his name from Prince Carl to King Haakon VII, and gave his son the name Olav.

Although it is past nine, we see a group of Norwegian hikers setting out with their telemark skis strapped onto their backpacks.

'Well, they're prepared for the worst, whoever they are,' Annabel comments.

I help myself to a heaping plate of *kjøttkaker*, potatoes and vegetables. If we're not as tired as the last few days, we're definitely as hungry. Someone has left *Dagbladet* on the adjacent dining table. I reach over for the newspaper and read the headlines. 'Who's Cameron Diaz?' I ask Annabel.

'She's a famous actress. You're really, *really* out of the loop, aren't you Andrew? What's it say?' Annabel's curiosity momentarily overwhelms her dismay at my lack of knowledge.

'Gives her salary for her next film.' I shrug, no longer interested in reading the article. 'Seems Norwegian folk heroes of today are measured by their financial success. It didn't seem that way ten years ago.' I look out the window. 'Damn!'

Outside it begins to snow heavily.

'Uhhhhh,' I groan.

'What's the matter?'

'I can't get out of bed,' I whimper, 'and my legs won't budge.'

'The other day when I told you the same thing, you said I could take a bus to Bergen and wait for you there,' Annabel reminds me.

'I was joking.'

'There's a road here. You could probably hitchhike out.'

Hitchhiking doesn't seem like a bad option.

'Look, it's not surprising we're feeling the effects of walking several hours a day with heavy backpacks,' Annabel says with a more conciliatory tone. 'It's not like we do this every day.'

'We lead sedentary lives at home,' I complain.

'No we don't. We exercise a *minimum* of an hour a day but I'm in an office all day and you're sitting at your computer writing.' She looks over at me. 'Or at least you're supposed to be sitting at your computer all day writing, and not water-skiing, fishing or lobster diving.'

'Well, now we're putting in a working day of walking.' I spread the map over the bed to examine what we face. It's overcast and the view out of the window still looks as if we could be in Siberia. 'We're heading down today, Annabel, nineteen kilometres. Down is bad.'

Tending to her healing blister she looks over her ankles at the map.

I point at the topographical chart of Jotunheimen. 'We're going down to where it's actually coloured by green bits.'

'Good!' she replies. 'Everything we've been walking in since Memurubu has been either brown over mountains or white over glaciers.'

'But today, today we reach green!' I add triumphantly.

I flop back on the bed. 'Annabel, you're going to have to find someone else to finish the trip with. I can't go on.'

'Oh for heaven's sake. This walk was your idea.'

'I'm too old for this.'

'We've met eighty-year olds hiking around.'

'They're Norwegian. I'm not.'

'They were in gumboots! On Galdhøpiggen! They weren't complaining.'

'So find yourself an eighty-year old Norwegian in gumboots.'

'Okay,' she says, 'where's it hurt?'

'Everywhere. My back feels as if someone just grabbed me

and wrenched the top half of my body in the opposite direction to the bottom half.'

She starts laughing as she wraps her ankle in tape to protect the blister. 'You're just one big, non-coping mess today, aren't you?'

'How much punishment can a body take?' I ask, rhetorically. 'Can you imagine,' I say dramatically as I snuggle under the duvet, 'we're actually intentionally, and of our own free will, going to launch ourselves back out into that snow and ice and rain, and walk nineteen kilometres in the cold carrying heavy backpacks. We need our heads examined.'

'It's not raining . . . ' she looks out the window, ' . . . *that* much.'

'This reminds me of Scott's diary in the Antarctic where he says he's getting weaker and weaker every day.'

Annabel replies slowly, 'You don't have lead poisoning.' She dresses and leaves me lying under the duvet. 'I may be gone for some time,' she says, paraphrasing Oates when he walked out into the Antarctic cold.

I really don't want to get out of this big, comfortable bed covered in a fluffy, warm duvet when all I can see out the window is mist, bits of glacier and occasional glimpses of a frozen lake covered in snow. I get out of bed and stare outside. It's so desolate and quiet it's lovely. In fact, I've decided I can hardly wait to get out there.

Our boots are perfectly dry for the first time. We pack our backpacks and at the front door I ask, 'Could you help me put my boots on? I can't bend over enough to reach my feet and do up my shoelaces.'

'Pitiable,' Annabel mumbles as she bends down to do up my shoelaces. A year ago she had to help me do everything, even put on my underwear. But walking, as well as swimming, is one of the best things one can do for an injured back. Five months after my accident, in November, I went off on my own for a month to walk from Lukla to Everest Base Camp and back. I had promised myself, while lying in hospital, that I'd get well enough to trek in the Himalayas before Christmas. There were many times the target had seemed unrealistic, and even when I flew off, Annabel wasn't sure I'd cope with the long flight let alone the trek. Yet when I came back, the stiffness in my back had largely gone after four weeks of walking.

It's the first day in Jotunheimen that's been warm enough to set off without wearing gloves. A couple of hours later, we pass two tents beside the path. The campers, the only people we have met today, are just waking up although it is midday.

'How's it been?' I ask.

'Cold and wet.' They are from Poland and have taken the same route as us but didn't climb Glittertind because of the bad weather. 'It's so light we sometimes walk until midnight and then sleep in, like today. We were woken up several times during the night because of the icefalls from the glacier. They rumble like thunder.' They point at Smørstabbreen Glacier hanging over us. 'We have been free camping everywhere except at Spiterstulen where they chased us to the site one kilometre from the lodge. We have two more weeks in Norway but we want to see some sunshine,' the only one of the four who can speak English says emphatically.

The silence of these steep-sided mountains is awesome. Although everywhere around us there are glaciers, there is indeed less snow underfoot and more rock. Before us are the tops of the Hurrungane Mountains, jagged peaks and steep protrusions too high to have been crushed smooth under massive glaciers. Underfoot is either bedrock, scraped flat by the glaciers, or crushed boulder gardens where the weight of the glacier has smashed the rock into giant jigsaw pieces.

We sit by a turquoise lake formed by a small dam. Five sandwiches and a chocolate bar later, as I relax lying back on a rock, I tell Annabel, 'I really like walking.'

She starts laughing.

'No, I do,' I reiterate. 'Except first thing in the morning when I can hardly move my bones.'

'Oh really?' she replies.

Descending below the dam it suddenly becomes warmer. There are fewer and fewer patches of snow to trudge through and the first ferns are good signs of things to come.

'We've hit the "green" area depicted on the map,' I inform Annabel. There are grasses around us, and the first flowers too. We hear birds singing. When we left Leirvassbu this morning it was like Siberia, and now suddenly we are in the Scottish Highlands. We come across the first isolated trees and more flowers, and then enter woods protecting a thick carpet of yellow buttercups and purple cranesbill. Winter avalanches have flattened swathes of birch trees, allowing in the sunlight. I pull out my mountain flora reference book and start looking up the names of the flowers I used to know but have forgotten, like reacquainting myself with the names of good friends. A bewildering variety of saxifrage, cinquefoil, buttercups, campion, chickweed, orchids, butterwort, lousewort, delicate speedwells, gentian primrose and forget-me-nots are evident everywhere. I've never seen such an abundance of flowers in Norway before. It must be because the weather has been so cold and the early blossoming flowers are late.

'It's like entering a secret garden,' Annabel suggests enthusiastically. 'You can smell the flowers. And just listen to those birds singing.'

It becomes very warm and we stop to strip off layers of clothing. Down the steep 'V' of Utladalen Valley are lines of waterfalls tumbling into the valley. Several U-shaped valleys cut into the main gorge, which is narrow and has mountains on either side rising vertically a thousand metres.

The last stretch of the route through the dense meadow birch and blueberry birch forest seems to take forever. Unlike the previous huts, which we spotted a good hour before we reached them, we come across the Skogadalsboen DNT hut unexpectedly as we exit the forest into a clearing. At the same time, the sun comes out, illuminating a thick mantle of yellow flowers. It's as if summer has finally arrived.

I look at Annabel and a smile spreads across her face. 'This is more what I expected,' she says looking around her.

It *is* a postcard-perfect scene: the sun is bright, the greens iridescent, the sky suddenly blue, the festival of colourful flowers impossibly perfect.

Annabel says, bending down to smell the profusion of flowers, 'It's as if we'd walked out of winter this morning, had an hour of spring, and now we're in mid-summer. It's amazing.'

'It's like that in Norway every year when winter changes to spring and then summer; it happens so fast you'd hardly know it's happened.'

Utladalen Valley

The Utladalen Valley, despite its proximity to the Sognefjord at the bottom of the gorge, was originally colonised from the mountains, not from the sea. People have lived in this area for several thousand years. The first farmers, who settled here some 3,000 years BC, were originally hunters following the reindeer herds. They combined farming with trapping and evidence of their presence are the wild reindeer pit-traps, of which there are still many scattered around the valleys.

Because there are no roads, there's a distinct sense of isolation here at Skogadalsbøen. We walk towards several staff sprawled on a wooden deck in various states of undress, soaking in the sun's rays. Lars, the manager, tells us, 'Because it's been raining in Oslo for months, they think it's raining everywhere else, so we probably won't have many visitors tonight.' He nods and looks at the spectacular scenery around us. 'I've been here for seventeen summers now and this is what I live for: three summer months running this hut.' He is slight, tanned, has thinning blonde hair, refined features and an easy laugh.

'And the rest of the year?' I ask.

'Work as a financial consultant.' He explains, 'But every summer I rent these facilities from DNT and run it as a business and try and turn over a profit.'

'How do you bring in the supplies?'

'Helicopter, three times a year.'

'And all the staff here work for you?'

'Some of them have been here longer than I have.' He shrugs. 'For us, it's a way of life.'

I'd happily spend my summers here too, on evenings like this, with the fresh mountain air, the spectacular view down the valley, the surrounding Alp-like peaks, never mind the flowers. Lars seems particularly relaxed and if he's running this as a business, it certainly doesn't seem that way. He leads us in to the reception and shows us two glass paperweights on the counter. 'Feel how heavy they are.'

'They're like lead weights,' Annabel says.

'Lead crystal.' He laughs. 'Two Czechs came here one day and stayed for a couple of hours while their clothes dried in the drying room and then gave me these glass paperweights in exchange.' Like many Norwegians, Lars' English is perfectly colloquial.

'Their packs must have weighed a ton if they were disbursing glass paperweights to every Norwegian who did them a favour,' she comments.

The dinner is the best we've had so far, the vegetables varied and fresh, lamb with garlic. Even the water is noticeably good. After dinner, Annabel and I sit outside on a deck basking in the last rays, lazily admiring the view far down the deep valley before the sun dips below the mountains towering overhead.

'What do they call that long, thin flag?' She points at the tall, white flagpole flying a variation of the Norwegian flag that flutters in the breeze, amidst verdant grass, brilliant flowers, green pine and birch forests.

'In Norwegian it's called a "*vimpel*". Don't know what it's called in English.'

'It's like a medieval flag from when knights jousted.'

Alone in the six-bunk room at almost midnight, it is still bright outside our window, and quiet. Annabel lies in the lower bed of one bunk, I am in another. She asks me what I can recall from reading the night before, but I am already dreaming of flowers.

The sun is up and the birds are singing and it is a sunny, clear blue sky when I go outside for a pee. It's also three in the morning, I realise, looking at my watch.

'What do you want to do this morning?' I ask some hours later when I have woken again and can see Annabel lying there with her eyes open.

'Nothing,' she replies.

'Seriously.'

'Seriously,' she laughs. 'I don't want to think about it for an hour.'

I head outside and watch as Lars hoists the Norwegian flag, not just the *vimpel*. 'On days like this we are so proud to be Norwegian we have to put up our flag,' he tells me. There are a lot of proud Norwegians in Norway, flying a lot of flags during the summer; sometimes it seems as if every home or hut has to fly the flag as a matter of course.

A hiker dripping with perspiration removes his pack and asks Lars for a beer despite the early hour, and then collapses on the grass outside after exchanging a few words. I can't quite place his accent. After breakfast Annabel and I see the same hiker passed out in the sunlight on a stone wall. Lars whispers to me that he's a Finn and he's just re-hydrated his dehydrated body with several beers. A knife, considerably longer than the ones Norwegians carry, dangles from his belt.

In the sharp light I can see a herd of reindeer moving on the brilliant Maraldalsbreen Glacier on the opposite side of the valley. It's such a spectacular setting we decide to have a rest day and spend another night here. Annabel wears her running shoes, which give the blister on her heel a chance to fully heal. With only a lightweight day-pack each, we decide to climb the mountain behind us. There are two crumbling stone cottages 100 metres above our hut, surrounded by a pasture thick with yellow buttercups and purple cranesbill. We cross a bridge spanning a peaceful turquoise pool and head up the Skogadalen Valley before abandoning the path to climb up Uranosa, aiming for the 1,427-metre summit. We clamber steeply on bare, wet rock festooned in moss with a small waterfall slithering alongside.

From the top of Uranosa the air is so sharp we can see far up steep-sided Skogadalen Valley, Uradalen Valley and all the way down the Utladalen Valley to what must be the mountains lining Sognefjord and perhaps even beyond. The Utla gorge is so precipitous Lars told us, only six people have ever walked up to Skogadalsbøen along the bottom of the entire Utladalen Valley. From the perspective of this peak, it is readily apparent why. This is one of the deepest valleys in Norway, a continuation of the glacier-gouged 200 kilometre-long Sognefjord, stretching into the heart of the Jotunheimen. We are surrounded, in our immediate vicinity, by some fifty peaks over 2,000 metres high and scores of hanging side valleys with streams toppling several hundred metres into the gorge.

On the summit, we shelter from the breeze behind a large boulder and eat our packed lunches, treating ourselves to a row of chocolate. With bellies full and the sun lulling us, we fall asleep on a soft bed of reindeer moss to the vague rumble of rivers and waterfalls far, far below.

An hour later we awaken to gradually make our way down the mountain. Annabel takes the lead but with my tender knees I have to prod and probe my way down, assisted by my scavenged walking stick. I stop often to take photographs of glacier poppies with spectacular mountains, glaciers and valleys as a backdrop. It takes me longer to get down than it did to climb up.

'What happened?' Annabel demands when I finally reach her near the bottom.

'I can't go any faster, my good knee hurts so much every time I step down.'

'Didn't you hear me calling?'

'No.'

'I was worried about you, I thought your knee might have collapsed or you'd fallen over the edge.'

After a shower at Skogadalsbøen, and despite the sunny weather outside, I sit by the fire in the living room and search through a stack of old DNT annual reports looking for English entries. William Cecil Slingsby is a regular contributor and, as were other wealthy young Englishmen of the time, a frequent visitor to Norway. Although Norwegians nowadays are known for their love of the outdoors, it was the visiting British anglers, huntsmen, mountaineers and hikers who inspired Norwegians to take to the mountains as a form of recreation.

In the 1881 DNT yearbook, Slingsby comments: 'Some Vandals have proposed to put little steamboats on Tyin, Bygdin and Gjende, but if this ever be done, I will visit these haunts no more. The very thought . . . on Lake Gjende, makes me shudder.'

I read the entry aloud to Annabel.

'If he could see the accommodation at Memurubu now, and the boat ferrying tourists backwards and forwards on Lake Gjende . . .' Annabel comments.

'He'd shudder.'

'I reckon.'

I read another of his entries where he wonders, 'When will the ladies begin to climb Stolsnastind and Knutshulstin instead of the hackneyed Galdhøpiggen, or rather in addition to it? My sister's ascent of Glittertind in 1875 I am glad to see has led other ladies to follow her example.'

Sitting comfortably in front of the fireplace with another DNT yearbook, this one from 1893, I read Slingsby's comments about this area: 'We saw as is usually the case on the wooded heights above Utladal, plenty of fresh traces of bear.'

But there are no bears now, or very few. The closest thing to a bear is Lars' Newfoundlander dog lying in the sun like a black bear rug.

Slingsby describes Skogadalsbøen, presumably the two tiny stone cottages above this one, as 'this most comfortable and luxurious of alpine huts'. He should see the hut now.

Slingsby is not only struck by the beauty of the mountains and the luxury of the *seter* huts, but also by the loveliness of the young Norwegian women on their mountain farms looking after the cows for the summer.

I read the history of this hut – how DNT, in 1870, with a membership of only 600, decided that a refuge should be built here, although it wasn't until 1883 that the money was set aside for its construction. In 1886 a builder in Lom, a community on the other side of Jotunheimen, agreed to build the hut, transporting the material by horse and sled over the mountains during the winters.

After dinner, Annabel and I wander around outside, too reluctant to give up this perfect summer evening. Eventually we turn in to the six-bunk room, which we have to ourselves again. She opens the scavenged paperback and begins reading by the light coming through the window. Wafting on the breeze, the stillness of the midsummer night is punctuated by the rushing sound of waterfalls and rivers . . .

'Andrew William . . . Are you still awake?'

When I hear my name, I manage to wake up, barely.

'What's been happening?' Annabel tests me.

'Those . . . strange, furry creatures with red eyes . . . are in the room . . . '

'That was ages ago. What's happened since then?'

'I don't know.'

Patiently she gives me a quick synopsis of what's happened and then continues reading.

Sometime later I hear Annabel rustling in her sleeping bag.

'I'm still awake,' I mutter.

'Of course you are, dear.'

I look at my watch. It's six in the morning.

Lars sees me heading out to the toilets with a particularly wicked bed-head.

'Fried eggs and bacon for breakfast?' he offers, sitting on a bench reading a week-old newspaper.

'Sure.'

By the time Annabel and I stumble in for breakfast with my hair plastered down so I look less like a punk hedgehog, Lars has cooked us bacon and eggs with fried tomato, wild mushrooms and toast.

A Dutch couple sits with us at our table. 'The Norwegian coffee is terrible,' one of them sputters.

'That's because you like it so strong in Holland the spoon stands upright in it,' I reply.

'No,' he corrects, 'we like it so strong the spoon melts into the coffee.'

When we say goodbye to Lars and the staff sitting outside basking in the sun, Lars informs us happily, 'It's still raining in Oslo.'

After an hour and a half of fast-paced walking, we come across a solitary young Englishman sitting on a ridge of rock with a commanding view down the valley. We greet him, talk, and then sit down next to him.

'Hope you don't mind us plonking ourselves right next to you when there's all this empty space to occupy,' I comment, too late for him to say no without seeming like a grump.

'No, not at all. I've been camping alone and I hardly meet anyone.'

'Neither do we,' Annabel says laughing.

'But you're in a hut every night,' the Englishman says.

She indicates me with a nod of the head. 'He's too tired to talk to anyone else by the time we get to a hut and it's the best I can do to get him to utter a few monosyllables to me.'

We talk for a while and then the Englishman leaves.

When he's out of earshot, I confess, 'That's how *I* usually travel around: on my own. It's a lot more fun being with you even if I'm not a bundle of energy in the evenings or a conversational guru.'

We both enjoy walking in silence and tend to leave a certain amount of physical space between us. But to guarantee Annabel keeps within hailing distance, I keep the chocolate. Unfortunately the temptation as Guardian of the Chocolate is far too great and an hour later, with the chocolate burning a hole in my pocket, I secrete a row into my mouth without sharing it.

Crossing a remaining drift of snow, a ptarmigan pretends it is injured and flies pathetically in front of us, distracting us from its nest. It flutters helplessly until we have crossed the patch of snow, and then it capably flies back to the top of the snowdrift where it probably has a nest.

Walking and hiking can be addictive. If I could, I'd spend at least a month walking with a heavy backpack every year. This annual, solipsistic migratory passage through mountains and forests is my own way of meditating, sorting through the mental baggage accumulated during the year. Along with swimming daily, these long walks have helped me to recover quickly from my spinal injury last year.

For the first time since Heidal, pine roots obstruct the path. As we descend, we see evidence of dead pine trees and they become increasingly numerous the further we go down the valley. 'What's happened here?' Annabel asks when I point the dead trees out to her.

'The aluminium factory in Øvre Årdal. It's the fluorides or something.'

We walk into the flat area that is Vettismorki. Several turf-roofed huts straddle a brook. There is a new, self-service hut here but I didn't bother collecting the standard key from the DNT offices in Oslo. I didn't think ahead. We locate the charming hut and can look inside, but despite searching in obvious places, can't find the key.

'Perhaps there's someone around in one of the huts,' I suggest, sitting dejectedly on a plank of wood in front of the brook. So as not to frighten anyone with my unkempt appearance, I elect Annabel to go and search.

'Well?' I ask Annabel when she returns twenty minutes later.

'Found a woman sunbathing outside her father's hut but she doesn't know where he keeps the key to the hut either.'

We sit pondering what to do. Although it's a warm, sunny evening, it's also a long walk to the next accommodation.

Giving up the search, and to compensate for our lack of success, we finish our chocolate.

Then we see the woman that Annabel had spoken to approaching us – brown as a berry with a shock of blonde hair, wearing a scant bikini and a big smile across her face. 'One of the owners of the huts here has arrived back, and he had the key, so I can open it for you,' she volunteers, apparently as happy as we are that she can let us in.

Inside, the new cabin is spotless, with fresh wild flowers thoughtfully left in a bottle on the table by the previous occupants. There are food supplies, two wood-burning stoves, a kitchen, a living room and dining room combined with wooden furniture, and three bedrooms with two bunk beds complete with duvets and pillows in each.

'Amazing,' Annabel keeps repeating as we walk around the hut. 'It's incredible,' she repeats, 'there's a heap of dry and tinned food in the cupboards. Do we just help ourselves?'

'Write down what you take, and then before we leave, we add up the bill and put the money in the envelopes provided and drop it in that metal box.'

'And people don't cheat?' she asks.

'Nope.'

'That's almost as unbelievable as finding such a fine, well-equipped hut all to ourselves in the first place.'

'Norwegians wouldn't cheat the DNT hut system any more than they would stomp on their grandmother's grave.'

Three full buckets of water have been left conveniently beside the kitchen counter. We boil a pot of water over a gas stove and mix in a package of hot chocolate powder from the supplies on a shelf, then sit outside nursing the hot drink, more than satisfied with how the day has worked out.

'Stick with me baby,' I say, looking through the hut's guest book as we stretch out in the early evening sun.

'Stick with you?' Annabel laughs. 'Better you stick with me. If it weren't for my effort going around seeing if anyone else was in the other huts, we wouldn't be sitting here right now drinking hot chocolate.'

That keeps me quiet for a while until I see an entry, which I read out loud.

'*Kjære Gud . . . vi har hatt det så godt.*'

'What's that mean?'

'Dear God, we have had it so good.' It's not the first time I've heard that heartfelt sentiment expressed by a Norwegian. They've got a point. Looking around us at the blue sky, the mountains with their cascading waterfalls, this clearing by a stream, the Norwegian *vimpel* flapping gently in the breeze, it's not hard to agree. In fact, the United Nations has just ranked Norway at the top of its 'quality-of-life index' measuring a nation's appeal by considering what its nationals can expect in life: health care, life expectancy and educational levels beyond just pure economic growth in terms of per capita income.

'Let's take a *tiki* tour,' Annabel suggests.

We wander around the clearing that is Vettismorki, the dozen wooden huts with turf roofs decorated with wild flowers. It is so warm it is almost hot. After a dinner of tinned stew, we sit outside on the steps and I read to Annabel an English entry in the Ingjerdbu hut's guest book made on 9 July 1995:

> Thanks so much for providing weary travelers with a beautiful place. We walked from Skogadalsbøen yesterday past Vormeli across the gorge from which our great grandmother and great-great grandmother emigrated in 1867. She, her siblings, and her parents came to western Wisconsin where they prospered. But Utladalen must have been in their hearts, as it is now in ours. *Tusen Takk for alt.*

> Edi Thorstensen

> Martin Thorstensen

'We passed Vormeli yesterday on the way down,' I remind Annabel. 'It was that tiny patch of open ground hugging the other side of the valley facing south where it catches the sun.'

'Amazing anyone would even think of farming it.' For a New Zealander from the South Island where farms are generally measured in hundreds to thousands, and even hundreds of thousands, of hectares, it must seem very strange to Annabel indeed.

'Arable land was in short supply in Norway before Norwegians started emigrating to America, so younger offspring of poor farmers had to farm increasingly inaccessible patches of land. In those days it was impossible to descend the valley from Vormeli so the inhabitants actually had to climb back over the mountains.'

'How do you know?'

'DNT has a self-service hut there. I read the description. The last person to farm Vormeli left in 1868.' Emigration to the USA began in 1840 and waves of immigrants peaked around 1870, 1880, 1903 and 1923. More than 800,000 Norwegians immigrated to America. Only Ireland had a higher proportional rate of emigration. Like the Irish, there are few Norwegians now who do not have a close relative living in the United States.

I find a sad entry on 3 August 1997 and translate for Annabel.

> Finally at Ingjerdbu again, on the anniversary of Jørgen's last tour to Vettismorki. Here in Ingjerdbu he had a lovely evening before he started off for home at Vetti, at 23.10. And he never arrived home. His death date was fourth of August 1996.
>
> But you ARE here Jørgen . . .
>
> Greetings from your daughters Marie and Ingjerd, they will be here soon.
>
> Thanks for the burdens that you carried
>
> Thanks for the memories we have got,
>
> Berit and your Gordon setter, Arak, who was with Jørgen that night

Lars at Skogadalsbøen told me that Jørgen Vetti was the man who had built this hut. It's not a DNT hut but part of the DNT system. It belongs to the Vetti family, and is a memorial to Jørgen, even if it does appear for all intents and purposes as if it was a DNT hut.

When it gets late, we light firewood in the iron stove and the warmth from the fire makes us sleepy. 'The only bad thing about coming here in the summer is we won't see the northern lights, the aurora borealis. I've seen them lots of times in Canada, but never as spectacular as here,' I tell Annabel. 'Once in Heidal, about October, I saw crimson red lights the colour of blood waving in the breeze like curtains seen from below.'

We head to one of the rooms and both take adjacent bottom bunks. Annabel opens the windows wide to let in the fresh summer air and wriggles into her sleeping bag. It's light enough outside to read from the novel without using the solar-powered electric light.

'What a perfect morning!' I exclaim when we wake up. Through the open windows we have pristine views of mountains and forests. It was so quiet during the midsummer bright night and we slept well. We sit on the porch steps in the warm light, sipping coffee and eating several steaming pancakes hot off the griddle, with margarine and honey melted on top.

Reluctant to leave, we clean the hut until it is as immaculate as we found it – chop wood for the wood-burning stove, fetch buckets of drinking water from the nearby brook, wash the floors.

Despite being mid-July, it's such a crisp autumn-like morning with no humidity in the air it seems we can see forever. We follow the brook out of Vettismorki, trying to avoid stepping on the buttercups that grow everywhere. Within a short time we reach the Vettisfossen Falls, the highest free-fall waterfalls remaining in Norway after other waterfalls were dammed or diverted for hydropower. Norway used to have nine of the highest waterfalls in the world. Now they have two.

The Vettiselva River spouts out of the top of a cliff, free falling 260 metres to the valley bottom. We drop our packs and walk timorously to the edge of the precipice. My feet tingle and I have a sensation of vertigo as I stare over the sheer drop to get a photograph of the whole thing, but it's difficult, even with the twenty-millimetre wide-angle lens.

'This was the last walk Jørgen made, from the cabin to his farm below,' I comment.

'I guess dying suddenly of a heart attack while walking home from your cabin is a pretty good way to go.'

'I dunno. Dying peacefully in your sleep would be good.'

'Thing to do, Andrew, is spend as much time as possible sleeping so you increase the odds of dying peacefully in your sleep.'

'I don't think so.'

'Didn't think you would.'

From the path descending from the falls, Annabel points out a tiny farm below. 'You'd wonder how they can farm that tiny patch of land.'

'They'll log a few trees from their forest, keep a few goats and/or sheep, a few dairy cows, a field for hay.' Most of the small-scale farmers have to have other jobs as a source of income and government subsidies keep them going. They get paid to cut their hay, and are given a subsidy for every animal raised. But they couldn't do that indefinitely if they were a part of the European Union, which is why Norwegian farmers and fishermen voted against joining the EU in two referendums; they're so protected by these subsidies they couldn't compete in the real world.

'It'd make a nice hobby farm,' Annabel says.

'Farms can only be bought by farmers, although the children of a farmer can inherit the farm, even if they aren't farmers themselves. The government determines the price based on the productive value of the farm, not on the value of the buildings. It's a government policy to protect farms as farms; otherwise wealthy urbanites from Oslo would buy up farms like this and use them as holiday homes and not bother to actually work them. Having said that, the Government had to change the rules recently because there weren't enough young farmers willing to buy these smaller, marginally productive farms and many of the smaller ones would just sit there and deteriorate. Now the rules have changed and if a farm is less than something like two hectares, you can buy it, even if you aren't a farmer.'

We descend the steep path to Vetti and encounter a group of French tourists who have bussed in to the farm at the top of the track and are now hiking up to the falls. The tour leader asks us where we have come from.

'Gjendesheim,' I answer.

'That's on the other side of Jotunheimen,' he replies.

'We've walked through the mountains.' The words come easily enough, but even as I impart this bit of information, I realise that's exactly what we've done and it seems a bit of an achievement.

'How long did that take?' he asks.

I count the days on my fingers. 'Eight days.'

At Vetti, we stop for waffles and coffee at the farm. It is Berit, Jørgen's widow, who serves us. She and her sister and mother are so nice we want to wrap them up and take them home. I let her know how much we enjoyed staying at their hut. She smiles, but says sadly, 'My husband had only finished it a short time before he died.'

Walking down the valley, Annabel looks up at the mountains tightly enclosing the farm. 'They must have darkness all winter when the sun wouldn't ever get over the tops of the ridges surrounding their farm, and then in the summer it rains a lot.' She continues down the farm road into the depths of the narrow gorge.

I dawdle, taking photographs of the fields of flowers.

'Rattle your dags!' Annabel calls when she sees me talking to some Dutch tourists. 'We've got a bus and a ferry to catch!'

Continuing along the farm road towards Øvre Årdal, the cliffs on either side are so impossibly steep I have to crane my neck way back to see the sky above. Although it is now midday, the sun still hasn't appeared over the rock face. The boulders at the bottom of the gorge are the size of mansions and are a reminder of how vulnerable we are should something as small as a pebble drop from above.

When I mention this to her, Annabel says, pointing at a cave on the other side of the gorge, 'There's a good place to shelter.'

'Yeah, but you'd have to cross a raging torrent first.'

'That's a point.'

We reach the parking place at Hjelle and hope from here to hitch into Øvre Årdal. Public transportation no longer runs along this dead end. There's another long, seven-kilometre walk remaining down the asphalt road and we've already walked several kilometres this morning down the gravel stretch. A tiny car with a couple sitting in the front drives by, the driver ignoring our outstretched thumbs. I read the license plates. 'Bloody Dutch!' I comment as they continue past us without stopping to offer us a lift.

'That's not very nice,' Annabel says, reacting to my expletive.

'They could have given us a ride.'

'It was a tiny car with only two seats, and the back was full of stuff,' she says, defending the tourists.

'Still . . . '

Twenty minutes later the Dutch driver returns, turns around in the road and pulls alongside us asking, 'Can I give you a ride?'

Annabel looks at me before replying, 'Yes, thank you.'

'Where are you going?'

'To Øvre Årdal.'

'I'm staying at the camping place down the road but that's okay, I can give you a ride to Øvre Årdal.'

Annabel was right. There's hardly any room in the car. We throw our packs into the back and I climb in with them while Annabel sits in the only passenger seat, up front.

He drops us off in the centre of Øvre Årdal, a major metropolis after our last two weeks in the mountains. We sit on a bench at the bus stop and watch the locals. 'Apart from the mountains, we could be almost anywhere in small-town America,' I comment to Annabel as the same Harley Davidson passes by for the tenth time in as many minutes.

'Look at the hoon-mobile,' observes Annabel, as a car with sawn-off muffler and jacked-up rear-end and fat tyres cruises up and down the one and only main street. There's an abundance of young girls pushing prams. One of them stands next to us, waiting for a bus.

'She's dyed her hair black!' Annabel whispers. 'You can see the blonde roots.'

'So?'

'Everyone else in the world is trying to look like a Scandinavian blonde and here they're trying not to.' Despite the jet-black dyed hair she has pale skin and when she turns around, startling blue eyes. Pulling a face, Annabel hands me a plastic bottle of Solo, a fizzy orange drink the Norwegian equivalent of a Fanta. 'Doesn't taste as good as the mountain water we've been drinking.'

Sognefjord

Because the bus to Bergen has no one else on board we take the two front seats, normally reserved for older passengers. The coach is immaculate, with plastic flowers in a vase on the dashboard. Cold drinks are available from a refrigerator beside the driver. On schedule to the minute, we pass Årdalstangen along the edge of the Årdalsfjord, a glacial extension of the sheer-sided Utladalen Valley we have just walked down. I've never seen this finger of the Sognefjord and am impressed by the sheerness of the flanking mountains. By contrast, the fjord's surface is smooth as a mirror. I see the backs of three whales break the surface and point them out to Annabel.

'Where?'

'Watch. They'll come back up again. You'll see their dorsal fins or the puff of spray as they breathe.'

'Are you sure they're whales?'

'The Norwegians call them *nise*. About the size of a small dolphin but they have blunt snouts unlike dolphins.'

'Like a porpoise?'

'Maybe they are porpoises,' I concede. 'I've never really known for sure and no one I've ever asked can enlighten me of the English equivalent.'

We don't see them again although we crane around in our seats to try to catch another glimpse. We pass plenty of tiny isolated farms; white wooden houses with mossy slate roofs squeezed on patches of pasture on the edge of the fjord with boathouses and small fishing boats hanging off moorings.

'What are they doing in the fields?' Annabel cranes around in her seat as we pass a small farm in the cramped space between the road and the fjord.

'Cutting the hay and throwing it over wires spread between poles to dry.'

'With scythes? It's medieval.'

'There's no other way. You can't get a tractor on a tiny patch of sloping land like that.'

'I don't know how they can make a living at it, although I saw the same thing in Switzerland about a decade ago.'

'A bit of hay, some goats or sheep, a cow or two, supplemented with some fish and a lot of government subsidies. It's a political decision to encourage people living in the rural areas to stay there. Otherwise, much of Norway's farmland would revert back to wilderness. Many of the coastal and island settlements would probably slowly die as the younger generations moved to the cities. Besides, Norway's economy is basically export-oriented: oil, fisheries, natural gas, metals, timber products, shipping. Most of that is based along the coastline so that's another good reason to spend so much money on bridges and tunnels linking these isolated communities.' We pass another four white-haired Norwegians laboriously throwing cut hay over strands of wire.

It had always surprised me to witness the incredible capital outlays invested in the infrastructure in the rural districts, especially the north, when Oslo and Bergen seemed to require so much roadwork themselves. More recently those overdue improvements seem to be happening into the cities too, but for many years rural areas were a priority. Oslo and Bergen definitely do not acquire the lion's share of government spending on infrastructure and both cities levy tolls on traffic entering their municipal boundaries, not only as a sensible deterrent to traffic to minimise noise and air pollution, but also as a local source of funding. It reflects the Norwegian sense of fairness that expenditure in the cities came only after massive investments had already been made in the rural areas. Now Oslo has a new airport and a fast train to and from the airport, but both were long overdue.

We stop at Fodnes where a ferry awaits. There are, or at least were, some 230 ferry services within Norway. But those numbers are dwindling fast with the construction of tunnels under the sea and bridges over it.

We exit the bus and climb onto the open deck of the ferry. Dozens of leather-clad bikers lie back and face the sun. On a day like today, with winding Norwegian roads through spectacular scenery, a motorbike would be an ideal way to travel. I linger, admiring the sleek machines, but I'm not tempted, not any more. I touch the bumpy, bony protrusion under the skin. Annabel was right; I can feel it. The radiologist told me when he showed me the CAT scans of the burst L–2 vertebra that I was lucky not to have been paralysed. I'm a couple of centimetres shorter than my medical indicated a year earlier, but apart from stiffness in the mornings, my recovery has been better than expected. The wrecked Suzuki, although repaired, sits forgotten in a corner of the garage.

The ferry leaves the dock and we cross the shimmering fjord towards Kaupanger. In the middle of the fjord, I see more whales and point them out, telling Annabel to watch where the seagulls are. This time Annabel sees them too and we search for more. They are easy to pick out when the sparkling surface of the fjord is like glass. On days like this, you want to grab every perfect instant and keep it forever close to your heart.

On the other side of the fjord, we re-board the bus and drive off the ferry through a three-kilometre tunnel opening out to a road lined with high fencing.

'See the fencing?' I point to the sides of the road. 'That's for elk, what us Canadians call moose, although the animal's not as big and doesn't have such massive *gevir*. I'm not sure what *gevir* is exactly in English; horns, I guess. The fencing is to prevent them from crossing the road here.' The elk, or moose, are not only a hazard to cars, but are also about the only thing stopping Norwegian trains nowadays. Norwegian State Railways, the NSB, have snow clearing down to such an art that even in the worst snowstorm, the trains continue to operate. But when the moose start moving along the railway lines, the NSB have to use heli-copters to clear the animals from the tracks ahead of the trains.

We slow down a couple of minutes later in Kaupanger where a bus waits by the road for us. We board the connecting bus, the only passengers, and are driven the short distance to the dock where another ferry awaits.

'It's unbelievable,' Annabel says.

'What?'

'The whole transportation network in Norway.'

When I first arrived here, travelling around Norway in the middle of the dark winter, figuring out cycling or hiking routes for tourists coming into Norway, I'd be scared I'd get off a ferry and the connecting bus wouldn't be there, and I'd freeze to death by the roadside. But there would always be a bus or a ferry waiting, even if I'd be the only passenger getting on. 'That's one of the best parts of Norway; you've got all this nature and yet it's so easily accessible by public transportation.'

The ferry reverses out of Kaupanger's natural harbour, postcard-perfect with its bowl-shaped hill of verdant farms, lines of cut hay drying in the sun, and neatly aligned rows of apple and cherry trees. Despite its northern latitudes, the Gulf Stream keeps the western coastline of Norway relatively mild all year.

The deck rumbles satisfyingly as we pick up speed. When I was a child growing up in Asia and Africa, our family often moved from one posting to another by Norwegian cargo ship. With its limited space for half a dozen passengers it was an ideal way to travel and to see the world, stopping for days at obscure ports to unload and load cargo. And it was probably then that I first developed a fondness for ships, and Norwegians. The Norwegian officers and seamen missed their own families and as surrogate kids, we had the run of the ship.

We find a couple of spare chairs on the deck of the ferry and, surrounded by tourists for the first time in eight days, hear other languages being spoken around us rather than Norwegian. Instead of *Dagbladet* and *VG*, we see copies of the *International Herald Tribune*. Norwegians are well read. The average Norwegian over fifteen years of age spends more than an hour a day reading newspapers. In fact, Norwegians read more newspapers per capita than any other nationality – an average of 1.8 newspapers per household. Perhaps this is because television as the rest of the world knows it, with its multitude of channels brought by cable and satellite, is still a relatively new phenomenon here. Like other small nations in Europe, I've always been impressed with the Norwegians' wide knowledge of current world affairs.

As we head into the main Sognefjord, I spot another pod of porpoises, but then we mistake several seals for porpoises until we get closer and see their rounded human-like heads and sad, dark eyes.

'Be perfect for sailing here,' Annabel observes, a keen windsurfer prone to heading out only when there are gale-force winds blowing.

'Until you want to moor; you'd throw your anchor overboard and it'd never stop dropping. The fjord's as deep as the mountains are high.' I look at the almost vertical cliffs on either side of the fjord. 'Picture a glacier a thousand metres higher than us, carving out the bedrock another thousand metres below us, extending some two or three hundred kilometres to the open sea. Imagine what that would look like!'

We see scallop farms along the shoreline – a new phenomenon – more seals, and yet more porpoises. I've never seen as many in one day; it must be the hot weather and the mirror-smooth water. The ferry lists around a corner off the winding, mighty Sognefjord, and heads down towards the entrance to the Aurlandsfjord and then, as if in a maze, it veers once again down the Nærøyfjord, the narrowest fjord in the world, according to the locals. We lean against the rails and survey the dark blue fjord bordered by green mountains bursting with waterfalls from melting snow and glaciers. The light is intense. Small farmhouses are nestled amongst patches of brilliant green pasture, overlooked by precipitous rock faces and the inevitable waterfalls that plunge like tap water gushing out of faucets only to disappear again into hidden crevices before plummeting vertically the remaining distance down to the sea.

In the afternoon light, the shadowy side of the fjord is dark shades of blue, the tops of the fortress-like mountains casting oblique columns of shadow down to the water. The other side of the fjord is still brightly lit, waterfalls sparkling in the sunlight as they tumble down vertical, craggy mountains to the occasional iridescent green ribbon of pasture at the fjord's edge.

A small collection of houses lies on the starboard, shaded side of the fjord. 'That's Dyrdal where the youngest person in the community is supposed to be more than eighty.' A few minutes later, on the sunny flank of the mountains, we pass the farm Styvi and the old postal route path that formed part of the communications network between Oslo and Bergen from 1660 until 1860, when steamers were introduced.

The danger to many of these farmhouses is as much from avalanches coming down the *other* side of the fjord as it is from above. Some farmhouses have massive stone walls on the *lower* side of the farmhouses, not above, to protect them from the blast of wind in front of an avalanche coming down the other side and *across* the fjord. People at Gudvangen have told me those winds have knocked herds of goats right across the fjord like so many skittles in a bowling alley.

'It's hard to believe we were still in Jotunheimen this morning. It's been such a long, perfect day,' Annabel reflects as the ferry skirts around a cruise ship to dock at Gudvangen, one of the major centres of tourism in Norway despite the fact that there can't be more than a couple of dozen permanent residents.

When I arrived in Norway at the end of 1990, the two main cities of Norway, Oslo and Bergen, were connected by road via this ferry. Whether you took the road over Hardangervidda Plateau to Hardangerfjord and crossed by ferry there, or drove down the Aurlandsdalen Valley and caught the ferry from Flåm to Gudvangen here, you had to stop and take a ferry.

I point out the wooden buildings some two hundred metres up the road. 'The old wooden Gudvangen Hotel used to be where the waterfront was, and the dock for the ferry. What we're standing on, all of this – the new hotel and restaurant, and on the other side of the river, the gas station – weren't here. It's all landfill, 11.4 kilometres worth of rock pulled out of the mountain from the tunnel when it surfaces briefly before another four kilometre stretch to Flåm.'

During the construction phase one winter, I was told that a Swedish couple had ignored the road barriers and driven into the incomplete tunnel after the construction workers had knocked off work for the weekend. The Swedes drove past the warning signs several kilometres into the tunnel before they realised their mistake and tried to turn around in water deep enough to flood the engine compartment and stall the car. They couldn't get the car started again and spent the night in there, cold and hungry but otherwise okay, until the construction workers returned on the Monday morning. There is much good-natured rivalry between the Norwegians and the Swedes and this might have seemed just another joke, but apparently it wasn't.

We have a choice of staying overnight here in Gudvangen, or continuing through the tunnel to Flåm or Aurland. Although it is only late afternoon, the sun has ducked behind the perpendicular mountains looming overhead and the narrow valley is already in shade. Despite Gudvangen Fjord Hotel owner's invitation to stay here for the night at his new hotel with turf roof and panels of glass over each bed to better appreciate the perpendicular view, we take the bus through the tunnel to sunny Flåm and then Aurland.

The only passengers, we hurtle into a strange tunnel underworld. The sunny day outside is abruptly shut out. It's an anticlimax getting off that glorious ferry ride and then driving through a pitch-black tunnel, the hissing of the compressed air brakes of the bus gasping for air like a dying mechanical monster. Signs illuminated by the bus headlights count off the kilometres to either exit. We emerge briefly into the sunlight only to duck back into another four-kilometre continuation of the tunnel.

This is the quickest road route between Bergen and Oslo. Instead of a two-hour ferry ride that was an integral part of the drive between Oslo and Bergen, and one of the most spectacular journeys in the world, it's a fifteen-minute drive through rocks; although the passenger ferry still operates five times a day during the summer. And now there's a new tunnel from Aurland to Lærdal – the longest tunnel in the world, something like twenty-five kilometres. The two ferries we took from Fodnes to Manheller-Kaupanger, and Kaupanger to Gudvangen, will only operate in the summer, basically for the tourists.

'Postcards for future tourists will be black with lines of tail-lights and headlights,' I exaggerate. The bus continues its smooth, wheezing ride into the depths of solid bedrock. Sometimes I wonder if those communities built around harbours will decline when these tunnels and bridges are built and traditional ferries taken out of service. The social fabric and economic life of an island will skew community existence towards the towns. With all the oil revenue Norway has got, it has the financial resources to build tunnels and bridges to the smallest communities, changing the whole way of Norwegian life, forever.

The bus curls around the flyover across the Flåmselva River, bypassing Flåm itself as we enter another tunnel. I ponder the fact that Norway's character has emerged from its rugged terrain and fragmented coastline, and that the isolation imposed by its mountains and fjords strengthened its traditions. We exit the tunnel and cruise the new highway skirting the fjord to Aurland, now just a few easy minutes past Flåm.

With the sunny weather, the tourists seem to have come out of the woodwork. They line up at the tourist information counter in Aurland, hoping to find accommodation, but there are no more hotel rooms or huts available. Only by phoning ahead from Årdal to the helpful tourist office here have we been able to book a room in a private house. We walk up to the house perched on the hillside overlooking the fjord and ring the doorbell. Despite the cosy exterior, this is no quaint bed and breakfast with a charming four-poster bed. Our tiny room is in a corner of the semi-finished basement.

We don't want to remain in the room on this perfect summer evening so we walk the short distance back to the centre of Aurland where we sit at an outdoor restaurant nursing a beer each, while waiting for a hastily ordered pizza.

It's so warm we could be in southern France – in fact there are times in the Norwegian summer when the temperatures exceed that of the Mediterranean. Young Norwegian girls dressed identically in low-cut jeans and skimpy, halterneck tops reveal expanses of tanned, flat midriffs sparkling with pierced bellybuttons.

The Norwegian attitude to sex and nudity seems entirely wholesome. In front of our house in Oslo there was a nudist beach and every summer day there were plenty of healthy, normal Norwegians sunning themselves in the buff. Going topless is accepted as the norm rather than the exception at any beach. Their attitude seems to be that, after all, sex is healthy for you. Norwegian women, relatively speaking, are at ease with their sexuality, and a Norwegian woman is as likely to initiate a conversation with a man in a bar as vice versa. And yet, contrary to their reputation as Scandinavians, Norwegians are surprisingly conservative, especially in their attitudes towards the exploitation of women's bodies as objects of sex. Pornography and prostitution aren't as prevalent here as in other Western nations. Although there isn't outright censorship, commercialised sex and exploitation of women is frowned upon when it isn't illegal.

On the other hand, there is definitely censorship of violence on television and on films permitted to be shown in Norway. In North America, I never understood how one could see the graphic depiction of a person's brains being blown out in a violence-filled film and yet nudity was unacceptable. Nudity is perfectly natural. Seeing someone's brains being blown out in slow motion doesn't seem normal at all.

Reflecting their open attitude to sex, half of the young girls standing in the square are pushing prams, accurately portraying the fact that 50 per cent of children have single parents. Working women are entitled to a year's maternity leave; the first six weeks are taken by the mother, but the following forty-six weeks can be taken by either parent with 80 per cent of their salary paid. Fathers are also entitled to take two weeks paternity leave and although this is without pay, 80 per cent of Norwegian fathers elect to take the time off work to be at home during this period.

Nowhere else have I experienced such a profound feeling of equality between men and women as I did living here in Norway. From the time of the Vikings when the men left the management of their farms and communities to their women while they rampaged *berserk* over much of Europe, to Henrik Ibsen's theatrical dramas featuring strong-willed women, females have played a critical role in Norwegian society. Recently much of this empowerment has been enhanced by an informal quota system in Norwegian politics. In the 1970s many of the political parties voluntarily self-imposed a quota requiring that 40 per cent of the working members at various levels within their parties were women. In 1986 the principle of 40 per cent representation was applied to the cabinet. At that time Gro Harlem Brundtland was prime minister, and eight out of her eighteen ministers were women.

I suspected that, despite the attractiveness of Norway's extensive social welfare system, there was a downside to this affluence as well. Such is the cradle-to-grave social welfare system that even at death, a lump sum is given by the national insurance scheme to cover funeral expenses. Sometimes, it seemed Norwegians were so coddled by their privileged existence that they wouldn't be competitive in the cut and thrust of the international arena. While extensive social welfare states protect the weak, the infirm, the disabled, the single parent, they often don't necessarily promote excellence or private initiative either. This doesn't seem to be the case here however, as Norway is at the cutting edge in several industries relying on its technology-based, highly educated workforce; Statoil, Norsk Hydro, Kværner, ABB and Siemens are some of the better known companies that come to mind.

In the 1930s a Norwegian poet, Aksel Sandemose, came up with the Jante Laws, mocking the Norwegian psyche based both on envy and an anti-elitist principle. *Janteloven* are several 'laws' – philosophical dictums rather than enactments by parliament – expressing variations on the theme, 'Don't think you are better than anyone else'. Although Sandemose formulated his laws as a disparaging comment on the Norwegian sense of parity, the implication that all of us are equal appealed to me. In Norway, I never sensed the stifling, institutionalised hierarchy of Britain that I found objectionable after attending boarding school there. Apart from the Norwegian royal family there is no Norwegian aristocracy, and every member of the royal family goes to great pains to be of and for the people. The previous king, King Olav, was often seen skiing in the woods around Oslo, or taking public transportation. Consistent with the Norwegian disposition for equality, the Norwegian monarchy must be the only royal family in modern history to be elected by its common people. The present king, Harald, married Sonja, a commoner, and his son Crown Prince Håkon Magnus, in a Cinderella story come true, married Mette-Marit Tjessem Høiby, not only a commoner, but also a single mother. Crown Prince Håkon gave a speech publicly proclaiming to his wife: 'I've never been so much in love as I am with you.' This sense of equality – whereby a crown prince can not only marry a single mother, but she can also actually be welcomed into the royal family by the king and queen, as well as the Norwegian people – is the stuff Norway is made of.

Coming as I did from North America, I was inclined to view the Jante Laws as a positive reflection of Norwegian modesty, rather than a negative. I found it appealing that Norwegians have this down-to-earth sense of humility. By contrast, North Americans can have an overblown awareness of their own importance and self-worth to the point of arrogance. Admittedly, being an outsider, I was blissfully ignorant of the subtleties of stratification in Norwegian society, but overt opulence certainly didn't fly in my face either. There were no Rolls Royces or Ferraris, most Mercedes were taxis, and the finer homes weren't that different from the average.

Admittedly the mentality reflected in the Jante Laws doesn't necessarily nurture those who are gifted, or willing to take a risk and break out from the herd mentality. It sometimes struck me that compared to the people in other Western nations, Norwegians aren't particularly ambitious. But perhaps this diffidence was preferable to a puffed-up sense of self-worth. In a welfare state where so much is provided free by the state and there is such overall security and protection, financial success isn't as highly valued as the quality of life – including free time, family and enjoying the outdoors. Except in the sports arena, I never noticed amongst my Norwegian peers any particular drive to succeed or compete.

Even as a newcomer who could barely speak the language, starting up two adventure companies in Norway was relatively undemanding because the competition simply wasn't there. But being an employer wasn't particularly easy either and some-times it seemed that as an employer, I had all the responsibility while my employees had none. Employees are entitled to *feriepenger*, or holiday pay, equal to about a month's salary. If ill during a holiday, an employee has the right to take an equal number of days off later. If ill for three days starting on a Friday, then the weekend is also taken as sick days. Even if a child is sick, a parent can take up to an additional ten days off during a calendar year.

While these requirements made it more onerous to run a busi-ness, I was also amazed at the ease with which funds were avail-able to help start up Askeladdens Eventyrreiser, a limited com-pany. I was given two grants to assist my adventure company on the basis that I was providing employment in regions where the economic opportunities were fewer than the urban areas.

I never felt sorry for anyone in Norway, and I wasn't envious of anyone. Residents in Norway are entitled to virtually free health care, education, housing for pensioners, home nursing and house-help facilities. But the Jante Laws mentality is no longer as prevalent in Norwegian society as it was in the 1960s and 1970s. While still protecting the less intellectually or physically talented, Norway is keeping up with the real world. Recognising that it can't realistically remain economically isolated forever, Norway is far more amenable to encouraging excellence and private ini-tiative and enterprise these days. For one thing, the punitively high income taxes have dropped in recent years.

Staying out of the European Union, Norway has probably not incurred a net loss economically; in fact in the shorter term it has gained tremendously by hoarding its considerable wealth to itself. But politically, despite its history of involvement in international affairs and leadership in the United Nations, Norway's role in the world's political arena will be reduced to that of a small and wealthy, albeit independent, nation. Norwegians have a Lutheran sense of fairness and perhaps because of their own fairly recent history, identify with the political underdogs and the economically deprived of the world. While Norway was one of the first nations to recognise Israel after World War II, they balanced the equation more recently by advocating on behalf of the Palestinians. Being idealistic, rich and neutral, Norway's influence still extends far beyond its borders and yet at the same time, the country seems sheltered from so much of the political and economic turmoil in the world.

Annabel and I sit at an outdoor table, sip our seven-dollar beers, and study the young girls who giggle as two noisy hoon-mobiles park directly in front of them. The local boys, all wearing soccer gear, get out and lean against their cars, adopting a cool demeanour, although with their blonde hair and hairless, youthful faces, they look more like innocent altar boys than potentially tough hoodlums. So many of the girls have natural good looks they could easily earn a comfortable living as models in America and become rich. But nose jobs, breast implants and face-lifts are not a part of the average Norwegian's life; there's an unaffected modesty these naturally good-looking people have and it appealed to me from my very first holiday in Norway, some years before I came here to study. Norwegians are essentially a good-natured, down-to-earth, outdoors-oriented people and their most obvious failing, if it can be called that, is their naiveté.

Not so long ago, and it persists to a certain extent even now in the countryside, two Norwegians bargaining for the price of something would bargain in the opposite way than expected. The price asked by a farmer for a sheep, or a carpenter for a service, would be deliberately set too low and then countered by a higher offer from the purchaser. The seller would never deign to ask what he really wanted, starting instead at a lower price. The buyer would understand this and suggest a higher price until a price was agreed to. In modern Norwegian society, the price asked is the price expected to be paid. There certainly is no expectation of a buyer bargaining downwards! This cultural difference perhaps explains why Norwegian businesspeople seem so rigid in selling their products or services for the price demanded.

Watching the teenage antics of the youngsters it is apparent, even here in Aurland, at the end of the longest fjord in Norway, that there is a mixture of genetic stock. In the mountains and valleys, Norwegians tend to be consistently very fair-haired and light-skinned, more like the Swedes. On the coast there is more of a mixture; more of them have brown or black hair, their skin is less fair and brown eyes are more prevalent. This is apparently a result of centuries of interaction with people from the south. The Norwegian Vikings brought back the 'best' women from their rampages in Ireland, England and France, and so probably did generations of merchant sailors working in the shipping industry. And residing in Bergen were mostly well-behaved Hanseatic traders from Germany, as well as shipwrecked sailors from Portugal and Spain settling in small coastal communities.

Not only are the coastal Norwegians different in looks to their compatriots inland, they are also very different in character. I found the coastal Norwegians far more gregarious and open to outsiders; they have a reputation even within Norway for being talkative, and those living in Bergen are supposed to be masters of conversation. My own experiences didn't prove the preconception wrong.

Although Gudvangen was already in shade from the tall mountains enclosing it, Aurland is still bathed in sunlight, even after we have finished our pizzas. We walk to the bridge over the river and watch several sea-trout fishermen fly-fishing upstream. 'We'll head up that valley back into the mountains the day after tomorrow. It's a fantastic three-day walk up to Finse, Norway's highest railway station,' I promise Annabel.

'And tomorrow?'

'That's a surprise.'

It's past eleven and the direct sunlight by the turquoise river disappears, but higher up the mountainside a farm and its fields are washed in the intense, yellow, evening light. The dark blue waters of the fjord are calm, precisely reflecting the wooden hull of a boat against an inverted image of mountains.

Back in our room, we leave the window open to the still, silent summer evening. Annabel reads the novel aloud until someone on the balcony upstairs plays traditional folk melodies on a Hardanger fiddle accompanied by an accordion. The haunting music reminds me so much of my years living in Norway, some of the happiest, and saddest, years of my life. The plaintive tune enhances another perfect Norwegian night I never want to let go of.

Stigen Farm

Waterfalls plunge mysteriously out of the overcast sky. By mid-morning patches of blue begin to show through the clouds riding the tops of mountains. Annabel phones home to New Zealand. She talks for so long I have to signal from the dock that the catamaran from Flåm is arriving.

A few minutes later we are in the cockpit of the cat where the captain sits comfortably in his skipper's chair, his forefinger and thumb playing delicately with the joystick that directs the cat's jet engines. His young son sits proudly in the co-pilot's seat. These jet-propulsion catamarans have become an essential transportation link in the coastal communities and fjords of Norway, providing fast, comfortable service as commuter planes would in other parts of the world. With a coastline of almost 3000 kilometres excluding the fjords and some 50,000 islands, boats – and these days fast catamarans – have always been a necessary means of transportation.

The Norwegian guide picks up the microphone and announces in three languages – English, French and German – that the farm Stigen, or The Ladder, is ahead of us. Another guide makes the same announcement in Japanese. 'This farm is 300 metres or 1000 feet above the Aurland Fjord. It is called Stigen because the path going up is so steep they used a ladder. When the taxman came, the farmer raised the wooden ladder. It is said that a rope tied his children to a stake in the garden to make sure they did not fall off the cliff.' Within a few minutes the catamaran slows down and I explain to Annabel that this is where we are getting off.

We disembark on the tiny wooden dock and as the catamaran backs away some twenty goats invade the dock. Passengers watch curiously and take photos as we trip over the goats besieging us. We remove the food we brought for lunch and leave our relatively inedible backpacks under a tarpaulin, weighed under several tyres lying on the dock, and then start the climb on the steep path, followed by the entire herd of goats. A sign warns us not to look down.

'Are you sure this is the right trail up?'

'Yes.' I'm not sure at all.

'Well that's good because it doesn't look very well used.'

She's right, the path is overgrown with grass. 'I guess once you're up there, you're up there, and you don't bother coming back down unless you really have to,' I reply hopefully. 'It's not as if you'd carelessly traipse down 300 vertical metres and then row a few kilometres down the fjord just to fetch a pound of sugar you forgot, or casually drop in to the local Saturday-night dance to see if anything was happening. You'd have to row some distance and descend and climb 300 metres every time you wanted to do something besides stay at home on the farm.' That explanation for the overgrown path keeps Annabel happy. 'Besides, the goats don't have any problem following us up and they must know what they're doing.' It's as if we are leading a long caravan. We try to shoo them away but they just stand patiently until we continue climbing again, and then they follow us.

The zigzagging path cuts into a stone overhang where a gate held in place by a boulder stops our progress. I try to open the gate but it doesn't budge. Instead, I climb over it. Annabel follows. She straddles the gate but doesn't quite get over.

'Keep going,' I encourage. 'Once you've got your . . . '

'Centre of gravity,' Annabel interjects.

'Once you've got your . . . centre of gravity over the top . . . you'll be fine,' I observe as she manages the obstacle with more finesse than I did.

Without the goats we continue climbing steeply up the rocky path through wild flowers sprouting precariously from the mountainside. Against the posted advice, I look down and experience a momentary sense of vertigo. I wouldn't want to climb this path in wet weather or during winter. In places the bare rock of the path angles perilously to the outer edge. It had been chilly down by the fjord, but now we are steaming with the effort of walking up the garden path to this farm. We both peel off layers of clothes and eventually crest a rise. 'We're only halfway there.'

'And they live here all year round?' Annabel replies, resting a hand on a knee, staring up ahead of us.

'Six months of the year. They've got another home down by the fjord in Fresvik, around the corner as the boat goes.'

The overcast sky has broken up and the patches of cloud passing by create a moving kaleidoscope of sunlight and shade. This sense of motion gives a heightened awareness of the sculptured aspect to the scenery as different sections of mountain and fjord are spotlighted in the shifting sunlight.

Finally, we climb onto a small ledge of land where several humps of hay are piled. Two goats and then a dog seek us out and refuse to leave us alone. The dog barks to begin with but soon wags its tail and dances circles around us as the pair of goats nibble our legs and bootlaces, hoping to find something reasonably edible.

Hege has been raking hay in the field. It's the first time I've met her. Introducing herself, rake in one hand, she's obviously strong and very fit. She'd have to be. There's no need for exercising in the gym when you live on a farm where just stepping out the front door means exerting yourself to climb back in again. Two tousle-haired young boys with mischievous smiles come over and shake hands politely, introducing themselves as Une and Brede, before running off. Contrary to the guide's memorised spiel, the children are not tied by rope to a stake in the ground. Far from it – they play by hurtling themselves as fast as they can down the steep, tiny patch of cut grass to somersault into a pile of hay. Mind you, if they misjudge the haystack, they've got a long way to go.

'They used to have fourteen kids,' I joke to Annabel when Hege yells up to her partner Dee to come down. 'These are the only two who survived,' I whisper. She jabs me sharply in the ribs with her elbow.

Hege had already warned me on the phone that they'd have to spend the day bringing the hay in.

Dee descends the steep gradient from the old barn perched almost vertically above us. He carries what looks like a giant toothpick over a shoulder. Like Hege, he is wiry and fit-looking. 'Welcome to Stigen,' he says with a noticeable southern drawl, a broad smile and a twinkle in his eyes.

'You're American?' Annabel asks.

'What'd you expect?' he chuckles.

'A Norwegian.'

'Uh-uh. Sorry to disappoint you, but I'm a farm boy from Missouri.' He laughs easily, like Annabel. They invite us in for a coffee. Although the farmhouse can't be more than twenty metres away as the crow flies, it'd be a scramble getting up there.

'We'd rather help you in the fields,' Annabel replies quickly. She loves the smell of mown hay and wants to get working and out of her role as a tourist hiking through Norway. 'What do we do?'

'Well, we've cut the grass, it's dried, and now we have to pile it in haystacks and then get it up to the barn,' Dee says, surveying their handiwork.

Although the barn isn't further than thirty metres from where we're standing, measured horizontally, it's probably twenty or thirty vertical metres higher as well.

'How do we carry the hay up there?' I ask, staring at the barn with my head bent back.

Dee laughs. 'The first years here I carried it all up by pitchfork in hard-pressed bales, one load at a time.'

I can't even begin to imagine doing that.

'Then I got smart and used a cart. After that experiment, I dragged it up on a tarpaulin. Now I'm really smart and I've reverted back to the old farming techniques and use this.' He kicks the giant toothpick he carried down. 'They might have used a horse back then, but the basic technique is the same.' He sees the look of puzzlement on our faces. He slides the sharp end under the nearest pile of hay until it protrudes from the other side.

Then he attaches a wire leading from the barn through a shackle at the thick end of the pole, tosses it over the haystack, pulls it down over the back of the hay, then loops the end of the wire over the thin end of the pole, drawing it firm. As we watch, he climbs back up towards the barn.

'You can help me if you like,' Hege tells Annabel, and then turns to me. 'You climb up to the crest and signal to Dee when we're ready.' She grabs the slack wire and walks diagonally up the steep field to where a steel rod pokes from the ground. She throws the wire over the rod. 'The rod is to "steer" the haystack so that we can manoeuvre it in place to pull the hay directly up to the barn,' Hege explains. She leans back against the steel rod to keep it in place.

A gas-powered winch starts up.

I scramble after Dee up to the crest where I see him standing beside a mobile winch that's powered by a gas engine, mounted on a sled that's bound to a boulder. I'm out of breath just climbing the short distance without carrying anything. Hege gives me a thumbs-up and I pass the signal on to Dee. He puts the winch in gear and the wire tightens around the steel rod. When the slack is taken up, the haystack moves with a jerk as the wire on the giant toothpick tightens over the mound of hay. Like a giant hairy troll out for a stroll, it moves diagonally across the clear ground towards Annabel and Hege. When the hay reaches them, Hege signals me to stop, and I relay the gesture. Dee disengages the clutch and Annabel and Hege remove the steel rod from the ground so the wire is free. Now the troll climbs vertically up the hill.

'Simple but ingenious,' I admire aloud when Dee turns the engine off. 'But I still don't know how you manage this when it's just the two of you.'

'You get used to it. These mountain farms are known for wearing farmers out, so you have to learn how to work it without breaking your body in the process. You'd never get a tractor on a steep slope like that, even if you managed to get a tractor up here in the first place. You've got to be clever,' Dee admits. 'This gas-powered winch mounted on a sled pulls itself to wherever I need it, like a horse used to do in days gone by.' He looks around. 'It's a never-ending task though. All the time I see things that have to be fixed, mostly old masonry, especially on the path up here. But I can't fix that massive stonework on my own and I have to accept that one day it'll all crumble down the mountainside.'

The next time the troll-like haystack comes gliding up the hill, the two boys ride the hairy creature up to the barn while the two goats and dog follow Annabel and Hege to prepare the next haystack for manoeuvring.

We work like this for some hours – Dee operating the winch and descending with the giant toothpick-pole, Hege and Annabel raking the hay into heaps, and me pitchforking the hay into the barn when I'm not relaying the haystack's movements up to Dee. Annabel is in her element. 'It's so perfect here,' she says when we take a break.

'When I'm here, I don't want to be anywhere else.' Dee looks around thoughtfully. 'How about a lunch break?'

We walk up to the barn, past a fenced-in area with a multitude of thriving vegetables, to a shelter Dee has built on heavy stone foundations. 'This was the original house. I've made it into a kitchen and outdoor dining area now for our guests.'

'What have you got growing there?' I ask, studying the beds of vegetables.

'All kinds of salad greens and vegetables like cabbages, cauliflower, broccoli, garlic, onions, peas, beets, carrots and tomatoes. I've forgotten exactly.' He looks more carefully. 'Brussels sprouts, red cabbages, strawberries, Chinese cabbages, mints, lots of herbs, rye. I'm sure I've left some out, but we produce everything we need here and it's all organically grown.'

I admire the healthy crop. 'You never lose your harvest due to frost?'

He appraises the leafy crops and laughs. 'No, but the maddest I've ever seen Hege was when we found the goats had broken into the garden and eaten most of the vegetables. She wanted goat for dinner that night.' He chuckles again at the thought.

'But you still keep them?'

'We used to milk them twice a day and make cheese but this was too binding and there was no time to take people for hikes in the area. It also meant I had to come here and climb up to the barn to feed them all year-round. So we've decided to let the kids do the milking.'

'The kids do the milking?' I ask incredulously.

'Goat kids.'

'Oh.'

'Besides, we're taking in more guests now and guiding them on long walks in the mountains so we're not always here, even in the summer. But two of the billy goats can carry twenty-five kilos of supplies on their backs, so they're still useful. One's called Jens, the other Sherpus.'

'So you've got everything you need.'

'There's even a library boat that comes around to all the small villages and isolated farms like us.'

'You don't have television?'

Dee laughs again as if I had asked a stupid question. 'Apart from photovoltaic cells for lights, we don't even have electricity. Until I got that gas-powered generator recently for the winch, I did everything by hand. The only electrical tool I've had is a battery-powered drill.'

'How'd you recharge that?'

'Take it down to our other home in Fresvik and charge it there.'

'You carry the battery all the way down the mountain and then climb back up here with it?'

'It's still easier than using a hand drill.' He looks around. 'Have you seen Une and Brede?'

'They were jumping from the loft into the pile of hay to flatten it so I could get more in, but I haven't seen them for a while, although I think I heard them playing over there.' They seem to be able to play and amuse themselves endlessly. You couldn't hope to meet nicer children. The brothers seem to be having a whale of a time living on this farm despite its isolation and being deprived of computers, computer games and television. They are definitely going to be one-offs.

'Where?' Dee asks.

I point in the vague direction where I last saw them.

'Okay, they're playing on the trampoline.'

'By the cliff?' I ask.

'There's no other flat area big enough to put it.'

I have this image of them making a mistake when they bounce on the trampoline, rebounding into the air and free falling some 300 metres down to the fjord.

We sit down at a table soon covered in home-made bread, goat's cheese, smoked sausages and meat. There's also home-made wild raspberry and wild blueberry jam, wild bee honey and rhubarb juice. The main meal for Norwegians is *middag*, literally translated as 'midday', the only hot meal of the day, and nowadays served at four or five in the afternoon in urban areas but still served at noon on the farms. Dee calls the boys over from where they are still successfully bouncing and somersaulting on the trampoline a couple of metres from a sheer drop down to the fjord. A chicken-wire fence makes sure they don't take a flying 300-metre leap, although I suspect the boys are as sure-footed as the goats.

'Annabel and I brought our lunch with us.'

'Don't be ridiculous,' Hege says. 'Unless you'd rather eat store-baked bread and processed cheese?'

When the two boys overhear we've brought 'store-baked bread' and 'processed cheese' with us, their faces register avaricious delight.

'Do you want some?' I ask as I pull out soft white rolls, processed cheese and vacuum-packed salami.

Une and Brede scoff the processed grub as eagerly as Annabel and I tuck into Hege and Dee's home-made food.

Hege says ironically, 'It's a treat for them to have store-baked bread and packaged cheese and meat. They call it *butikksnadder*.'

'Which means?'

'Shop treats.'

'It's amazing anyone even thought of farming way up here in the first place,' I comment, stuffing goat's cheese and a crunchy home-made bun into my mouth.

'Prehistory, this land was originally cultivated by hunter-gatherers who came over the mountains some 5000 years ago. There are plenty of old reindeer traps that have re-emerged after the last glacier retreated. Taken from that perspective, it doesn't seem so crazy to farm a piece of land like this. The first cultivators didn't climb from the fjord up to here, but were already living in the mountains, trapping and hunting, and this was a good patch of land for a base. Norway was such a poor country every scrap of potentially arable land was cultivated. All along this area there were mountain farms.' Dee points across the chasm of the fjord to a promontory on the opposite mountainside. 'You can see two farms over there that have been abandoned, although they still hunt there sixty years after the last inhabitants left. The farmers used everything that might be productive, even cutting down the trees to sell as firewood. The goats kept eating the saplings and ringbarking the bigger ones so there wasn't much left of the forests here either. Sixty years ago you probably wouldn't have seen any trees along here at all. There's an old steel aerial cable out there from earlier this century that was used to transport firewood down here from a farm that's even higher up than this one.'

'But you live in Fresvik during the winter?' Annabel asks.

'Now we do. We still come up here in the winter to feed the goats with hay and of course feed the Christmas *fjøsnisse* with porridge and butter . . . ' Dee replies.

'The what?'

'You know – the *julenisse*. They're little gnomes with white beards and red noses and cheeks. You have to give them porridge with a dash of butter at Christmas to keep them happy. They always eat it. At the midsummer ceremony they used to have to light fires on different parts of the farm to satisfy them too, and the bonfires had to be big enough for the flames to leap.'

'Must be scary coming up here in the dead of winter,' I comment.

'Once I came up in the middle of winter and heard this horrible screeching sound coming from the barn. Couldn't make out what could howl like that until I saw it,' Dee replies. 'It was a lynx and it must have been looking for a mate because it wasn't scared of me at all. It was making a heck of a noise. I've lost two goats to lynx.'

'Where are you sleeping tonight?' Hege asks, changing subject. 'You'd be welcome to stay here.'

Annabel and I look at each other. Before we came here I didn't realise Dee and Hege had started taking in guests, otherwise we'd have invited ourselves. 'We'd love to stay over.'

'Only if we don't interrupt you bringing in the hay,' Annabel adds. 'We'll finish the job with you.'

'You don't have to do that.'

'We want to,' Annabel asserts. 'I love working in the fields, the smell of the cut hay . . . ' I know it reminds her of New Zealand when she used to spend all her time out at a farm training with her horse. Beautiful as Bermuda is, we don't have anything remotely resembling this.

'Only thing is, you'd have to leave tomorrow. It's Une's birthday and I've promised to take him fishing. We're leaving in the morning for three days,' Dee explains.

Dee, Hege, Une and Brede are characters straight out of a Norwegian fairy tale, except if you read it you wouldn't believe anyone could actually live this life. But they not only look as if they lead a fairy-tale existence, they *are*.

'Fishing in your little rowboat? Where are you going?' I ask.

'Camping along Nærøyfjord,' Dee replies.

I guess when you live way up here you don't go down to the dock to go fishing for the evening. When you live at Stigen and go fishing, you go for three days and make the walk down to the dock worth it. 'What do you catch?' I ask.

'Brede wants to catch sharks. He caught a little one once.'

We bring the rest of the hay in, the boys jumping from the loft in the barn to flatten the rising mound of hay so that I can pitchfork more in. Occasionally they ride the hairy troll up the steep hillside, laughing delightedly as Dee tows the haystacks up with the giant toothpick and winch.

When we finish getting all the hay into the barn, Dee shows us around the farm. He has built two small guesthouses, both perched on the edge of the cliff.

'What kind of guests do you have?' Annabel inquires.

'Mostly Norwegians and only nice people,' Dee responds.

'Consistently?'

'Yep.'

'How do you manage that?'

'The climb up here has something to do with it. By the time most people arrive at the farm and they've got even more mountains towering above, they're feeling pretty humble.'

We left our toothbrushes and sleeping bags in our packs, not expecting to spend the night. 'There's plenty of sheets and blankets,' Dee tells us, but Annabel wants her toothbrush in her toilet bag. I volunteer to get it. I look forward to the walk down and climbing back again.

'Would you mind taking these two goats down with you?' Dee asks. 'The two following you around don't belong to us, they belong to the twenty-odd other goats from the neighbouring farm you saw at the dock. The farmer has rights to let his goats feed on the land between the dock and the gate under the cliff overhang. Somehow these two goats found their way up here, despite the barrier.'

Using their mobile phone, I leave a message at the Gudvangen Fjord Hotel that we won't be spending the night at the hotel.

Annabel goes back to the main farmhouse to help Hege with dinner while Dee gets the boys ready for bed.

'We'll have a warm beer and a cold shower ready for you when you come back. Take your time and enjoy the walk!' Dee calls after me. 'And I mean it.'

Descending the path is almost the equivalent of walking along the edge of a high diving board looking at the water immediately below. Down the fjord, towards Aurland, a swathe of evening sunlight illuminates a farm and its lush surrounding fields as intensely as a spotlight on a darkened stage. It's almost supernatural the way the light remains fixed on the one farm for the entire duration of the walk down to the dock.

Surrounded by twenty goats, I open our packs and remove our sleeping bags, my toothbrush and Annabel's toilet bag and then begin the walk up. Twenty goats, plus the pair that followed me down, pursue me. I feel like the Pied Piper leading a long line of bleating kids and goats up the narrow, overgrown trail. This time I manage to properly open the gate in the middle of the cliff ledge, but I have to shut it quickly behind me to stop the goats from following. I feel like a heartless parent abandoning the two faithful goats that have followed me everywhere, as they stare, thoroughly astonished that I'd dump them.

Taking my time ascending, I stop frequently along the path to savour the scenery. A cruise ship appears around the corner from Flåm and Aurland, cutting a wake through the stillness of the fjord. The ship, which must be huge, is dwarfed by the size of the mountains looming on either side. As I zigzag up the path I speculate whether the passengers can see me. I wave at the boat and see a flash from a camera.

Perhaps one day when our knees have completely given in, when we're retired and rich enough, Annabel and I will take a cruise ship up this fjord too. That would be nice. But it will be sad too, remembering when we were younger and able to climb this steep path up to Stigen. And who will be living at Stigen then? Will Dee and Hege still be climbing up here? Will Une or Brede be running the farm? Or will the path up have finally collapsed into the fjord and the farm have been abandoned?

I write in my notebook, then look up and am suddenly aware of the long drop in front of me. For a few seconds I'm so dizzy I almost fall over.

When I reach the farmhouse again, it is late – the light is flat, the sky overcast and it is surprisingly cold. As I approach the farmhouse from below, I hear Dee singing to the boys in an upstairs bedroom.

Annabel comes out to greet me. 'We've all had showers, the kids are in bed and we're ready to have dinner. The shower's over there.' She points at a showerhead on the end of a long black hose hanging on a fence beside the vegetable garden. She has a towel in hand.

I strip naked. The air is cold. 'Where's the hot water?'

'You must be kidding?' she replies laughing.

'Dee said a cold beer and a hot shower.'

'He said a *warm* beer and a *cold* shower.'

'Are you sure?' I turn the water on and test it with a finger. 'Oh boy, it's not just cold, it's bloody *freezing*.'

'Don't be such a wimp.'

'Where's the water come from?' I ask, already shivering and covered in goose bumps although I haven't poured any water over me yet.

'From a waterfall somewhere up there.'

'From a melted glacier, no doubt.' I hold my breath and extend the showerhead over me. 'Aaggghhh.' I pass the shower to Annabel and soap myself then rinse off.

'Let me get a photo,' Annabel says as I quickly towel myself dry. Inside the farmhouse it's cosy and soon I'm thawed out from the warmth radiating from the wood-burning cast-iron stove heating the entire house. This living-cum-dining room is tiny; one wall is lined with books, another dominated by a window facing the entrance to the Aurlandsfjord where it meets the Sognefjord, the other window overlooks the fjord towards Aurland and Flåm. I approach the main window, as close as I can get with the dining table in front of it; the sensation is the same as leaning against the window of a 100-storey apartment building. I can't even see the ground in front of the farmhouse, just the fjord.

Hege advises me, apropos of my complaining about the temperature of the shower, 'If you think that was cold, try it in the spring or fall. Right now the water's as warm as it ever gets.'

I'm thirsty from the climb and in the tiny kitchen help myself to a glass of water from the tap. It's like a fire hose. 'You sure don't have problems with water pressure here!' I shout, covered in water that's splashed up from the sink.

'It's hardly surprising. The source is 150 metres up and 800 metres away,' Dee yells back.

On one of the bookshelves I recognise two books by Gary Zukav. '*The Seat of the Soul* – did you like it?' I ask.

'Yeah.'

Annabel says, 'I saw him on "Oprah Winfrey" the other day.'

'Never seen the "Oprah Winfrey Show", but I've heard of it,' Dee says.

'You're as bad as Andrew; he thinks she's called Winifred Oprey.'

I sit at the table and admire the interior. 'Was it like this when you moved in ten years ago?'

'It hadn't been lived in for a while and it was falling apart. The windows had been left open, the glass smashed, the chimney leaked. We had to redo the windows, stripping them and soaking them in linseed oil and turpentine. I rebuilt the chimney; carried every one of those bricks up here myself.'

Hege says, 'He used to be two metres tall and 200 kilos.'

'Not only did I carry the bricks up here, I rowed them over from Undredal.'

Dee serves me warm home-brewed beer. 'We used to keep goats in Undredal during the winter. We had a small plot of land on the hillside and a tractor, until I rolled it on top of me. Punctured my lung, broke my ribs. Stay away from machinery now. In Fresvik we have a motorised three-wheel moped, but no car.'

'And no television? Not even in Fresvik?'

'No time for it. Although in the winter if there's a stormy Sunday night we might go to Hege's school library – she works there as a librarian – and watch a video on the television there. I give a yoga course in the winter that keeps me busy but I've always got lots of projects on the go.'

'And your children don't miss television?'

Dee points at a wooden mobile hanging from the ceiling. 'These are billy goats and a troll I carved.' He stands at the table, reaches up and lifts a candle from the dining table, holding it up to the mobile. 'See the shadows of the troll and the goats on the wall opposite?' Although it is late and overcast outside, we can barely see the silhouettes. 'I make up stories for the kids and do a shadow show on the wall. That's our favourite thing to do here in the evenings when it's dark in the fall. They still love it although I must have done it hundreds of times.' He puts the candle back down on the table and slices a piece of the goat leg then passes it to me. 'Try some dried, salted and sugared goat.'

'Don't the kids, I mean your children, mind?'

'Une had a pet kid goat but after one and a half years he started head-butting the others so much we butchered him; but we made him into sausages out of respect.'

'And do you eat other meat?'

'We have one and a half shares of a red stag each year, which I hunt.'

Sitting inside this restored farmhouse I admire the work Dee and Hege have done in restoring this farm and building the two new guesthouses. 'I can't believe you did this all by hand. No electric saws to cut the planks of wood?' I ask Dee, looking around me.

'Like I said, just the drill.'

'And you carried everything you needed up here on your back?'

'For the first five years, and then I built a pulley system. But most of the work was done before then.' He thinks and then says, 'Oh, and I had a gas-powered drill to put holes into the rocks for the steel rods when I was building the pulley system.' He looks at Hege and laughs. 'That's another story.'

'A gas-powered drill? That must have been heavy to carry up here.'

'It was.' Both Hege and Dee start laughing again.

'What happened?'

Dee, once he gets going, is a raconteur *par excellence*. 'I bought the gas-powered drill but the first time I tried it at the farm it wouldn't work. I was really angry that I'd carried it all the way up here and had to take it all the way back to the store in Voss, a full day's trip. I put the drill in my pack ready to take down to the dock. The next day, Hege went down to meet two Englishmen who wanted to come and visit us. They had rowed over from Undredal. She knew there were two bags of goat feed down there on the dock, waiting for someone to carry them up. She removed the drilling machine from my pack up here and took the empty pack down to the two Englishmen so they could carry the two bags of goat feed up here.

'I woke up at four the following morning to walk down to the dock with my pack. Then I rowed to Undredal in the dark to catch a ride on a boat with railway workers heading to Flåm at five in the morning. I took the Flåm train up to Myrdal, and then took the Oslo–Bergen train to Voss and went back to the store where I had bought the drill. I was so angry I'd bought this piece of equipment from them, carried it up to the farm, and it never worked. When I told them the drill was useless, they asked to see what was wrong with it. I opened up the sack and there was twenty kilos of goat feed.'

Annabel and I have a choice of sleeping in the extra bedroom in the main farmhouse, or in one of the two new huts Dee has built on the edge of the cliff looking straight down to the fjord. We choose the nearest hut and stand outside in the chill, brushing our teeth and admiring the view. It is cold and the sky is overcast with heavy clouds again, but a vestige of light clings tenaciously to a patch of mountain.

'It's so quiet up here. We can't even hear the waves of the fjord lapping on the rocks, we're so high up,' Annabel says.

I spit over the edge and a gust of wind carries it out over the fjord until it disappears from sight. The slight breeze stirs the leaves on the trees behind us. 'It reminds me of Nepal, with the steep farms and paths, the goats and chickens,' I say.

'It's like a fairy tale.'

'Except this is real.'

Aurland Valley

Hege, Dee and the boys say goodbye in the morning. Dee has used the mobile phone to request one of the passing catamarans to pick us up. We give ourselves half an hour to get down to the dock but it's a race against time as the cat approaches. By the time we reach the fjord, twenty-two bleating goats surround us. Pulling our backpacks out from under the tyres I remember the two pieces of leftover pizza wrapped in aluminium foil that we had saved from dinner the other night. 'Damn, those kids would have killed for that.'

Annabel pushes a goat away from her. 'No kidding.'

'No, I mean Une and Brede.'

The fast catamaran cruises in, blunt bow nestling against the wooden structure. We have to keep the goats at bay with our walking sticks so they don't clamber on board. The cat reverses out from Stigen's diminutive dock and one of the most famous farms in Norway. Almost every cruise ship that comes to Norway glides up the Aurlandsfjord below the little white farmhouse sitting conspicuously on the mountainside.

The clouds clear away and a strong breeze blows as we disembark at Aurland. Unfortunately, we've missed the early bus that would have taken us to the start of our hike today. In one of the Aurland grocery stores we buy food to take with us on our walk, including a container of juicy, bright-red Aurland strawberries, which we are too greedy to wait to eat. I don't know what it is about Norwegian fruit, but the taste is much better, more intense, than fruit from southern climes. It's as if the long summer nights and cooler temperatures, the slower ripening process, somehow give that extra flavour to whatever grows here.

I borrow a large piece of cardboard from the friendly tourist office opposite, scrawling on it 'Vassbygdi'. We stand beside the road, Annabel's backpack hidden discreetly behind mine, munching on the succulent strawberries, thumbs stuck out, hoping for a ride. Hitchhiking is not part of Norwegian culture and I'm not optimistic we'll get a lift.

The sun comes out and the last fragments of cloud from yesterday and last night are quickly blown away. The weather forecast for bad weather today has been completely wrong.

We have barely eaten half the strawberries when a car approaches, and as I stick my thumb out it stops beside us. The automatic trunk flips open and we shove our packs into the boot, then hop into the back seat. Driving alongside the river the driver tells me he is on his way to work at the electrical power station at Vassbygdi, but he has to drop his son off at his aunt's house, past the electrical station, at the entrance to the Aurlandsdalen Valley walk, ten kilometres away. Perfect.

Driving just outside Aurland we pass several sea-trout fishermen casting their fly-fishing lines out from wooden walkways built out into the river or cantilevered around boulders.

'This is one of the two main roads between Oslo and Bergen,' I say to Annabel a few minutes later as we enter a tight tunnel.

'Hard to believe.'

The road is so narrow we stop several times to let cars coming from the other direction go by. To the right, on the other side of a lake surrounded by almost vertical bedrock, the road zigzags above us, in and out of the wall of rock. 'That tunnel has only one lane. You have to wait at a traffic light outside until it's your turn to go through,' I tell Annabel. The rock face on both sides is impressive evidence of the brute force the glaciers had in sculpting this landscape. I've almost become blasé about these incredible natural monuments left over from the last Ice Age. Soon there will be a new tunnel twenty-five kilometres long from Lærdal to Aurland, and that will then become the best route between Norway's two largest towns, rather than the one we're driving on.

We bypass the turn-off for Oslo and continue a short distance up the valley. 'That was lucky,' I say after the driver has dropped us off on a gravel road linking several small farms and a couple of houses. 'We couldn't have had a better ride. Now we need to find out how to get the next scheduled bus to take our packs up for us so we don't have to carry them today.' I look around. 'There's a shop down there selling hot dogs in the parking area where the bus turns. I could ask them to look after our bags and put them on the bus.'

'Doesn't look open.'

'I'll be right back.' I walk down the dirt lane to where a blonde-haired boy saunters beside a collie. The dog is the spitting image of Lassie the television dog. 'Do you live here?' I ask in Norwegian.

'Yes,' the boy replies in English. He points behind him. 'I live in that jello house.'

'No yoking?' I tease, but he doesn't get the yoke. 'What's your name?'

'Erik.'

'Do you know when the shop lady opens, Erik?' I ask in English, burying my linguistic pride.

'He's a shop man.'

'Well, the shop man, do you know when he opens?' I repeat.

'Two o'clock. He lives in that . . . '

'Jello house?'

'No, the white one.'

'And the bus going up to Østerbø arrives at what time?'

'Three o'clock.'

The shop man probably opens up for the hikers coming down the valley from Østerbø. The early ones would be here around two at the earliest, if it's the six-hour walk the map suggests.

A girl riding bareback on a large farm horse clip-clops up the gravel drive and Lassie runs away with his tail between his legs. 'He always does that,' Erik says, slightly embarrassed. The horse clops by; the girl and Erik studiously ignore each other.

'If I hid our packs in the bushes here, when the bus comes this afternoon, would you put them on the bus for us?'

'Yes.'

'I'll give you fifty kroner.'

His eyes light up at the suggestion. He waits while I walk back and relate to Annabel what the plan is. We are almost down at the bus turning area when a bus unexpectedly arrives. I wave frantically and run down the dirt road as fast as I can, weighed down by the heavy pack. The bus driver waits in the middle of his turning loop.

'Are you going to Østerbø?' I ask, panting with the effort. That would be a bit of luck if he were going up there.

'No, I am going to Aurland.'

Damn.

'But this bus is going up to Østerbø later,' he volunteers.

'It is?'

'Yes, this is that bus, and I am that bus driver,' he says with a triumphant smile.

'Can you take our packs now and keep them in the bus until you get to Østerbø?'

'Yes, I can.'

'Yes!' I advise Annabel when she arrives. She removes the chocolate and our lunch packs and we slide our packs into the baggage compartment under the bus.

We pay twenty-five kroner for each pack and the driver shoves the backpacks to one side so that he'll remember they aren't to be unloaded before the afternoon trip to Østerbø. He drives off in a cloud of dust.

Looking glum, his arm wrapped around the collie, Erik sits on the doorstep to the shop man's closed hot-dog stand. I walk up to him. 'It's all been arranged, but thanks anyway.' I give him a fifty-kroner note and he almost falls backwards.

Annabel and I stroll up the farm road again. 'Fantastic. We have a six-hour walk ahead of us, it's all uphill, which is good for our knees, we've got chocolate, lunch, there's plenty of water on the way, and look at the clear blue sky . . . and to top it all, we don't have our packs!' I say enthusiastically.

'It's so peaceful too.'

'In New Zealand they'd probably have heli-tours ferrying people up to the top so they could walk down,' I harp in an unkind dig at Kiwi tour operators and their exploitation of New Zealand's wilderness.

The path is straddled with a mass of wild flowers thicker than we saw coming down to Skogadalsbøen. We pass through a shut gate and into a birch forest where patches of sunlight filtering through branches spotlight the psychedelic shag rug of flowers. In this steep-sided valley that twists and turns, there isn't a hint of a breeze and it is becoming very hot. We pass several large boulders under which sheep lie panting in the heat. I strip down to the waist, wearing only shorts and boots. Annabel, with a bit of encouragement, takes off her shirt to cool down too.

The walk up the Aurlandsdalen Valley is as spectacular as you'd expect one of Norway's best-known walks to be. Perhaps because of the cold summer, and the bad forecast for the day, we don't meet many hikers coming down. Occasionally we find hikers sitting on the rocks, faces turned to the sun like sunflowers. Norwegians, especially along the west coast, are prone to stopping in their tracks when it's sunny and angling their faces up to the sky to catch those rare rays of sunlight.

The path takes us alongside deep clefts, almost under waterfalls, over summer pastures, past abandoned farms, back down to the river, under cliff overhangs, beside still pools full of trout with swifts scooping their beaks in the water to drink, over ridges and up alongside rushing turquoise waters frothing over boulders. Every turn in the path is a postcard view and everywhere there is an abundance of yellow, purple, white, blue and pink flowers. I've never seen so many wild flowers. It is all heartbreakingly beautiful. We stop for a break at what used to be a farm until it was abandoned in 1922 and has now become a summer *seter*. In one of the old buildings, smoke filters through the roof and out the door. Inside is a huge copper cauldron containing a bubbling, brown, gooey mass. 'What's that?' Annabel asks.

'Goat's cheese.'

'But there are mostly cows outside.'

'They mix the goat's milk with cow's milk so the taste isn't as strong.'

After an hour's break, we continue the steep climb. Sections of the path have been cut out of vertical rock. As spectacular as the walk is on this absolutely perfect summer day, it's a bit of a relief when the valley broadens and we finally see our destination at the end of a lake.

Aurlandsdalen Valley has always been an important route from the fjords and the west coast to the interior. The modern road through the Aurlandsdalen Valley was developed in the 1970s. Because most of the road below Østerbø is carved through numerous tunnels, the major road link between Bergen and Oslo has been invisible throughout our walk, until this last hour. Feeling the effects of our hike, we collect our packs from outside the gate of the lodge where the bus driver placed them.

'Everyone leaves their packs outside and unattended like that?' Annabel asks incredulously.

'Yep. And those heading down will have had their packs taken there by bus and left outside the shop man's hot-dog stand.'

We've been walking for six hours, plus an hour sitting down for lunch at the *seter*. Nina, the hospitable manager of Østerbø Fjellstove, leads us to an outbuilding and shows us an immaculate room with two beds. We both collapse on a bed each and put our feet up against the wall. My feet pulsate against the wooden planks.

'Feels like my feet are on fire,' I admit to Annabel.

'Good.'

'What?' I ask.

'I said "good",' she replies honestly, turning to look at me. 'I wasn't going to say anything if you didn't, but my feet feel like I've been walking on a bed of hot coals for the last hour.'

'I hate to admit this, but four years ago I did the walk from here down to Vassbygdi and back up again in the same day, and I don't remember feeling anything like this.'

I go for long walks by myself when I have things to work out in my head. Sometimes I take a Walkman and listen to one tape, over and over. Then I don't listen to the tape again, but keep it aside, almost like a diary. Whenever I want to remember my thoughts, the smells, sights, sounds and feelings during that walk, I listen to the tape. On that particular day walking up and down the Aurlandsdalen Valley, it was one of my last days in Norway. I listened to Michael Bolton. Now, listening to a Michael Bolton song from that tape I can recall every nuance of my frame of mind that day. Once, going around the Annapurna Circuit, I listened to Celine Dion. Another time I climbed Kilimanjaro listening to The Eagles. Whenever I hear these tapes now, I can recall almost everything about those walks, those stages in my life, far more effectively than the memory-jog photographs or even a written diary provide. But there is no need for painful soul-searching on this trip. I'm content with where I am, and whom I'm with. I'm focussed on the here and now and it feels good.

'You mean you wouldn't go back down now?' Annabel asks.

'Are you crazy?'

'You know what your problem is, don't you Andrew?'

'What?' I ask, sitting up.

'It's a one-syllable word beginning with "a" and ending in "e" and it's got a "g" in the middle.'

'And I'm admitting it; I'm too old for this. I'm getting a day job.' The sharp pain has gone but my feet are numb now, like they've been chopped off at the ankles. 'How many flowers did Nina say there were in this valley?' I ask, flopping back on the mattress, feet propped against the wall.

'Between six and seven hundred.'

After long, hot showers, we dress and hobble over to the main building where several candles burn in the reception area even though it is a clear, brightly lit evening outside. 'It's a Norwegian thing,' I explain to Annabel. 'Like the heated shower floors. Makes things cosy.'

Nina lends us a flower book. From the photos we recognise flowers that weren't so obvious in our own book on mountain flora. Starry saxifrage, snow gentian, alpine speedwell, alpine milk vetch, northern wolfsbane, spotted orchid, melancholy thistle, to name just a few, become more obvious in this book illustrated with photographs.

At dinner, we once again demolish a tray heaped with so much good food it doesn't seem possible for two people to consume it all. As I waddle out of the dining room, Annabel comments on the line of thermoses and the bits of paper stuck to them with sticky tape. 'They're to be filled in the morning with tea or coffee, and the attached notes indicate whether it's to be with sugar or milk,' I explain.

Outside in the warm summer evening, we trundle around briefly before collapsing on our beds where Annabel reads aloud from the tacky novel.

Despite being sorely tempted to dive back into bed after breakfast, it's good to set out walking again in the fresh air with a sky as clear as yesterday and the ringing sound of cowbells amidst waterfalls.

'Remember anything from last night's reading?' Annabel asks as we set out for what is described as a seven-hour walk to Geiteryggen hut. We have left our packs to be carried by vehicle so we are walking once again with a minimum load.

'Um, not really.' I dreamt of flowers again; pastures full of flowers. I have a thing about flowers. Last year when I broke my back, I was on morphine for almost a week, and kept hallucinating about the flowers I'd planted in my garden. I was frantic that Annabel had to water them to keep them alive.

'I read the first paragraph and then asked, "Andrew William . . . are you still awake?" and there was no answer. You've missed the best part.'

'And we're not even halfway through the book.'

'Halfway? We're almost finished!'

'We are? So what's been happening?' I ask.

For the first half an hour of our walk, Annabel summarises what's happened in the novel to keep me up-to-date.

'How do you recall all the detail, names and everything?' If I'd read the novel, I doubt I could reconstruct it with so many facts. She astounds me with her ability to remember things. At home, Annabel keeps all our friends' and acquaintances' phone numbers in her head. Same with our calendar of appointments; we don't keep a diary. If I am asked out, I have to ask Annabel what we're doing on that date to see if we are free.

An hour later we're walking on drifts of snow left from the winter as we climb back into the mountains. Two Norwegians sun themselves beside the path on a promontory overlooking the valley. From here we can see the road and the transmission lines carrying electricity from the turbines in Vassbygdi to Oslo.

Halfway, we stop at another hut, Steinbergdal, where we stock up on more chocolate bars.

On the other side, higher up on an expansive snowfield, I see a huge herd of reindeer. 'Must be a hundred of them.'

'Where?'

I point them out to Annabel. 'They're easy to see, small dots running across the snow, fleeing something.'

'Three,' she says finally.

'Three! What're you talking about? There's a hundred up there! You can't even see them.'

'Typical guy thing. You see three reindeer and it immediately becomes a hundred.'

'It *is* a hundred.'

'I see three.' I watch her, puzzled, as she pulls the outer edges of her eyes and continues to look in the direction of the reindeer.

'What're you doing?'

'I can see better doing this. I'm not wearing my glasses but I can refocus my eyes by doing this'

'Are you serious?'

'Yes, I can see lots of reindeer now.'

'Told you.' I look up at the dots, no bigger than specks of pepper on the white snow. 'Couple of big males and lots of young ones and oh, look, there's an albino. It's got conjunctivitis.'

'Very funny.'

Like children playing hopscotch, we hop over stones strad-dling a small stream. When we cross to the other side, we stop and take off our socks and boots and let our feet cool in the water. 'Your blister seems better.'

'It's fine now. Your knees seem better and you're not taking anti-inflammatories or using your knee brace.'

'We're getting used to this. What's your favourite flower?'

'Dunno. What's yours?' she asks.

'The tiny blue gentian.'

'Why?'

'I like the intense blue colour, and it seems so tiny and vulner-able.'

Although it's getting late in the day and we are walking through more and more banks of snow, it is warm enough to take off my shirt. We are above the tree line again, walking on rein-deer moss and snow. Coffee-bean-sized rabbit droppings form deep craters where they have melted into the snow.

After six hours of walking, I catch up to Annabel and ask her, 'If we measured on a scale the pain our feet were in yesterday as a ten out of a ten, how painful are your feet today?'

She continues walking for a while then answers, 'I'd give it a three out of ten.'

'Sounds about right.' She starts singing. When she sings, I know she's happy.

We come across the first hiker since Steinbergdal hut. Her pack towers above her head and she's fully clothed; she even has rain gear on. A tent and a foam pad are tied on the sides of her pack. I look as if I'm going to the beach – bare-chested, my T-shirt stuffed in the pocket of my shorts. I walk a respectful distance, then turn around just in time to catch her turning around to stare at me.

I catch up to Annabel. 'My feet are a good, solid five now. If we don't get to the hut soon they'll be a six.'

'It's a slippery slope once they go beyond a five.'

The path joins a gravel road beside electrical transmission lines and soon we see our destination – Geiteryggen, a couple of large, two-storey buildings beside a lake. Just inside the front door, we find our packs lying on the floor next to a weighing scale. I hoist my pack onto the scale: just under twenty kilos. Annabel's is just under seventeen. Weighing our packs, we realise how lucky we have been not to have to walk with our packs these last two days. A colourful character behind the reception counter assesses us with an expert eye; Jan Eira, the manager, welcomes us and glee-fully informs us that it's raining in Oslo.

'What's with these Norwegians so concerned with the weather in Oslo?' Annabel asks as she leads the way up the stairs to a small double room with a washbasin.

'Norwegians are preoccupied by the weather, mostly because it's bad. If you phone anyone in Norway long distance, they'll ask you what the weather is like. Oslo's supposed to have better weather than most parts of Norway, so I suppose when it does rain in Oslo, they're happy everywhere else.' I open the windows over-looking the lake with bright, white banks of snow surrounding it. We both collapse on the beds and prop our feet against the wall again. 'We walked twenty-four kilometres uphill today,' I report.

'No wonder I hit six just as I took my boots off and stood in front of reception.'

'And tomorrow we've got another seventeen kilometres, but it's uphill a lot more, through snow, and we have to carry our packs.'

'And now we know how much they weigh.'

Annabel fills the aluminium washbasin from a tap out in the corridor and puts the basin on the pine table, shuts our door, and washes herself. Balancing on one foot, she reaches up with the other foot, puts it in the basin to wash and splashes water about the room. I ask her, 'Why don't you put the basin on the floor and just stand in it? Be a lot easier.'

She looks at me with surprise, as if I had discovered some intrinsic truth about the universe, and takes my advice while telling me, somewhat sheepishly, that her hair *is*, after all, blonde.

After a dinner of *lapskaus*, a stew of diced potatoes, carrots, leek, sausage and any meat leftovers from the previous day, we walk around the lake. Although the ice on the lake has melted, there are banks of snow some metres deep. The sky has been clear all day and the air is cool and crisp, but the sun is still warm. The light is intense and sharp. I wish I could capture this special light in a bottle and keep it for some dark, gloomy occasion in the future.

We walk around the back of the hut where a tame baby reindeer wanders into the kitchen and is promptly shooed out by the staff. Three lambs wait on the doorsteps until the reindeer comes back out. They move around as a herd, the long-legged reindeer thinking he's a leggy sheep, or more likely, the three sheep thinking they are stubby versions of a reindeer.

Jan comes out of the kitchen with bottles of milk and gives Annabel a bottle to feed to the baby reindeer. Living at this hut since his parents started managing it in 1966, Jan confesses it's the coldest summer he can recall. Five years ago he took over from his parents managing Geiteryggen hut and, like Lars at Skogadalsbøen, pays DNT 90 per cent of the income from the beds. He makes most of his profit providing meals and services; campers who sleep in tents but eat in the hut and buy lots of chocolate are most welcome. Jan is a Sami, what many people call a Lapp. His small herd of reindeer are remnants of the herd his parents once managed but gave up because they were losing more of their animals absconding each year to the herd of wild reindeer. Some 40,000 Sami live in Norway, still surviving off their reindeer herds, although many, like Jan, are now involved in tourism.

'We saw reindeer on the way up here,' I update Jan when Annabel has finished feeding the baby reindeer.

He cross-examines us as to exactly where the reindeer were, which direction they were heading and how many there were.

'A hundred.'

'Three,' Annabel says.

'Any wild animals around here?' I ask, diverting from our blatantly inconsistent observation.

'I found bear shit and bear tracks some weeks ago but never saw them. The government wants to reintroduce wolves. Three generations ago my ancestors went out on skis to kill them and now the government wants to bring them back. Even if the wolves don't kill the reindeer or sheep, they make it impossible for sheep farmers and reindeer herders. Once our animals smell wolves, they're gone.' Jan's English is perfect, if colloquial, probably a result of growing up in a DNT hut where there's a constant flow of tourists. In the dead of winter, Jan tells us, when the hut is buried in fifteen-plus metres of snow, he takes his tame reindeer to shopping centres and hotels all over Norway. Listening to him laugh, it's easy to understand why he's been typecast as Santa Claus. It wouldn't take much make-up or padding, maybe just a white beard, to make him look the part.

Later in the evening I read an entry in the guest book made on 14 March 1999. There's a long, three-page description written by a Dutchman of how a party of two Dutch and three Germans set out for Kongshelleren hut despite the prospect of a snowstorm and a warning from Jan not to go. Caught out by the blizzard, they lost their way and had to dig a snow hole to survive. Jan radioed the other hut to check whether they had made it, but when they hadn't arrived by midnight he realised they were probably in trouble. The Dutchman describes hearing snowmobiles and then seeing their headlights as rescuers went searching for the cross-country skiers.

He wrote:

> I'm not gonna bore you with the lessons learned, but I can't stop saying one. We people have intellect, knowledge, can make everything we ever dream of, have money, can move mountains . . . but we must RESPECT nature and weather, because we people are NOTHING.
>
> I've left my heart in Norway.

A whole bunch of us left our hearts in Norway.

We wake up to another glorious morning with no clouds and a sharp crispness in the air. Already, the Norwegian flag is flying proudly from the flagpole.

'You feeling okay?' I ask Annabel at breakfast. Despite the bright day, the dining room tables are laid with burning candles.

'Why?'

'Usually you've eaten slices of bread *before* you make your lunch packet.'

'Ah, slices of meat and cheese, pickles and herring for breakfast and lunch are starting to wear thin.'

'Even the goat's cheese topped with jam?'

'Even that. Wish I had some Marmite.'

Jan offers to take us to see some Stone Age shelters where he has found flint and spearheads. The boulders that formed this cave have long since fallen away but the remains of the prehistoric people's toolmaking, and collections of animal bones, remain.

Jan walks us to another point of interest. He has a deceptive way of walking: long, lanky strides, as if he's barely moving, hands hanging casually by his sides, shoulders hunched forward so there is a minimum of movement. His legs and feet hardly seem to be in motion, even as they fly over the boggy terrain. I suppose this economy of moving parts is how the Sami used to keep up with their reindeer herds for hundreds of kilometres, before they had snowmobiles. While I'm hopping and jumping, jogging and running after him, Jan glides effortlessly over the terrain. Even Annabel has difficulty keeping up with him. I notice from the streams trickling on either side of this hump of rocks that we have once again crossed the watershed between eastern and western Norway.

On the way back to the hut we pass the Geiteryggen, which, Jan explains, doesn't mean the literal translation of the goat's back, so much as holes in a ridge. The ridge has been scoured smooth by an ancient glacier and then, some time after, stones grinding into the softer bedrock had carved several circular holes. In one of these open-sided potholes, painted in red against the side, are the words '*Denne er ca. 4 m dyp*'.

Jan laughs. 'My father did that. It says, "This is about four metres deep", but he doesn't know how deep it is.' He shrugs. 'It could be one metre deep or six, but the sign keeps people happy.'

We thank Jan for his hospitality, pack our backpacks, then set off, skirting the lake until we are onto the deep snow on the other side and crossing a massive snow bridge. Annabel is well ahead as usual, so I know the snow will probably hold my weight too. When I catch up to her, I ask, 'Tell me about the book last night.'

'I finished it.'

'You did? What happened?'

'I read you the more exciting bits but you fell asleep again and then when I finished the book, *I* couldn't sleep. It was so light out-side . . . ' she replies.

'An American woman I met this morning told me she had counted fifty-three fields of snow between Geiteryggen hut and Finse, where we're heading.'

'Andrew, what qualifies as a "field" of snow? Could it be just a small patch?'

'Dunno.'

'What do you reckon those depressions in the snow over there are?'

'UFO landing spots,' I answer.

She looks sceptically back at me.

'Okay, how about where reindeer have slept? The heat from their bodies has melted the snow.'

Walking steadily upwards in absolute silence, we occasionally meet a Norwegian or two coming down, but no one seems to be going up. We climb ridge after snow-covered ridge and keep thinking optimistically that we're approaching the last one when we perceive another. The air is so clear it seems we can see for-ever and distances are difficult to judge.

We think we're approaching the highest point on another ridge when I look up and see a field of snow, and beyond what looks like another ridge a hundred metres in the distance. But the ridge isn't a hundred metres distant at all; it's actually the top of the Hardangerjøkulen Glacier some fifteen kilometres away. The air is so translucent the distances are totally distorted. When we reach the top we can clearly see the entire distant glacier with a long descent between. Behind us are the peaks in Jotunheimen and the tops of Hurrungane we walked through going down the Utladalen Valley.

At an area of broken rocks amidst the snow, we sit down to rest and take in the spectacular view extending hundreds of kilometres. Behind Hardangerjøkulen Glacier is Hardangervidda Plateau, the Roof of Norway, stretching into the distance. There aren't any waterfalls up here and it is so quiet, all I can hear is the wind blowing by my ears. Annabel snaps off a row of cold chocolate and hands it to me. We silently suck on the chocolate while admiring the scenery. There's nothing as satisfying as sitting on top of a mountain on a clear day and surveying the landscape below with God-like omniscience. Sometimes I am amazed at how far our own two feet can carry us, simply by putting one in front of the other, over and over again.

'We're lucky it's so clear. I've never seen it like this. Even on a perfectly clear day there's usually clouds hanging above the Hardangerjøkulen Glacier, especially in the summer, but today there's nothing, except far to the east where it's raining in Oslo.' I look around at these bare rocks surrounded by snow and glaciers, and spot a tiny, isolated gentian. It touches me to see these fragile lives surviving in such a harsh environment.

We descend through snow, past the emergency hut of Klemsbu, down bare rocks, over more snow bridges and eventually through a mountainside resplendent in lush grass and wild flowers. I glance over at Annabel, waiting for me beside the path. 'What's wrong?'

'This time next week we won't be together any more.'

I put my arms around her and kiss her.

'I'll miss you.'

'I'll miss you too, having a buddy to hike with and someone to read to me every night,' I reply with more meaning than my glib response might suggest. For two people who were so fiercely independent before they met, it's amazing how much we've come to rely on each other. The more I get to know Annabel, the more respect I have for her. This trip to Norway is our second big holiday together and it may seem a superficial and even a selfish trip down memory lane for me, but Norway was an important part of my life. There are feelings about our past that we have to deal with, together. Earlier this year we were in New Zealand visiting her family and friends and hiking some of the trails there. By going back to her country, meeting her friends and family, I understand Annabel so much better. I appreciate her willingness to come here to Norway.

Descending for some time we reach Finse six hours after leaving Geiteryggen hut. There are no roads here, besides the closed-off old railway supply road, and therefore no traffic. How magical places seem when there is no road traffic.

'Recognise the place?' I ask.

'The Bergen to Oslo railway line?'

'We came through here three weeks ago on the train.'

'It's greener now and almost all the ice on the lake has melted.'

Despite carrying our packs all day, we're both in good shape. We wait for an oncoming train to pass before we cross the railway tracks.

'Looks old,' Annabel comments.

'It's the local cycle train. They use it to transport cycles, backpacks and passengers doing the cycling trip over Rallarvegen, the old railway supply road the railway workers used to transport materials when they were building the Bergen to Oslo railway.'

'Which is what we're going to cycle?'

'If we don't first go up to the glacier tomorrow.'

'How long will it take?'

'Two days to cycle down to Flåm.'

We clamber up to the railway platform and cross to the unconventional Finse 1222 Hotel, which has a suspended railway carriage as a corridor to connect two buildings. Finse 1222 Hotel, named because it is 1,222 metres above sea level, is located right on the station platform, the highest in Norway. The fact that there is a railway so conveniently close by, and no road, makes the hotel a rather special place. A poster on the front door warns of polar bears. When I first saw that polar bear warning sign at two in the morning on a cold February night ten years ago, the alert hadn't seemed so far-fetched. That was my second month in Norway and everything about the country seemed to make a lasting impression on me. I recall leaving Bergen almost in the middle of that winter night, the train winding its way alongside the fjords, up the tortuous, silent valleys, past frozen waterfalls, into the mountains. I sat by the window and stared at the scenery. It was a clear night with a full moon hovering over mountains, glaciers and lakes so completely covered in snow it appeared to be a cottony, soft, vast blue snowscape. There were no rocky points of reference and, being far above the tree line, there was just a gloriously empty, frozen panorama. I felt my heart bursting with the magnificence of it.

Periodically the train disappeared into snowsheds only to re-emerge into a scene that seemed increasingly imposing. It was one of the most fantastic sights I had ever witnessed and it seemed bizarre to be sitting in the warmth and comfort and security of a train in the midst of something that looked like the dead centre of Antarctica. The analogy wasn't far wrong. Polar explorers, including Captain Scott and Sir Ernest Shackleton, visited, if not trained, at Finse. Scenes from the ice-planet Hoth in the Star Wars film *The Empire Strikes Back* were filmed here.

When the train stopped at Finse at two in the morning, I stepped out of the railway carriage into frightening subzero temperatures and howling winds. I made my way into the hotel through a tunnel on the platform carved out of a snowdrift fifteen metres high. Inside I was greeted by the spectacle of three railway workers in overalls – two dancing, thumping around arm in arm on the timber floors, while the third played the fiddle. Several empty and not-so-empty glasses of beer were assembled on a long wooden table. This out-of-the-ordinary experience, like so many in Norway, was etched into my psyche, another episode in my love affair with the country.

At that time Finse was still a major staging point for the railway workers stationed here to maintain the railway tracks, particularly in the winter. Not so long ago, a thriving community lived here, but now a new tunnel eleven and a half kilometres long has been completed just west of Finse, avoiding the section of the railway renowned for the worst snowdrifts. With the completion of the tunnel, there's less need now for the rotary snowploughs and the snow-removal teams, and Finse is depopulated, another community sacrificed to progress.

It's hard to believe as Annabel and I enter the lobby of Finse 1222 that it is in fact a hotel, much less one of the most luxurious of its time when it was built just before World War I. The interior is decidedly rustic with a stuffed reindeer and polar bear in front of plate-glass windows overlooking the blue lake and the glacier on the other side. We shower and wash our clothes in the room, return to reception and order a beer before walking through the high-ceilinged lounge with its flanking walls of plate-glass windows hinting at its exclusive heritage. Finse was one of the most fashionable destinations in Europe, on a par with Zermatt. The guest register included royalty and the rich and famous from all over Europe at a time when the world's attention was on the heroic exploits of the polar explorers and it was considered *de rigueur* to take a train to a place evocative of the Arctic.

There are many black-and-white photographs on the walls depicting the interior of the same elegant lounge, still easily recognisable, although large, exotic ferns decorated the room in those more exclusive days. We walk out to the balcony where we take off our sandals and rest our feet against the railing, taking in the view. It feels good to have walked here, to shower in scalding hot water, and now to sit with our feet up, cold beer in hand, gazing at the floating remnants of ice on the lake and the snow-covered glacier with its foot of blue ice. To the left of the new tunnel, the old railway line skirts the lake. Much of the track is buried under snowdrifts left over from last winter. A child toboggans down a field of snow piled high over the defunct track.

Several years ago, the previous manager of this hotel offered to let Kirsten and I stay two successive Easters at a tiny hut, Ravnaberg hut, thirteen kilometres from here, about 1600 metres up on the edge of the Hardangerjøkulen Glacier. The hut, both Easters, was totally buried under several metres of snow and the only thing giving it away was the tip of the metal chimney sticking through the snow by a few centimetres; nothing else was visible in a landscape consisting entirely of snow. We had to ski cross-country from the hotel, locate the solitary, snow-covered hut – not an easy task – then excavate the snow from outside the door to clear a tunnel to get in. There was a small iron stove for warmth and plenty of wood in what was essentially a luxurious snow cave.

In the middle of the week-long Easter break, there was a blizzard. Drifts blew all night into the excavated cavity we had dug and the outward-opening door was pressed in by cubic metres of snow. Fortunately one small window above the gas stove opened inwards. We opened it to a wall of snow and I began shovelling the snow into the hut, filling black garbage bags, one after another. When I had enough space to crawl out the window into a miniature snow cave, I continued shovelling snow back into the hut until I hit sunlight. Then I re-excavated the original tunnel back down to the door.

One bright morning, needing to pee, I put on my ski boots and, dressed only in my underwear, opened the door and climbed out through the tunnel. I turned around to see two telemark skiers descending the glacier. One stopped, conversed with the other, and then they both changed direction towards me. They were dressed in heavy Gore-Tex, goggles, woollen hats, thick gloves and packs on their backs. They skied down to me and stared incredulously at this bedraggled, bed-headed figure clad only in underpants and unfastened ski boots. As far as they could tell, the nearest hut was several kilometres away. 'What are you doing here?' one asked in English with an accent I deduced was probably German or Austrian.

They still hadn't seen the snow-covered hut. 'Taking a leak,' I explained truthfully, standing there for all intents and purposes naked.

It wasn't until Bonso heard their voices and came rushing out of the tunnel to protect me that they realised my 'walk', at least in my current state of undress, had entailed a distance of only a few metres.

Outsiders say Norwegians are born with skis on their feet. To be a famous cross-country skier, jumper or slalom champion is what many Norwegian children aspire too. Several times in Oslo I noticed teenage boys standing on the curb waiting for a bus. They went through this strange antic of standing on the curb, crouching down and then hurling themselves up and as far as they could into the street whenever there was no traffic passing by. I couldn't fathom what this aberrant behaviour was all about until a Norwegian told me they were practising ski-jumping.

I take a swig of my beer as we sit on the balcony of the hotel, facing the Hardangerjøkulen Glacier. Why does beer taste so good when it's expensive? You sip it as if you were swallowing liquid gold.

'Every few years, the population of lemmings explodes and they're all over the place,' I tell Annabel, apropos of nothing in particular. 'In Heidal, you could hardly go for a walk on those mountain ridges without stepping on one. On Lake Gjende, you'd see them swimming endlessly around in circles until they drowned. Here, you'd see them climbing by the thousands onto the glacier where their bodies remain, half-frozen, for years. Unless you like your 10,000-year-old glacier water spiked with little black bits of lemming fur and crunchy chunks of lemming bones, the water would be crap to drink.'

We head into the dining room, which is also evocative of earlier days when the hotel was the exclusive preserve of the elite. I eavesdrop on a young American talking to an older Norwegian couple. He speaks a few words of Norwegian but I can't quite figure out what his relationship to the Norwegian couple is. He seems to be familiar with them, and apparently their guest, so I presume he is an American of Norwegian ancestry visiting an aunt or uncle.

I point out the window at a rectangular patch of concrete beside the hotel. 'That's the foundation to a skating rink where the figure skater Sonja Henie practised. She won three Olympic gold medals in three successive Olympics and several world championships before she became a Hollywood star.'

Norwegians are crazy about winter sports. They won ten gold, eleven silver and five bronze medals in the 1994 Winter Olympics at Lillehammer, the second highest tally of any nation. With a population of only four and a half million, I calculated that on a per capita basis the number of gold medals the Norwegians won in those Winter Olympics equated to something like 600 American gold medals. I'd gone to the Lillehammer Olympics thinking I'd have to fight my way through hordes of people and cars but no traffic was permitted within sixty kilometres. Trains ran every ten minutes, efficiently shuttling spectators backwards and forwards from Oslo. Over the next two weeks the trains ran twenty-four hours a day, every ten minutes, on schedule throughout the games, and if it seemed God was on the Norwegians' side, this was confirmed by the weather. It snowed heavily right up to and through the opening ceremony, but then two weeks of cold weather followed when there wasn't a cloud in the sky and the metres of fresh snow shone like diamond dust in the sunlight. I couldn't get enough of those Olympics. There was a wonderful atmosphere and a sense of intense pride amongst Norwegians that their small nation was at the centre of the world stage. And then, as if drawing the curtains, it snowed heavily again during the final closing ceremonies.

After dinner we walk around Finse, examining the retired rotary snowploughs and the railway museum. The buildings that once housed hundreds of railway workers have been sold off and there are plans to turn one of the old railway buildings into a jazz hall to hold festivals. Walking beside the lake, we see the water flowing out to the east. Not only have we climbed back into the mountains again, we've crossed back into the eastward-flowing watershed.

Annabel stares intensely at the glacier across the lake. 'Are those reindeer?'

A dozen reindeer move over the side of the glacier. 'Ten to fifteen thousand wild reindeer live there up on the Hardangervidda

Plateau,' I reply. 'There are Stone Age caves over there on the other side of the lake from when Stone Age hunters followed the reindeer north as the continental ice sheets started receding. There's flint in the caves and arrowheads that come from Bømlo, an island south of Bergen, dating back some seven or eight thousand years.'

The egg-like summit of the glacier is covered in snow. During World War II, German soldiers occupied Finse with plans to make an airfield at the top of the Hardangerjøkulen Glacier so that heavily loaded bombers could use the slope of the glacier to help take off. The elevation above sea level meant the planes wouldn't have to climb any higher, they'd just have to maintain their height until they reached Britain, which meant they could carry heavier loads of bombs. Fortunately, the first Luftwaffe aircraft crashed on takeoff from the top of the glacier and disappeared down a crevice.

Rallarvegen, the old Bergen—Oslo supply road

The smell of bacon wafts through the lounge as we walk to the dining room. It's another buffet breakfast, similar to the others, but here we have bacon as well as the usual offerings.

The young American shows up late, eyes puffy. He stands at the buffet table and I make an offhand remark to the Norwegian woman he is with. We chat; I ask whether he is a visiting nephew.

'No, he is our daughter's boyfriend,' she replies in Norwegian.

'Where's your daughter?'

'Studying in the United States, where they met. She has a summer job there so she couldn't come home, but we're showing him Norway.'

'You picked up some Norwegian,' I comment, turning to him.

'*Ja, litt,*' he replies.

She asks me in Norwegian, 'Where are you from?'

'Canada,' I reply.

'But you speak Norwegian.'

'I was married to a Norwegian and lived here for five years.'

'But you're not married to her now?'

'No, I left Norway four, five years ago.'

'*Ja vel,*' she says, but I can see the question is at the tip of her tongue.

'Although it's a Western country and similar in many ways,' I continue, probably answering her unasked question, 'there are still cultural differences to bridge. It's not so easy for a foreigner to settle in Norway; it's a tight social community and there's the language barrier.'

She raises her eyebrows and nods. 'The divorce rate of Norwegians married to foreigners is very high,' she admits. Although her prospective son-in-law has learnt a few words, she adds quickly in Norwegian, 'And that's what I'm worried about.'

I shrug my shoulders in commiseration. 'Even two societies like Norway and North America, which seem so similar, are in fact culturally quite different. It's often emotionally hard for a Norwegian to leave Norway forever, and it can be difficult for a non-Norwegian to fit in here. They have to decide which country they're going to live in, which language they'll speak, and where they spend their Christmases. Suddenly things that would be taken for granted when both individuals are from the same place become major issues.' I finish loading my plate with bacon, scrambled eggs and toast and join Annabel. When the mother sits down, I overhear her repeating the conversation to her husband while the American boyfriend-in-law heaps his plate high with bacon and eggs and everything else, oblivious to the controversy I've just rekindled.

I had found it unexpectedly difficult immigrating to Norway. In the evenings, I took government-sponsored Norwegian language classes. Most of the other students were refugees, at that time from war-torn countries in Africa or Asia, although more recently Bosnians have become the latest wave of asylum-seekers. One night an Ethiopian asked the Norwegian teacher whether, if he moved into the house or apartment next to her, she would come over and introduce herself or bring him food to welcome him. She replied honestly, no. He said that he and his classmates couldn't understand how Norway gave so much foreign aid to countries in Africa at a national level and to them as refugees, but wouldn't as individuals knock on a new neighbour's door to welcome him into their country. It's not a criticism levelled so much at Norway as any Western European or North American urban community.

Mind you, she was living in Oslo and I'm not sure that same reaction would apply to all parts of Norway.

There were times living in Oslo, especially during the winter, when I would meet the same neighbours and greet '*hei*' as we passed; a simple, polite acknowledgement of the other person. More often than not, I wouldn't receive a reply, despite the fact that I might pass by that person every day. Years later, I realise the diffidence didn't reflect their negative attitude towards me, as I had thought, so much as their inherent reserved nature and their sense of personal space.

It was hard to get to know Norwegians, especially during the winters when it seemed they hibernated. But when I did manage to break through those barriers of reserve, I had friends for life. Now, having left Norway, I'm surprised at how many of what I might term 'acquaintances' consider themselves close friends, and have kept in touch with me over the years. One, Lars, has this uncanny ability to phone me at critical points in my life when I would most like to talk to somebody. It's as if we had some kind of mental telepathy going between us.

Norway's National Day is 17 May, the anniversary of the day in 1814 when the Norwegian constitution was laid down and Norway declared itself independent from the union with Denmark. Although it was a short-lived independence – Norway was forced the same year to accept union with Sweden – its existing constitution remained in force. This is the day all Norwegians express their pride in their country, dressing in *bunad*, their traditional costume, and waving the Norwegian flag. Finse is one of the collecting points for the more outdoors-oriented Norwegians to wave the flag. Camping in tents or even igloos made of snow and ice, they congregate here by the thousands and ski under a cluster of flags to the top of the Hardangerjøkulen Glacier. It's a fun occasion and moving to see how strongly Norwegians feel about being Norwegian, but it also served as a reminder to more recent immigrants like myself that we weren't, and never would be, really Norwegian.

This nationalism is more quaint than objectionable. Not having bullied the world for a millennium since the Vikings went rampaging around Europe, the Norwegian flag doesn't have the bad connotations of colonialism. Seeing the thousands of flags on 17 May, or raised on a flagpole outside a typical home on any fine summer day, isn't a sinister sign of an impending bout of aggressive imperialism or grotesque ethnic cleansing. Inside the atrium at the Royal Christiania Hotel in Oslo is a Norwegian flag that must be several storeys high, and yet there is no negativity linked with this display of national pride.

Annabel and I had hoped to do a guided-walking tour of the Hardangerjøkulen Glacier but the weather has clouded over and there are no other participants to persuade the guide to march over to the foot of the glacier.

'Shame we won't be able to do some glacier-walking on the blue ice,' I commiserate. 'Although we'll be walking across the Folgefonna Glacier in a week, we won't be on blue ice.'

The ten-day hiking tours I offered stopped here for two nights, spending a day walking on the glacier. I recollect one of those first trips. 'I had a group of British clients with one member who insisted on asking everyone what they did for a living, but would refuse to answer the same question, saying he worked for the British Defence Department and what *he* did was top secret.

'While he was tall and thin, his wife was rather short and fat. He had an annoying habit of criticising her every time she did or said anything, and of questioning me on whatever decisions I took. If I said, "Okay, we'll take a break here", he'd say, "Why not over there?" If I said, "We'll stop to have lunch now", he'd say, "Why not in an hour?" Whatever he was told to do, he challenged. This went on for a day until I lost my patience and told him that the guide makes the decisions, and as I was the guide and there wasn't a need for another guide, he'd have to abide by me. We were here on the glacier, all roped together, with Mr Top Secret following directly behind the local Finse glacier guide who was leading the way. I was at the end of the rope with a seventy-year-old quadruple coronary by-pass patient tethered in front of me so that I could keep a watchful eye on him. As we started climbing on the blue ice, with snow bridges filling some of the crevasses, the local Finse guide instructed everyone to make sure they stepped exactly in his footprints. Of course this was effectively saying to Mr Top Secret, "Don't step where I step!" Well, he didn't do as he was told. One second he was there, and the next he'd disappeared down a crevasse. It was his sturdy wife, to whom he was still attached by the safety rope, who was primarily responsible for preventing him from falling to his death.

'Suddenly the dicky-heart client in front of me doubled over, bright red in the face. I thought he was having another heart attack. As fast as my ice crampons would allow I scrambled up to him. "Are you all right?" I asked. "Yes," he replied, trying to hold back the laughter and hissing, "Somebody should pass a knife up to his wife so she can cut him loose." No one did, but we felt like it. After Mr Top Secret was pulled out of the crevasse, he was strangely subdued and well-behaved for the rest of the trip.'

We've arranged to rent a couple of mountain bikes, and for our heavy packs to be carried to the next hotel, Vatnahalsen, by the bike train so we'll cycle with only our warm clothes and lunch packets in the panniers. Magnus, the bike-shop manager, adjusts our bikes. His hair is so blonde it's white. Tall, broad-shouldered, narrow-waisted, with a strong jaw, high cheekbones, deep-set blue eyes, flawless complexion, full lips and a visible set of gleaming white teeth, he'd be a Hollywood heart-throb on a par with Brad Pitt, if only the American public knew about him. Unlike Hollywood film stars though, he seems totally unaffected.

We set off cycling Rallarvegen, the old supply road. Constructed by the railway workers a century ago when they were building the Bergen to Oslo railway, the 'temporary' road was so well made it still exists.

From a passenger's point of view, this stretch was one of the best parts of the railway trip, alongside these lakes facing the Hardangerjøkulen Glacier. But one of the challenges in making this railway was not only the construction of it, but also the maintenance required to keep it clear of snow in the winter. The low-pressure centres moving from the west coast meant that there was a constant battle against strong winds and heavy snow. Despite the fact that much of the railway line up here is, or was, sheltered by snow fences and snowsheds, intermittent gaps provided tantalising glimpses of the spectacular scenery. Now, the ride through the new eleven-kilometre tunnel to the west of Finse completely blocks out this magnificent landscape.

The child we'd spotted yesterday evening is back tobogganing down a snowdrift covering the railway tracks and the adjacent supply road. Although it is almost the end of July, and relatively warm, it's like stepping into a fridge whenever we have to get off our bikes to push through deep drifts of snow. In all the summers that I offered weekly five-day mountain-bike trips along this route, I can't ever remember it being as snow-covered as it is now, this late in the summer.

A couple of hours later, at Fagernut hut, a handy stopping-off point for lunch, we encounter a family of Norwegians – father, mother and five boys with a white Pyrenean mountain dog. The father's and the oldest boy's bicycles pull home-made two-wheel trailers. I examine the intricate work that has gone into making the trailers: a sturdy, steel frame mounted on bicycle wheels, fitted with a spare wheel, metal tubes for holding fishing rods and even custom-made frames to hold a workbox, axe and shovel. Inside the main frame are coolers, boxes of food, tents and everything they need to cycle over the old railway supply road spanning the Roof of Norway. The family, we are told, has planned this trip since last summer, and the father, Jarl, a farmer from southern Norway, spent the winter welding together the trailers. Despite the robust steel frames, one trailer has a cracked rod connecting to the bike and Jarl has had to jury-rig scavenged pieces of wood to support the shaft. They have cycled from Haugastøl, a stretch that is relatively easy compared to what we are about to do.

'It amazes me they have managed to reach this far,' I marvel as we watch them set off. 'There were some long patches of snow we had to get through and it was difficult enough for us without having to drag those heavy trailers behind us. The trailers must weigh a hundred kilos each.'

We mount and dismount our bikes as we alternate between cycling downhill over a gravel track and pushing the bikes awkwardly through deep, slushy snowdrifts left from the winter. We come across two stretches where we can't imagine the family successfully pulling the two trailers. One is a very steep incline over snow, and the other is a narrow ridge of snow, about a hundred metres long, with steep drops on either side. The path cut by previous bikes at the top of the snow ridge will be too narrow for the wider trailers to pass along.

Halfway along our route, we stop at Hallingskeid where the mountains open up to a rolling vista of flattened peaks. There are only a few scattered huts here and it seems totally isolated now, yet this was an historic marketplace centuries ago for traders from the west coast and farmers from the interior. I point out to Annabel the DNT hut where I stayed with my sister and her husband when they came to visit one June. There was still enough snow for us to ski cross-country. At the end of a week, they had a flight to catch back to Bermuda. The train stop for Hallingskeid is inside the nearby snowshed. Unfortunately, we miscalculated the climb from the hut to the snowshed and missed our train by minutes; the next one was an express that wouldn't stop. Fortunately, inside the cavernous interior of the snowshed is a public payphone. I phoned up Bergen railway station, explaining we'd missed the train and that if my sister and her husband didn't catch their flight out of Oslo for London, they'd also miss their connecting flight to Bermuda, and that they had two young children waiting for them. I waited patiently as I was connected by phone to the train driver of the oncoming express train and then I explained the problem again. The train driver told me if we were waiting inside the snowshed with all our belongings in hand, he'd stop and pick us up. That kind of thing can happen in Norway.

Cycling alongside a lake, we enter a tunnel hewn roughly into the bedrock under the railway line, to emerge on the other side at the top of a dramatic gorge with a plunging waterfall. Along this stretch of the old supply road carved into the sides of the ravine, there are vertical drops down to the surging mass of the icy, glacier-fed torrent. With the stony, uneven gravel surface and the steep decline it's always surprised me that there haven't been more accidents here. I notice now that there is a railing along the most dangerous segments.

Alongside another two tranquil, deep-blue lakes, connected by a plummeting turquoise waterfall, we cycle up the last stretch of track and reach Vatnahalsen Hotel, perched like the proverbial eagle's nest on a promontory overlooking the valley. As we lean our bikes against the hotel, the Flåm train descending from Myrdal on the Bergen to Oslo line stops at the Vatnahalsen platform to deposit our backpacks.

'Good timing,' Annabel comments.

Both my ten-day hiking trips and the five-day biking trips stopped at the Vatnahalsen Hotel for two days. This is one of my favourite places. 'Before we go to our rooms, I want to show you something,' I tell Annabel. We ignore our packs on the platform and I lead her across the Flåm-line railway tracks to a cliff face with a perpendicular drop into the Flåm Gorge. It's a dramatic view of a stunning valley.

'There's the continuation of the Flåm line way down there where it comes out of the tunnel on the cliff facing us and goes further down the valley, and over here, part of it does a corkscrew turn right underneath us. We'll cycle down the valley tomorrow, then return here on the train in the afternoon. It'll be a fantastic day.'

We pick up our packs off the railway platform, hoist them onto our shoulders and walk through a yellow buttercup-strewn lawn to the hotel. '*Takk for sist*,' I tell Jannet, the daughter of the previous owner and now co-owner and manager herself. Norwegians aren't great at saying 'please'; in fact there is no literal translation of our English 'please' except for their equivalent of 'be so kind'. But Norwegians will say 'thanks' or even 'a thousand thanks' for everything. It would be considered bad manners for us to meet each other now, for example, and for me not to thank Jannet for the last time I stayed here, even if it was five years ago. Jannet gives us the bridal suite, a large bedroom with an *en suite* living room. 'I must have moved up in the world, I never even knew they had these fancier rooms,' I comment as we move in.

When planning my tours and getting confirmation of the numbers, I would fax to Jannet's father the details of my group's dates of arrival and departure, and never get a reply. When I followed up with a phone call I was inevitably told it would not be a problem, and it never was. But it was a nerve-wracking experience to have guests about to arrive and not have any written confirmation of their bookings. What I began to learn is that for Norwegians, their word is binding enough. They deliver what they promise.

Annabel luxuriates in a bath, then when she's finished she pulls the plug and watches in amazement as the archaic plumbing system drains the water out of the plughole and directly onto the floor, flooding the bathroom before the water flows down a drain in the middle of the floor.

At dinner we are once again served a tray heaped with food, and yet we almost demolish the entire larder-sized offering.

'Have some more,' Annabel suggests facetiously.

I lean back in my chair. 'Couldn't, I'm stuffed.'

Despite my confession to being stuffed, when the dessert arrives I manage to tuck into it with the gusto symptomatic of someone who's been on a hunger strike for a month.

'How can you eat yet more when you said you were already stuffed?' Annabel demands, not unreasonably.

'It's the compartment theory.'

'The compartment theory?'

'I used to believe, and this evening's gluttonous performance would confirm it, that the torso is divided into compartments. The meat, potato and vegetable compartments go here.' I pat my budding stomach. 'However, chocolate, desserts and ice cream go into separate compartments up here.' I indicate my chest area. 'As you've probably noticed, you can very often feel full in your stomach but very rarely up here.'

'So that explains how you can be stuffed one minute and then eat a litre of ice cream the next.'

I waddle to a far wall to show Annabel photos of the hotel before it burnt down in 1942. Like so many of the traditional wooden hotels in Norway constructed during the tourist boom at the turn of the nineteenth century, their histories are brief. Inevitably most of them accidentally burnt to the ground, to be replaced with less ornate structures.

When the Germans occupied this place in World War II they didn't adhere to the rule of cutting logs for the iron stove short enough so that they would fit entirely inside. One night the ends of the burning logs sticking out the front of the oven fell onto the floor and burnt the place down. There are photos taken in 1953 of the rebuilt hotel, and also of the new wing, built during the awful architectural epoch of the 1970s. Unfortunately Norway is littered with buildings constructed during this utilitarian phase after World War II when the country was poor and still reconstructing, especially in the north where the occupying Germans razed entire towns to the ground. As Norway prospers there is serious talk about destroying some of the worst of the pragmatic but totally unattractive buildings. With a finer sense of architectural traditions, even family houses being built nowadays combine the best of modern architecture with long-established influences.

Upstairs at reception Jannet asks, 'You haven't met two of our other guests, Mr and Mrs Kirby?' She introduces us to an elderly couple sitting in a corner of the lounge drinking tea. 'They've been coming here ever since I can remember.' She asks John and Marion, 'When *was* the first time you came here?'

'In 1936. My father brought me here as a boy,' John replies proudly. 'He loved Norway.'

'And how many times have you been back?' Jannet asks.

'To Vatnahalsen? At least twenty times.'

'And what brought your father here?' I ask.

'*His* father. He loved Norway too, so it must be a genetic thing. I have photocopies I recently made of the letters my grandfather wrote to my father during his holidays here in 1889, if you'd like to read them.'

'That would be great,' I reply. 'We're going down to Flåm today but we'll be back this evening. Love to read them then.' Better than listening to Annabel's story about the wolf-men with red eyes.

'My father loved the Fretheim Hotel down in Flåm as much as he loved Vatnahalsen, but he'd roll over in his grave if he saw what's happening now.'

'Why?'

'It's so commercialised and there's too many tourists. That's why we prefer Vatnahalsen. There's no road here, no dock either, just a railway platform, so the main tourist artery bypasses us, except the passengers from the cruise ships that come for after-noon tea and crumpets.' He laughs. 'Marion and I have been com-ing here for so long we're an institution; the conductors recognise us and don't bother asking us for our tickets. They used to hand-write the tickets in the old days.'

'You've got seventeen of your photographs in the railway museum, so it's not as if you haven't done anything for the free train tickets,' Jannet says in her perfect English.

'Well yes, but Norway's a special place and the Norwegian people are so nice,' Marion replies. 'Last year I had a nosebleed when we were staying here. There's no road, so Jannet called the railway workers up at Myrdal. We got up to Myrdal and they used one of their yellow work engines, used for laying tracks or repair-ing the Bergen to Oslo railway line, to take me all the way to the hospital in Voss. I can't imagine the British railways doing that!'

'And you still go hiking every day?' I ask. They must be well into their seventies if not more.

'John's more interested in photographing flowers. He's become a bit of an authority. Knows them all although sometimes I wish we could just go for a walk instead of photographing every flower we pass.' Annabel looks pointedly at me. 'We have a list of all the flowers from Hallingskeid to Vatnahalsen that we've seen and photographed over the years.' She indicates the *Mountain Flowers* reference book I have sitting on my lap. 'He's got quite a few that aren't in there.'

'You can look at our list of flowers too if you want,' John offers kindly. 'I have them in our room. I'll ask Jannet to make a photocopy of the list and the letters my father wrote so that you can keep them.'

A sprightly Norwegian enters the lounge and begins to play the piano. Jannet tells us his name is Eivind Solås, apparently a famous musician and comedian on Norwegian television. 'He's come up here to be inspired and compose music. He was the house pianist for our guests in the 1950s and 1960s.'

When he finishes playing he comes over to say hello. 'Has anything changed here since you played for the guests?' I ask him.

He looks around the lounge, then laughs. 'No, not even the furniture, although the piano needs tuning.' He goes back to the warm sunlight outside and soon has half a dozen Norwegian guests howling with laughter.

'Have you seen Huldra at Kjosfossen Falls yet, Andrew?' Jannet asks.

'No,' I reply, puzzled at her question. 'What are you talking about?'

'The last two seasons they've had Huldra dancing to piped music on the rocks by the falls.'

'They're turning it into a Disney World,' Mr Kirby groans.

'We'll let you know what we think tomorrow,' I say to Jannet, 'when we come back up with the train.'

Annabel and I go outside to a blue sky brushed with sweeping streaks of pink, orange and red. Even the snowy tops of the mountains seem to radiate a luminous orange hue.

'This is the first night I'm not hurting,' I acknowledge. 'I could go for a run, except I'd have to watch out for the hulders.'

'What on earth are they?' Annabel asks.

'They're mythical female creatures of the underworld who lure men into the mountains where they disappear. They look like very beautiful women and the only way to recognise a hulder for what she is is by her cow's tail, which she tries to hide. Of course, by the time you've seen whether she's got a cow's tail or not, it's usually too late to do anything about it.'

The Norwegian fairy tales – especially of Huldra, one of the hulders – caught my imagination, partly I guess because I happened to be one of Huldra's easy victims. Now when I see a pretty

Norwegian woman, like our waitress tonight, I don't bother looking for her tail; I simply avert my eyes so I can't be lured.

Flåmsdalen Valley

We get on our bikes after breakfast and cycle to the first of the twenty-one hairpin turns in the gully immediately below the hotel.

'Ow, ooh, ouch!' I exclaim as I ride down the rocky path. The appropriate body parts are still tender from yesterday's cycling. We get off and walk our bikes down the hairpin turns, the route so steep that if the front wheel hit a rocky protrusion you'd go over the handlebars.

Dwarfed by the cliff face of the mountain, the Flåm train toots like a toy locomotive as it climbs up the steep gradient and disappears into a tunnel. This must easily qualify as one of the most spectacular train rides in the world. It took twenty years to build the twenty-kilometre line, incorporating twenty manually excavated tunnels, several hairpin turns and a couple of corkscrew loops actually within the mountain; a feat of engineering impressive even by modern standards. All but two of the tunnels were excavated by hand.

'You can smell the flowers and the freshly cut hay,' Annabel says as we stop on a small bridge. Emerging from the narrow defile of hairpin turns and into the Flåmsdalen Valley, it quickly becomes warm as the sunlight rises over the top of the mountain and shimmers on the turquoise Flåmselve River, illuminating a field dense with yellow buttercups interspersed by patches of blue or purple. Once again, I stop to savour the magnificence of the sharp light, the colours, the smells, the sound of the roaring river splashing over rocks.

We coast by a goat farm pungent with the odour of goat droppings, to a bridge spanning the river. A plaque in the middle of the bridge is a poignant reminder of an eighteen-year-old German who fell off the bridge while taking photographs on 16 July 1994. Just like some of the rafters on the Sjoa River, his body was never found. It was the dangerous hidden undercuts in the rocks and the rapidity with which the glacier-fed rivers could become raging torrents even on sunny days that persuaded me that I didn't want to continue with the rafting business. That last summer, after three fatal accidents on the river that involved other rafting companies, we sold our rafts and equipment and folded up the business. We had been lucky not to have fatalities, but the risk was always there.

There is a sense of sadness that pervades this beautiful corner of the river where the falls tumble down into a tranquil, deep blue pool. Annabel and I pick wild flowers and put them in a jar beside a wooden cross, inscribed simply with the young German's name. I have passed this shady glen a dozen times since that tragic date and there have always been fresh flowers in the glass jars by the cross overlooking the pool of water.

Across the other side of the falls is an old farm. It has a barn and fields of grass and wild flowers that have been cut and hung to dry on wires strung between wooden poles. I take a dozen photos from different angles, and each photo could be the cover to a photo calendar. The pastures are so full of starry chickweed that from this side of the river they look like they have a dusting of snow. At an old bridge where we used to have our picnic lunches on our walking tours, I look to see whether a single mountain queen flower is still growing precariously on a rock in the middle of the river. It is still there, and it's like meeting an old friend.

At a small, artificially made dam that forms a weir across the river is a sign: 'Warning: Bathing and other sea activities are not allowed in this area because of dangerous enorents underneath surface.'

'Enorents?' Annabel looks at me quizzically.

'Norwegians do have mythical creatures living in their lakes, bit like the water-logged equivalent of trolls, but I think you'll find that "enorents" is probably the English word "currents".'

We pick wild raspberries covered in a coating of dew and our fingers are soon stained red. They are so flavourful, like doses of raspberry concentrate. We also find the occasional patch of wild strawberries; tiny versions of the farmed strawberry, smaller than a peanut, but compensating for its diminutive size with its formidable burst of taste, as if they too were flavour concentrate.

At Berekvam Station, the halfway point where the ascending Flåm train meets the descending train, a complete hillside is resplendent with giant daisies. 'I think these are oxeye daisies,' I tell Annabel. 'Strange how a particular section of hill will be completely covered by a specific flower.' We stop to take close-up photographs, with the valley, waterfalls and snow-topped mountains in the background. Beside the railway workers' hut a woman sunbathes while reading the newspaper. At the blast of the train horn she quickly puts on her railway uniform and hat, leaves the newspaper folded on her chair, and carries her red and green flags along the tracks to the railway switch.

Further down we reached the outskirts of Flåm and its quaint wooden church. Norwegian churchyards all seem to have flowers flourishing in front of every grave. I'm not sure whether the churchwardens organise this, or whether it's relatives of the deceased. Walking through the Flåm churchyard, I say to Annabel, 'Even in front of this foreigner's gravestone, there is always a bunch of thriving pansies.' The gravestone read, 'In memory of Owen O'Neil. 10-2-1965. He loved the Flåmsdalen Valley and died here 16-9-1982'. He wasn't even eighteen.

There is a preponderance of gravestones inscribed with the names Flam, Flaam, Flåm and Fretheim. Many of them say '*Takk for alt*' under the person's particulars. '*Takk for alt*' translates literally as 'Thanks for everything'. I've never really known what that infers. Maybe it's just politeness. What I think it means is a general expression of thanks, as in 'I've had a good innings; thanks to God, friends, relatives and everyone else who made life what it was'. I mean, Norwegians are constantly saying thanks so it's no surprise when they say thanks at the end of their lives.

Around the back of the churchyard we see Mr and Mrs Kirby sitting on a wooden bench in the corner of the graveyard. 'What are you doing here?' I ask.

'We took the train down and we always have our lunch breaks here. It's nice and quiet and no one bothers us. Maybe one day we'll be buried here,' Mr Kirby adds. I'm not sure if he's being facetious or not. 'It's deadly quiet here,' he adds with his distinctive smile showing a single upper tooth up front.

We cycle the remaining distance to the railway platform, souvenir shops, dock and the Fretheim Hotel. 'Holy cow,' I exclaim when I see the massive addition to the hotel. 'It's huge. No wonder Mr Kirby said his father would roll over in his grave.' We walk into the impressive modern foyer of the hotel and up the open stairs in the atrium to a glass room at the top providing a panoramic view of the gardens and fjord. 'But I guess it's not that bad,' I retract. 'There are huge numbers of tourists coming to Flåm now and they needed to expand their facilities; Flåm can't remain a sleepy backwater forever. It's hard for people like the Kirbys who have been coming here for years, but there are plenty of places in Norway that are just as beautiful where the mainstream tourists don't pass. Flåm is so popular because the train, cruise ships and the main road between Oslo and Bergen all intersect here.'

Like Gudvangen at the end of the Nærøyfjord, Flåm has changed dramatically in the last ten years, especially since the expansion of the dock area and railway platform using all the rock excavated out of the four- and eleven-kilometre tunnels through the mountain to Gudvangen. Sleepy Flåm recently won an award for having the best-improved port facilities in North Europe and almost a hundred cruise ships now overwhelm the small community annually, carrying a total of 50,000 passengers and crew. Aurland, which includes Flåm and Gudvangen, is one of the richest counties in Norway, not only because of the large numbers of tourists passing through but also because of the hydropower generated from water falling through hidden tunnels that powers generators just outside the centre of Aurland. Most of that electricity goes to Oslo with a tidy royalty payable to the county.

'The main road from Oslo to Bergen used to be this little lane we're crossing now,' I say as I take Annabel's hand. 'When I first drove it a decade ago, it was a dead end that led to the tiny dock where you had to drive onto the ferry to Gudvangen. Now that they've built the tunnel to Gudvangen and the flyover bypassing Flåm into the tunnel to Aurland there is no government ferry service, although there is a converted ferry that carries passengers during the summer, along with a multitude of other boats working this lucrative stretch of fjord.' We walk onto the landfill of rocks excavated from the huge tunnels. Flåm's old railway platform and dock were, until recently, severely stretched to accommodate the tourists discovering Norway in increasing numbers every year. But the newly built shopping centre, souvenir shops and restaurants are in harmony with the local architecture, and if you didn't know any better, you'd never know that none of this existed ten years ago.

The Flåm railway platform, located conveniently beside the Flåm dock, is a hive of tourist activity with what seems like thousands of visitors about to board or disembark from boats or trains. This is peak tourist rush hour. An enterprising young busker in a traditional Norwegian *bunad* plays the accordion, cap on the boardwalk in front of him.

We hand our bikes in to the special cycle shed where they will be sent back to Finse. Then we board the train moments before it sets off on its twenty-kilometre climb, 865 metres up the Flåmsdalen Valley, winding in and out of the steep mountain walls to Myrdal where it connects with the Bergen to Oslo train.

As an indication of how things are changing in Norway, an institution as venerable as the Flåm Railway has recently been sold by the Norwegian State Railways (NSB) to Flåm Development, a largely community-owned limited company. While NSB is still responsible for safety and operations, the private company has taken over the business management and marketing of the famous spur line. It is in effect, Norway's first 'privately owned railway'. Newly refurbished carriages, and engines in natural green are the most obvious changes, as are the railway platforms, which have been extended to accept the trains' increased capacity. The trains can now carry something like half a million tourists. It will be, if it isn't already, one of the prime tourist destinations in Scandinavia. Norway, Europe's best-kept secret, is rapidly stepping into the limelight. The old days when this quaint railway spur line succeeded in attracting tourists despite itself, have gone. The Huldras at Kjosfossen Falls are a measure of the marketing and packaging efforts that have recently gone into making the Flåm line a major tourist attraction.

This is the steepest adhesion type railway anywhere in the world, with a gradient of one in eighteen over 80 per cent of the line. We sit on the right-hand side of the carriage and I take photos of the sunlit farms and fields and the church as we climb up the valley past the original Flåm village. The train ducks into the first of twenty tunnels, under which the Flåmselva River flows, and I pull Annabel to the other side of the carriage. As we climb higher we cross the river again through a tunnel and Annabel and I jump back to our original seats. Rather than traversing bridges spanning the river, the river is diverted under the railway through tunnels in the mountain. Across the valley is the Trolla avalanche, a leftover mound of snow at the foot of waterfalls tumbling down from Trollanuten. We exit out of another tunnel to a view of the twenty-one hairpin turns and several waterfalls with free falls of a couple of hundred metres. On this side a wire retaining net prevents rockfalls from above hitting the train.

The train slows as it exits the tunnel at the Kjosfossen Falls, then stops with a jerk at a water-soaked wooden platform where we disembark. We are at the bottom of waterfalls tumbling quite literally out of the sky onto a rock ledge above us, the water cascading and twisting down to a pool below. Norwegian folk music plays from hidden speakers. I stand at the front railing, oblivious to the spray of water soaking me. I played Arve Moen Bergset's music over and over again in my house in Ottawa for a year before I moved to Norway, and Kirsten. Even now, the haunting melodies have a profound effect on me.

As the music plays, a long-haired hulder in a flowing red dress rises mysteriously out of the rocks high above, almost out of the falls themselves, and begins a slow, teasing movement, luring us into the mountains and beckoning with her hands for us to follow. She seems to disappear into the falls and then almost immediately appears again, closer, beside an old stone structure. She gestures seductively, then disappears only to resurface in the middle of the falls. I get goose bumps watching the performance and listening to the poignant tunes played on a fiddle over the loudspeakers. At last Huldra disappears into the rocks, the music stops and the conductor ushers everyone back onto the train.

'What'd you think?' Annabel asks as we sit down and I shake the water out of my hair.

'It was tastefully done, not like Disney World at all. It's subtle and a part of Norwegian folklore. If tourists don't like it, there are a million other waterfalls in Norway where they don't have a Huldra tempting you into the mountains to the accompaniment of Norwegian folk music. Look at the tourists on this train; most of them aren't the kind of purists who would go hiking into the mountains. Anyway, this isn't even a natural waterfall; it comes out of a small dam at the throat of the lake above. Vatnahalsen means "the lake's throat".'

'I don't think half of them even saw Huldra dancing up there,' Annabel says. 'They were too busy taking photos of themselves against the backdrop of the falls.'

The hulder was so unintrusive that when the tourists return home, they'll develop those photos and wonder who the crazy woman was in the red dress dancing up there in the falls and maybe, hopefully, they'll be intrigued enough to find out what it was all about.

The train ducks immediately into another tunnel carved into the vertical cliff face and we begin a series of corkscrew 'turn-around' turns within the mountain with just the occasional glimpse down the valley, first on one side of the carriage and then the other. These shelves built into the rock face are several hundred metres above the bottom of the valley. Having reversed direction within the rock, we exit the tunnels and curve around to the Vatnahalsen Hotel.

I can never get enough of the Flåm Railway. I've done it so many times and yet as the seasons change, and the weather, there's always something new to observe. It's like a wonderful natural work of art: you can't stare at the different perspectives of the valley long enough. As we get off, a cycling couple gets on the train with their young son covered in bandages. The husband carries his son's bicycle, which has a wheel crushed beyond use.

Before we left this morning, we hand-washed our clothes and put them on the heated bathroom floor to dry. I carefully avoid treading on them with my sweaty feet as I step into a steaming bath after Annabel has finished. 'It's not the same thing,' I shout above the splash of tap water.

'What?'

'Not hiking all day. You don't get the same adrenaline rush of endorphins or whatever it is that makes us so happy when we're tramping under a heavy backpack. You know what?'

'No,' she yells back.

'I'm going to go down to the falls tomorrow and check out that Huldra. I want to know how she appears and disappears out of the falls like that.' I'm not concentrating on what I'm doing and I accidentally twist the chain to the plug with my big toe, making the water drain out as the hot water pours in. I'm unaware of this until Annabel comes into the bathroom.

'You've flooded the floor and soaked our clothes, Andrew,' she says calmly, looking at the pool of water inundating the bathroom.

I sit up in the bathtub and look over the edge. 'Whoops.' I quickly replace the plug. 'Don't know why they have bathtubs that drain onto the floor like that.'

We squeeze as much water out of the clothes as we can and place them on the heated floor again to dry overnight. At dinner, Annabel wears a plaid flannel shirt from the bottom of my backpack. I've worn this shirt on every single hiking or backpacking trip I've made in the last ten years. It looks a lot better on her.

After dinner, enjoying tea in the comfort of the sofas in the lounge, we mention the minor bathroom disaster to the Kirbys. Mrs Kirby laughs. 'John's done the same thing.'

I notice a bedraggled character in the lobby. His face is black, his white-blonde hair is grey, his clothes are black, even his blonde eyebrows are black. The only aspects about him still white are the whites of his eyes and his teeth. It takes me a second to recall where I have seen him before. It's Jarl, the father of the five boys and the owner of the two bicycle trailers full of camping equipment. We had just been thinking about them, wondering how they could possibly make it over those mountains and fields of snow. He has come into the hotel to collect a bicycle pump he lent one of the biking guests.

Annabel and I go outside and say hello to the family. They sit in the garden on a wooden bench, exhausted. All of them are grimy and covered in bicycle grease. Even the white Pyrenean mountain dog is shattered, lying under the table, dirty as the others. Annabel and I ask them how they climbed up some of the steep banks of snow, and how they managed to cycle towing their bike-trailers along the long snowdrift with steep drops on either side.

The mother of the boys replies in English, 'We emptied out each of the trailers and carried them across empty, then we carried everything that was in the trailers.'

'How much do the trailers weigh?' I ask Jarl, the father. The linking arms between both trailers and bikes have broken and are lashed with rope to branches. I don't know how they got them here.

'Fifty to sixty kilos in each trailer.'

The boys, who are aged between seven and sixteen, listen politely as Annabel and I grill the parents on the trip. The mother, Randi, tells us how she suffered vertigo on the ridge of snow and had to be helped across.

'Do you mind if I go and get my camera and take a photo of you?' I nip back to our room and on the way out buy five Kvikk

Lunsj bars for the kids from Jannet at the reception desk. I'm tempted to buy a beer each for pappa Jarl and mamma Randi but I've a sneaking suspicion they are teetotallers. A couple of things that they've said, and mamma Randi's cross pendant around her neck, plus the fact that they come from the coast down south where whole stretches of coastline are alcohol-free, dissuades me from buying the alcohol.

When I offer the children a chocolate bar each, they are hesitant to accept them until mamma Randi okays it. They thank me politely. They look like kids who have just survived the Blitz, but it's only the youngest one, Vetle Jarand, who opens his carefully, breaks off a piece and quietly eats it. I've never met such polite kids.

Apparently they are grimy because Vetle Jarand had five punctures today and they were all involved in fixing them. I examine the smallest bike and test the front wheel. It's as flat as can be. 'That's his sixth puncture,' papa Jarl tells me, shrugging his shoulders.

'Were the kids good?' I ask. I wonder if their epic summer holiday cycling over the roof of Norway has been a disappointment. 'I mean, did they enjoy it?'

Mamma Randi replies, 'We have been singing songs every night.' She surveys them proudly. 'I think they were very happy.'

They started their cycle last Wednesday and today is Monday. I look at the kids and although they are exhausted, I can see they really are happy. I admire them for taking on the challenge. The family reminds me of the stoic Norwegian pioneers who settled in North America. They continue on, a line of seven, pushing and pulling bikes and trailers, followed by their pooped dog, another two kilometres up towards Myrdal, where they will camp for the night.

Back in the hotel Mr Kirby hands us photocopies not only of the flowers he has identified here, but also pages from his grandfather's letters to his children written while he travelled around Norway. 'I'm sorry I don't have all the letters from his trip, but you might find these interesting, especially because you came by boat from Newcastle to Bergen, and if you are going to Ulvik and Odda.'

I look through the list of flowers and recognise many of the names, but not all of them. 'Wow, how many have you listed here?'

'Eighty-three,' Mr Kirby answers. 'But that list doesn't even include the clovers, stitchworts, tormentils, willows and birches.'

'Down in the valley below you'll also find monkshood, wood geranium, red campion and buttercups, which we haven't listed,' Mrs Kirby adds.

'Don't forget the others,' Mr Kirby butts in. 'Blue sow thistle, melancoly thistle, welted thistle, field scabious and vetches in yellow, blue and mauve.'

'There are angelica, meadowsweet, cow parsley, oxeye daisies, bedstraws,' Mrs Kirby rhymes twenty of them off as if by rote.

'There are probably three to four hundred flowers in the short stretch of this valley. We've found seventy that we can't find in England.'

'Were there any bears in the valley when you first came here?' I ask, diverting for once off the subject of flowers.

Mr Kirby gives a short laugh. 'I asked a Norwegian that once, and he said there were so many bears in the valley they made jars of jam out of them for the winter.'

For the second night the sky turns bright red; the summits and peaks brooding silhouettes against a smouldering backdrop. Even after we've gone up to our room, the sky remains crimson, wisps of mare's-tails catching the light. We leave the windows wide open to another dream-like summer night in Norway, high up in the mountains, away from everything.

Shuffling through the pages the Kirbys have given me I call to Annabel before she comes back out of the bathroom, 'Here's a letter written on 26 June 1889 by Mr Kirby's grandfather to his children; it describes the same boat trip we took from Newcastle to Bergen.' I read out aloud the account of boarding the boat in England and the detailed description of the trip over to Norway, written while he and his wife were staying at Smeby's Hotel in Bergen.

I start reading as Annabel slips under the covers.

> Bergen is quite a pretty place, mostly built on a peninsula between two arms of the sea. Around the head of one of these two arms are most charming old houses and warehouses, all gabled, all red-roofed, the warehouses having cranes under short projecting roofs. Behind the town were the high hills all around it. Seven of them, the Bergen people say, like Jerusalem and like Rome. Inside Bergen it is equally interesting, and mother and I enjoyed very much our walk along the principal street, the Strand Gade, and the market place, the Torvet.

'It probably hasn't changed that much since he was there,' I interrupt myself before continuing.

> Mother actually climbed a high hill called the Floifjeldet, and touched a large stone on the top which the guide books say only active walkers should do, which is not to be wondered at, for the path is very steep and rough and the hill is 800 feet above the town. They are busy making a wonderful, skilfully devised footpath, and when you and the boys go to Norway, you will not be able to estimate mother's achievement for all the rough ways will then be made smooth.'

'That part's changed. We walked up a nice wide path,' Annabel remembers.

I put the letter down on the bedside table and turn off the light. 'Strange to read this diary from over a century ago.'

There's no answer from Annabel.

I stare out through the large open window at the snow-capped mountains, and listen to the sound of water tumbling off them. It's already getting lighter. During the dark Norwegian winters I cherished memories of midsummer nights like this, and even now I can recall them at will. I snuggle next to Annabel under the duvet, feel the cool breeze drift through the open window, and listen to the ever-present white noise of waterfalls filling the eerie silence.

Annabel puts her arm over me. 'Look, it's snowed during the night.' I sit up. The mountains are covered in a dusting of white.

During breakfast we hear Eivind Solås composing music in the room upstairs.

'I'm going to see Huldra down at the Kjosfossen Falls. Want to come?' I ask Annabel.

'I think I'll just chill out here for a bit and read Mr Kirby's letters.'

The train driver laughs as I stand at the platform and stick my thumb out as if hitchhiking. It takes a couple of minutes winding through the corkscrew tunnels below Vatnahalsen before the train comes out at the viewing platform at the falls. I've already explained to the train conductor that I want to visit Huldra and he has radioed ahead to arrange it. It amazes me how informal Norway can be, how easily things can be organised. He instructs, 'Remain on the platform after the train has gone and she'll come down and get you.'

When the train stops, passengers bail out and most take photos of the falls or of themselves in front of the cascading water. Instead of watching the falls, I study the crowd. When the folk music starts there are only a handful who realise that Huldra has appeared. I overhear an American woman ask her husband, 'Is that for real?'

'Are you kidding?' he answers. 'It's just a mechanical dummy.' But he looks long and hard. When the second one appears by the stone building, waving her hands and beckoning us to follow her, he's not so sure.

It's the Norwegian spectators who get the most out of the performance. They know what a hulder is and, like myself, feel that seeing a re-enactment of this fairy-tale creature is something special. You could probably count on the fingers of one hand how many of the foreign visitors know why the woman in a red dress with the long hair is beckoning them up there.

After the train has gone, I wait. Sure enough, a few minutes later, Huldra comes scrambling down the side of the falls. Unlike the mythical Huldra, this one has a safety harness around her waist with a carabiner attached to a safety rope that's bolted to the rocks. She's not wearing her long red dress, just long woollen underwear and gumboots.

'*Hei, hei,*' she says in a human voice. 'Want to come up?' She hands me a safety harness and an extra set of rubber gumboots. I accept the harness but decline the boots and follow her up the slippery narrow path to the stone ruins. Hidden from view is a mobile construction hut in the centre of the remains of an old building erected by the Germans during the war to house a turbine generator. The roar of the waterfalls is so loud I can barely hear her ask me to remove my muddy boots before stepping into the hut.

Inside is another hulder, wearing a long wig. I introduce myself to Ragnhild Sleireøyen and Silje Håvet. Their hut is warmed by an electric heater and is equipped with two sofa beds, a small dining table, a radio and a refrigerator and there are a pile of newspapers and magazines in a corner.

'How did they get this hut here?' I ask, admiring the facilities so cleverly disguised from view within the stone ruins.

'By helicopter.'

'Do you get a lot of visitors?' I ask.

'Just plumbers,' Silje answers seriously. 'Want something to eat? We haven't had breakfast yet.' She pulls a loaf of bread and condiments out of the fridge and pours me a mug of hot chocolate.

'You must freeze out there,' I comment.

'We have wool clothes underneath our red dresses. They get wet but at least we stay warm. It was worse last year when we first started doing this because we didn't have a nice hut, although we did have wet suits.'

'What did you think of it?' Ragnhild asks.

'I thought it was fantastic.'

She smiles. 'When I applied for the job I was sceptical, but now I think it's great and all the Norwegians I know think it's good. But it's kind of an absurd job getting cold and wet for ten minutes fourteen times a day, spending the rest of the time here in the hut. It's nice to get visitors like you.'

'Can you hear the music from up here?'

'Yes, but after a while you start hearing it coming out of the falls and you don't know if you're really hearing it or not. Sometimes I hear a complete orchestra playing and then I think it's the devil in the waterfalls luring me and I know I need fourteen days off. There are hundreds of stories of Huldra in this valley and a lot of people here still believe them. I meet old people who claim they have seen a hulder.'

There's a crackle from a radio as the conductor on the train coming up warns they are about to go into the last tunnel before the falls. The two hulders put on their red dresses and wigs and I follow them outside. Ragnhild crouches down low and then waits, squatting in a depression in the rocks. Silje signals to her, pushes a button mounted on the stone wall, and the music starts. I hide behind a wall and watch Ragnhild rise out of the hidden pool of water and dance on the rocks before she disappears by crouching back down in the pool. Silje in the meantime stations herself beside the stone wall and beckons to the train passengers below, then signals again as she disappears and Ragnhild rises out of the water and then ducks down too for the final time. The music stops. It seems to take an eternity for all the passengers to board the train. Finally the train disappears into the tunnel. Ragnhild scrambles over the rocks back to the hut.

'That's what we do fourteen times a day for fourteen days straight. Then we get fourteen days off. There are four of us hulders living all together in a house down in Flåm,' Ragnhild says.

Silje adds, 'The conductors tell us that a lot of the tourists don't think we're real. We've heard they don't even think the falls are genuine; they think those rusty steel pipes for the old turbines are used to recirculate the water and that it's turned off and on for the tourists when they come by. The last thing they think is that we and the falls might be authentic. Kind of sad . . . '

'Be sadder if you came to work tired and hung over. One little mistake . . . ' I comment.

'You'd only fall once,' Silje interjects.

On the wall is a hand-drawn calendar showing the weather they've had since the summer season began. Except for the last few days, it's entirely covered in rain clouds.

I have to wait for another train going down before I can board a train going back up. After a second performance I thank Ragnhild and Silje for allowing me to visit and I clip myself onto the safety rope to descend the rocks to the train platform.

Annabel is ready and packed by the time I get back. We say goodbye to Jannet, perhaps for the last time because, even if we come back here, she's hoping to sell the hotel. 'I want to work in Barbados for a while . . . sunshine, beaches . . . buy a car . . . '

Because I've been told it's a steep descent that can be dangerously slippery, I've asked Jannet to phone over to Mjølfjell Youth Hostel to find out whether anyone has walked from there to Ulvik this summer. The hostel confirms a few hikers have made it, despite all the snow.

I phone my friend Stephen to let him know we're on our way to Ulvik and that we'll meet him in Odda so he can guide us over the Folgefonna Glacier to Rosendal.

We say goodbye to the Kirbys and promise to keep in touch.

Standing on the platform waiting for the Flåm train, I hear the folk music echoing from the surrounding waterfalls, just as Ragnhild and Silje had said. But there's no possible way we could hear the music being played far down below at Kjosfossen Falls.

We board the train for the short ride up to Myrdal and as the train climbs past the spot where the cycling family, the Abrahamsens, were camped, we spot their tents, but no sign of them. Indomitable, they've probably cycled down to Flåm for the day.

Reaching Myrdal, we've hit the main artery for tourists in Norway. The more convenient front carriages are booked entirely by Japanese groups. Their guides are easily recognisable by the long sticks with little flags attached at the top that they carry over their heads. Tourists collect as those passengers who have just arrived on the Flåm line wait for the train to take them to Bergen or Oslo. Guides rush around with their flags, umbrellas or hands in the air, followed by their gaggle of tourists. I think I hear the baaing of a sheep until, watching and listening, I realise it's a member of a Spanish group with a noisemaker that sounds like a sheep. It's funny the first, second and even the third time, but judging from the expressions on the faces of the other Spaniards in the group, the joke has worn thin.

The Flåm train descends back down to Flåm and the Oslo to Bergen express takes its complement of passengers away. Suddenly there's almost no-one left on the Myrdal railway platform nestled into a ledge on a side arm of the Flåmsdalen Valley. Annabel and I have to wait for the next train, the slow local, which will stop at Mjølfjell on the other side of the tunnel, just west of here. We go inside the expanded and refurbished station and order a giant hot dog each, smothered in mustard and onions. Then we wander into the unstaffed souvenir shop where you could easily walk out with whatever you wanted. If you do want to buy something, you have to walk to the other end of the train station to beg the guy making hot dogs to take your cash.

On the platform I point up at the cleft in the mountains immediately above us. 'That's where I had hoped we'd hike today, to a self-service hut called Kaldevasshytta hut, and then down to Ulvik, but it's too difficult a walk in these icy and snowy conditions. We'd have to walk on parts of a glacier and the hut itself is on a tongue of rock between two lakes, which are probably still half-frozen. We'll take the train through the tunnel to Mjølfjell instead and walk to Ulvik over the mountains that way.' I've never done this walk before, only heard about it. The DNT guidebook's played-down description includes the advice that one should 'be careful at the edge of a steep valley' and that the route is 'impassable in the winter season'. DNT guidebooks are not prone to hyperbole, and I guess these understatements just hint at the reality.

When the local bicycle train arrives we board the old carriage and immediately are swallowed by another tunnel to emerge several minutes later at the top of a stunning and secluded open valley.

We get out at the next stop, Mjølfjell, which is not much more than a platform. Clouds have sneaked in overhead and it's decidedly cool again. We hoist our packs onto our backs having had two days' break from carrying them, and set off walking down a gravel road before turning right to cross a suspension footbridge over a fast-flowing stream.

I catch up to Annabel on the other side of the river. 'You know, I've been thinking.'

'Oh good.'

'I've just figured out where the word rucksack comes from.' She continues walking. 'It comes from the Norwegian *ryggsekk* which means literally "back sack".' I look at my watch. We're starting the walk after three and this is described as a six-hour hike, without breaks. There are some ominous-looking clouds scudding over the mountains. We'll end the mountain part of the walk no earlier than ten this evening but then we have another fifteen kilometres down a little-used road to get to Ulvik on the Hardangerfjord. It's not likely we'll be able to hitchhike at that time of the evening; all the farmers using the road will be in bed asleep. That means we'll walk into Ulvik at around two or three in the morning. I don't tell Annabel my concerns; it's a beautiful day, I haven't done this walk before, and for the time being, that's enough. Who knows, maybe we'll find a tractor beside the road with keys in the ignition.

We start climbing through birch forest and then ascend through the tree line where we continue climbing past small lakes with huts and then past a bigger lake. Soon there are patches of snow on the ground. The hot dog I ate at Myrdal keeps repeating on me, the fetid smell making me feel sick. I don't know why I insist on eating hot dogs because they always leave me with this uncomfortable feeling I've just put something inside me that I shouldn't have. Ignoring the putrid smell on my breath, I see at the head of the lake that we have to cross a stream swollen by the melting snow and ice. We attempt to find somewhere we can cross but the stream is too swollen. In the end we give up and sit down, remove our boots and socks, and put on our sandals.

'Okay. Ready?'

I sling my pack over only one shoulder in case I fall and tentatively put a toe into the water. I'm pleasantly surprised when I put my first foot into the fast-flowing stream. It doesn't seem as cold as I thought it was going to be. I put my other foot in and follow Annabel across.

The initial assessment of the water temperature proves to be totally misleading. Within a few steps the water is so cold it scalds. Halfway across the stream I can't feel my feet any more.

'Ooooo! Ow-ow-ow!' Annabel exclaims as she struggles to keep her footing on the slippery stones below the rushing water. At least it's not just me suffering. She's quicker than I am and soon she's on the other bank hopping up and down. 'Owww!' She doesn't normally complain as much as I do, so I know it must *really* hurt.

When I step out, my feet look like boiled lobsters. It hurts more when I get out than when I was in the freezing water. 'Fuck-a-duck!' I exclaim.

'Feels like I've been soaking my feet in acid!' Annabel grumbles, sitting down and vigorously rubbing the circulation back into her toes. 'The first few seconds in the water were fine, then my feet went numb and now they sting like they're burning.'

I flap my hands and try to stamp my feet without shattering them. 'There's snow directly above the stream and snow directly below it. This little stretch of water is just a momentary thaw in the ice.'

We put our woollen socks and boots back on. Our feet feel like stumps of wood to begin with as we start another climb through a granite gap. Where the rocky ground shows beneath the snow, it has clearly been ground smooth by glaciers. The striations flow down the valley we have just climbed. We reach a high ridge with views both behind us and in front. We are faced with another semi-frozen lake. We walk along its edge, crossing warily over a snow bridge that seems on the verge of collapse but at least provides an escape from immersing our feet in the freezing water of another stream.

'How do we get out of this valley?' I ask Annabel. Ahead of us is a dead end wall of vertical rock and plummeting waterfalls. It's been a spectacular walk but I'm concerned we've taken a wrong turn somewhere. Annabel has insisted she carry the map on this leg. I wait for her to pull the map out and we carefully cross-examine it. The path is shown as a broken black line on the map, but in reality it is non-existent. We occasionally come across the odd red 'T' painted on a rock not covered in snow, but so many of the natural features are snow-covered it makes map-reading a challenge. Whether we are beside a big lake or a small one is impossible to tell when the lakes are frozen with snow piled on top. I pull out my compass but that doesn't help much. 'We're supposed to continue in this direction,' Annabel points at the wall of rock facing us, 'and then hook sharp right down this gorge,' she adds, pointing at the map. The gorge is nowhere to be seen.

Looking up at the wall of rocks surrounding us I cannot see where our intended route could possibly be. By the look of things, we'll need climbing ropes to get out of here. I check my watch. It's already eight in the evening and heavy clouds have drifted in making it seem darker. We've met no one on the route and we're certainly not likely to now. In fact, we haven't seen any evidence that anyone has made the crossing; there are no footsteps in the snow. Somewhere we have to cross a pass and then begin a sharp descent . . .

We continue to climb towards the rocky walls of the gorge

closing in around us and then, quite unexpectedly, flanked by enormous vertical peaks, there is the hidden gorge at right angles to us. Climbing up here, the side valley was totally hidden from view.

'Holy cow!' I exclaim when we see the steep sides of the gorge we now have to descend.

We stop to rest on boulders overlooking the canyon. 'Impressive,' Annabel adds.

'Sure had me fooled. I was beginning to wonder how we were going to get out of here.' With a spectacular view down the valley, we open our *nistepakker* and eat our sandwiches. 'It's like the hidden entrance to Shangri-la. Thousands of years ago the glacier must have diverged here, exactly where we're sitting; one arm going down there, the other arm where we've just come from. Look, you can see the watershed between the two valleys is right there behind us, on that rocky bit of ground we just crossed.'

The valley below has a scary aspect to it, probably because it's getting late in the day, and cloudy, but also because of the huge walls of granite flanking both sides of the canyon. 'Can you see the path going down?' I ask Annabel. There are numerous banks of snow hiding what might have been a tenuous hiking route.

I hand three squares of chocolate to Annabel. She remains silent, as if she's thinking about something. 'Why are you so quiet?' I ask.

She shows me the 1:50,000 map of the area. 'Look at the contour lines delineating this canyon further down; they are just one big brown splodge, like a smudged thumbprint.' She examines the map carefully. 'The top of the mountains here are around 1400 metres, but the last contour line you can make out at the top of where it all gets smeared together is about 1100 metres, and the bottom one is 400 metres. We've got 1000 metres to descend with virtually a 700 metre vertical drop – well over 2000 feet on either side!'

With that thought we hoist our packs and with the walking sticks that we found at Gjendesheim to help us, begin to zigzag steeply down to the head of the valley. Waterfalls tumble out of rock walls, echoing up Fallet Gorge.

'You beauty,' Annabel exclaims at the dramatic chasm we are faced with.

At the bottom we are confronted with the more daunting prospect of walking along the narrow floor of the gorge, with numerous waterfalls plunging into mounds of snow left from the winter. We have to walk over snow bridges mined with dark holes where boulders have broken through into the swift streams flowing underneath. If we collapse through a snow bridge we wouldn't stand a chance of surviving, trapped in freezing waters under several metres of compacted snow. As if hidden weaknesses in the snow bridges underfoot aren't enough, black boulders embedded in the snow after plunging a thousand metres from above present an added danger. If one rock the size of a clenched fist hit us, we'd never know it. At least it would be relatively quick compared to falling through a chink in a snow bridge and drowning, or freezing, to death.

Until now we've made good time. Our knees don't hurt and even the descent to the bottom of Fallet Gorge was easy enough. But now our progress slows to a snail's pace as we try to gauge where we can walk across the angled snow bridges with the least prospect of dropping through. Compounding the problem is the icy surface of the compacted frozen snow. Crampons would have been a good idea to prevent sliding because if we do we slip, it'll be hard to stop our descent until we hit the stream at the bottom. Between snow bridges we struggle over sharp-edged boulders the size of cars. When I turn around to see where we have come from, the right-angle gap we've just descended is invisible. Climbing up the route we are descending must be an intimidating prospect, faced with the steep sides and apparent wall of rock and waterfalls at the end.

The valley opens up and the path becomes more obvious; soon we are walking by two small lakes with a couple of huts nearby. 'It'd be wonderful to come up here and spend some time fishing,' Annabel says. Smoke drifts out of the stone chimney of one of the huts, but otherwise there's no evidence of anyone being here. We select a boulder at the lake's edge to sit down on and finish off our sandwiches, then suck contentedly on another row of chocolate squares.

'Anywhere else in the world and a setting as perfect as this would be famous. There'd be hordes of tourists coming to see this and yet here we are all alone, a crystal-clear lake full of trout, waterfalls all around us, vertical cliff faces towering above . . . ' Annabel waxes unusually lyrical.

After the second lake we have to climb again and then descend into the defile where the mountains on either flank tower seven hundred metres vertically above. I study the mountain on the right-hand side. 'If you took a running jump off that overhang up there, you wouldn't hit anything till you smashed into the bottom down here,' I say.

'Good place for static parachute jumps though,' she replies.

'Bungy jumping too.'

'You'd have to hope your equipment worked because if it didn't, there wouldn't be much left; not even enough to match your dental records.'

'Maybe your fingerprints.'

'You ever been fingerprinted?' Annabel asks, squinting at the towering ledge far above us.

'Nope. So all that would be left of me that would be of any use for identification would be the titanium screw in my tibia.'

'At least you'd have *something* useful left . . . '

The gorge is so narrow there's little light. It's nine o'clock, overcast and a bit spooky. 'This wild canyon would be the kind of creepy place the three giant trolls sharing an eye would lurk, waiting for the smell of a Christian. There's no protective sunlight now at all.' This is the kind of time and place when I wish I wasn't such an avid reader of Norwegian folk tales.

We continue walking down the valley, tired and hungry.

'These mountains remind me of the Canadian Rockies,' I break the silence as we safely exit the opening to the valley. 'Look at all the pine trees up there.'

Getting more tired now by the minute, we slosh our way

through a boggy birch forest, our feet continuously getting soaked in mud and water. Suddenly we're confronted with several cows across a small stream, partially hidden in a glade of birch trees.

'Thank goodness, the first signs of civilisation,' I say, relieved. The cows look at us in as much surprise as we look at them. Maybe they thought we were trolls out for a stroll. 'Look at their coats,' Annabel says admiring the sheen on their hides as we slop through the water towards them. 'They look like chocolate.'

From Annabel, that's a major compliment.

In a meadow in the birch forest I find a beautiful orchid. 'Must be the speckled orchid we've been looking for. There are clumps of them all over the place here. Aren't they beautiful?'

Walking the path seems to take forever before we reach a gravel road. It's ten now and the light is fading behind a solid wall of grey cloud shutting off the late summer evening sun. When we turn to look at where we have come from, and the formidable walls of vertical rock, I wonder how we've escaped through the gauntlet of trolls unscathed. It is unearthly quiet now that we've come out of the gorge, removed from the echoing waterfalls. We check our map and walk along the gravel a kilometre before we hit a sealed road. Each square on the map is a kilometre and there are several squares to Ulvik, but that doesn't count the squiggles within each square. Some squiggles in the road cross the same kilometre square three times. 'We've got a long walk before we reach Ulvik,' I hint as we stop at a stream to rehydrate.

'Mmm, that's better,' Annabel says as we swallow a litre of water each.

'Let's take a rest,' I say, removing my pack and letting it thump to the ground like a sack of potatoes. It is absolutely still, without a breath of wind, not even a slight hint of a breeze. Suddenly I'm very, very tired. It's been okay up to now coping with the fatigue, but the prospect of trudging down a bitumen road for fifteen kilometres, or whatever the distance is, is too much for me to even contemplate much less face up to.

Annabel is made of sterner stuff. 'We've got to keep going otherwise we'll never get to Ulvik tonight.'

'Maybe if we just wait, a car or a farmer on a tractor will come by.'

'Like pigs fly. Come on, let's go.' She sets out, determined to get to Ulvik even if it kills us.

I drag my pack behind me, refusing to put it on again. Annabel turns around when she hears the scraping of the aluminium frame against the bitumen.

'That's not what external frame packs are made for,' she says when I catch up to her.

'I can't carry it on my back any more. Besides, the North American Indians used to drag their belongings behind their ponies just like this.'

'You're not a North American Indian and you're definitely not a pony.'

I can't bear the thought of this ignoble end to a spectacular walk. I lean the pack against the guardrail on the curve of the road and, giving my grunts maximum volume, lift the pack up and heave it onto my back again. I pull the waist strap tight, then shove my walking stick horizontally under the bottom of the pack and grip it with both hands, trying to take some of the weight off my aching shoulders. I trudge behind Annabel like a truculent child. Despite the overcast sky that threatens to rain, it's still light and the scenery, no longer the stark chasm we've walked down, is soft and gentle, green, with pine forest and pastures dotted increasingly with red barns and white farmhouses. Annabel stops to talk to some cows curious enough to come to the side of the road. Then she sets off and I'm left behind in her wake again.

We've walked perhaps half an hour when I vaguely hear a car and turn around in time to see a big, squat, top-end BMW purring by. I stick my thumb out enthusiastically but the car glides past. 'Germans,' I mutter, dropping the expletive, as I read the license plate. What are Germans doing here? This road doesn't go anywhere.

Annabel is thirty metres ahead of me. She sticks her thumb out as she hears the car murmur by. I watch incredulously as the brake lights brighten and the car slows down. Then I see the white back-up lights shine brightly as it reverses up the hill to Annabel. I lumber down as fast as I can in case she accepts the ride without me.

The boot opens automatically and the large driver gets out to help Annabel with her pack. I catch up just as her pack goes into the cavernous boot. 'Hi, I'm with her!' I exclaim, out of breath, in case there should be a misunderstanding that there are two solitary hikers who don't know each other on this lonely stretch of road. I enthusiastically slip my pack off my shoulders and have a momentary pang of panic when I realise the enormous external frame won't fit in. We have to rearrange the driver's fishing rods and gear in the boot before we can massage both our packs into the relatively cavernous space. Then we open the back doors and jump in the car. I feel grubby sitting with my sweaty shirt sticking against the leather seat and ignore my muddy boots staining the clean pile carpet.

'You are going to the camping place in Ulvik?' our driver asks in a thick accent as we roll silently down the hill to the quadraphonic tunes of Phil Collins. His wife, equally as bulky even viewed from the perspective of the back seat, is silent.

'Uh, no,' I try and remember the name of the hotel. 'The, um, Brakanes Hotel,' I reply uncertainly.

'Where is that?' he asks.

'Somewhere in Ulvik.' I sniff and realise Annabel and I absolutely reek. If I can smell us, I wonder how bad we must smell to the Germans.

'I can find it for you. Where have you come from today?'

'We've walked from Mjølfjell, on the Bergen to Oslo railway line.' We tell him about our hike. He has been fishing at a lake further up the road. They are heading back down to their hut they have rented for two weeks. 'You are lucky, there is no traffic on this road. We are coming here for five years and there are few cars. We like Norway very much; it is very beautiful,' he continues. 'We are driving here from Germany every year since the first time.' We float down the road quietly, comfortably ensconced in these luxurious leather seats. *This* is the way to travel. Already the points in my shoulders where the pack's straps have been rubbing are starting to feel better. I prod Annabel and give her a thumbs-up sign and a wink.

As we wind our way down towards Ulvik I prod Annabel again and point out the window at the view of the basin-like valley. A mirror-smooth bowl of water looks exactly like a lake but is in fact a tiny offshoot of the mighty Hardangerfjord. Small wooden farmhouses and barns dot the basin of pastures and orchards. On the far side, behind the hilly peninsula enclosing the glass-like water of Ulvikpollen, are mountains covered in snow.

We descend into Ulvik. The first two hotels we drive to are not the Brakanes Hotel. Finally we drive to the front entrance of a very swish hotel. 'This is the Brakanes,' our driver says, reading the sign. He stops the BMW in front of the covered entrance and I look into the luxurious lobby. Although it is almost midnight, there are well-dressed guests milling around.

'Did you reserve a room?' the German driver asks with a hint of doubt.

'Yes.'

'But it is late, maybe they do not have room for you,' he says, providing me with an excuse, clearly not believing two muddy, smelly backpackers are going to be staying at this fancy, and no doubt expensive, hotel. 'You can stay with us in our hut. It is very big with extra rooms.'

'Thank you. I'll just jump out and see if they have kept our reservations.' I had asked Jannet at Vatnahalsen to telephone ahead to tell them we'd be late arriving. The receptionist takes one look at me as I approach the counter and says, 'Mr Stevenson?'

'Uh, how did you know?'

'You look as if you've just hiked here from Mjølfjell. We weren't expecting you until after midnight.'

'Oh . . . ' I reply, slightly taken aback at this welcome anticipation of our arrival. 'Well, we're here. Do you still have a room for us?'

'Yes, and dinner, because we knew you'd be hungry. I can send it up to your room.' She gives me the room key and I rush back to the BMW. 'They kept our room for us.' We extricate our packs from the fishing rods in the boot and thank the German couple for giving us a ride and their offer of hospitality. With our hiking clothes, boots and legs spattered in mud from the bog at the end of the trip, carrying our bulky packs, we lumber into the lobby looking totally out of place amongst the well-dressed guests who turn to stare.

Annabel grabs me by the elbow. 'Why didn't you tell me?'

'What?'

'That we were staying in such a fancy hotel.'

'I don't tell you everything.'

'I can't believe it. I thought Ulvik would be like some sort of a port town and we'd be staying in some kind of . . . I don't know . . . hut.' We lumber under our heavy backpacks through the lobby attracting more stares from the guests who spot us.

In our room Annabel runs a bath. On the balcony I remove my muddy boots and socks, sweaty shirt, shorts and underpants, and wrap myself in a fleecy white towel. From the minibar I pull out a bottle of wine and open it, giving Annabel a full glass as she soaks up to her chin in bubbles. I sneak a slice of smoked salmon off one of the dinner plates the waiter brought up, and sit outside on the balcony overlooking the gardens and the fjord while sipping the wine. The water is so calm; even at midnight I can see the reflections of the hill on the other side of the protected inlet, and the mountains on the other side of the fjord. It's so quiet and warm and perfect. I hear Annabel singing and I know she's happy.

So am I.

Hardangerfjord

The curtains are open. Through the sliding glass doors we can admire the inlet of the fjord while lying in bed. The tranquil black water is speckled with raindrops.

It's drizzling quietly, not a lot, just enough to add a bit of atmosphere and dissuade us from jumping out of bed to continue our trip.

'You know what?' I ask Annabel, her face embedded in a soft pillow, barely visible.

'No, but you're going to tell me,' she murmurs.

'I don't want to leave this place.'

'Really?' she says, opening her eyes.

'Really.' I look out the French doors. 'The plan was to cycle to Odda today, but I don't feel very ambitious. We could stay here another night and take the bus tomorrow. I mean, it *is* raining today and it wouldn't be much fun.' As if Annabel needs any convincing, I add, 'We've had a pretty heavy schedule.'

The throaty roar of a seaplane engine coughing into life echoes across the inlet. From the reclining position we watch as it taxis smoothly on its pontoons from the dock just in front of our balcony out to the middle of the inlet, then with a roar of its engine it accelerates over the water at full power. At takeoff speed the pilot rocks the floats from one side to the other to release them from the surface tension of the calm fjord, and suddenly the aircraft is airborne and circling around in the bowl to gain enough height to fly over the hills and mountains surrounding us.

'Maybe if we stay in bed long enough, all the bus tourists will have gone by the time we go down for breakfast,' I suggest. 'I could read you another of the Kirbys' letters.'

'Okay.'

Lying in bed, I read a letter from Mrs Kirby, written when they were in Voss, just an hour up the road from here.

> Vossvangen July 1889
>
> We left the steamer Viking at Eide and waited in the pretty hotel garden until our Stolkjerre was ready.

'I think that's a form of horse and carriage,' I explain to Annabel before continuing reading.

> Then we took our last look at the beautiful Hardanger Fjord. Our road was a very beautiful one, first around a charming lake past Granvin then mounting zigzag fashion to the very top of a waterfall, which we crossed twice in the ascent, a lower and a higher fall. Our road was so far above a large forest it seemed we could have walked over the tops, so level did they seem.

'That route hasn't changed much either. I recognise the description even now,' I comment.

> In Voss we have had a very lazy day by the edge of the river and in the morning watched the old ferryman plying backwards and forwards. Some gaily-dressed ladies have just gone along the road with their towels and bathing dresses so there must be bathing somewhere in the river for ladies. We gave out some washing this morning and the women have been busily employed upon it and other washing at the lakeside. They rub and beat the clothes and then they boil them in great iron cauldrons under which they light a fire by the waterside. You see it all over the country.

'It's amazing to think that here we are reading Mr and Mrs Kirby's letters about their trip over 100 years ago; so much has changed and yet, in a way, not so much. From the description it seems like the farms and the landscape haven't changed at all.' I examine the handwriting. 'You can see where the nib of the pen has been dipped in an inkwell. And now we do it all by email on a computer. Who'll be bothered reading our email a hundred years from now?'

By the time we go down to breakfast we are almost alone in the restaurant.

I had arranged to rent two bicycles from the Ulvik tourist office. They've kept two bikes for us but I let the tourist officer know we've changed our minds about cycling to Odda and that we're staying here an extra day. 'Are there any good cycle routes we could do for the day?'

'You could cycle to the end of the Osafjord, it's just over the hill there.'

It stops drizzling and the sun comes out. Everything looks greener than it did before. I have been in Ulvik, and Hardanger, in the spring, when the apple and cherry trees are blossoming, one of the typical idyllic scenes depicted in photographic books and post-cards. We are too late for that now, but the profusion of flowers makes up for the loss as we cycle along verdant hills interspersed with white wooden farmhouses and ochre barns with beautifully patterned slate roofs. At the top of the crest of the hill, we look back over a panoramic view of this inlet off the Osafjord, itself an arm off the mighty Hardangerfjord. From this perspective the inlet looks exactly like a lake. Farms are scattered on the bowl-like amphitheatre surrounding the dark 'lake'. Wild flowers grow everywhere amidst the green pastures lined with apple or cherry trees and surrounded by pine forest, mountains, fjords, waterfalls and glaciers. While the fields and orchards of the farms are soft and gentle, and the mountains rough, harsh and hard, they are somehow perfectly matched – one counterbalancing the other.

On the old road running precariously alongside the Osafjord we discover raspberries, and then wild strawberries. The bushes are thick with succulent, perfectly ripe raspberries coated in fresh dew. We stop to gorge ourselves so often it takes some hours to cycle the nine kilometres to Osa. The dead-end road is old, in most places cut out of vertical walls of granite. Steel rods have been hammered into the side of the rock where the original road must have been cantilevered over the fjord; they are made redundant now by several recent tunnels hacked out of the rock. There is no traffic.

Across this narrow arm of the Hardangerfjord, tucked under opposing walls of rock, is an isolated farmhouse with a barn and a narrow strip of pasture along the water's edge. A small boat moored nearby is the farm's connection with the rest of the world. Norway's isolated farms such as this one are becoming exceptions to the rule as the extensive infrastructure of this country knits its cut-off communities into a central road network.

We cycle in the dark through a dripping tunnel and eventually reach Osa at the tip of the fjord – a collection of a few houses and some farms. It amazes me that a road would have been built here despite the obstacles presented by the vertical mountains.

There is a new water factory here and the water has been exported to the United States since 1994 where, we are told at a small kiosk, it is marketed as 'the best water in the world'.

'I thought "the best water in the world" was from Doubtful Sound in New Zealand,' Annabel whispers to me.

'What's "the best water in the world" mean?' I ask aloud.

'The purest. It has the least impurities. It's pure H_2O.'

A couple of large houses are evidence of a failed scheme in 1915 to harness the nearby waterfall and turn Osa into an industrial town. That probably explains why the road was built here in the first place and why there is almost nothing here now.

Although it begins to drizzle slightly again as we cycle back to Ulvik, we cannot stop ourselves from picking at particularly attractive clumps of raspberries. When we get back to the Ulvik tourist office I ask Annabel if she can deal with returning the bikes. She gives me a quizzical look, then recognises my body language and guesses correctly at the cause of my malaise.

'I hope you make it,' she calls after me as I scuttle off. 'You shouldn't have stuffed yourself on so much fruit, you know that always happens to you,' she yells indiscreetly after me.

It's touch and go. Another ten-second delay at the reception desk waiting for the room key would have been disastrous for everyone concerned. I'm still sitting on the toilet when Annabel arrives.

'You okay?'

'I'll be fine.'

The phone rings. Annabel answers it. 'It's for you – someone called Ulf Prytz.'

'Tell him to hang on a sec.' At Vatnahalsen, Jannet had told me her brother worked for Ulf in Spitsbergen. When I first moved to Norway, Ulf and I worked together to set up an adventure company. He had gone on to establish Svalbard Polar Travel. Jannet had contacted her brother in Svalbard, what we commonly term Spitsbergen, and gave Ulf my itinerary and the phone number of the Brakanes Hotel. Less inconveniently disposed, I write down dates and contact numbers before putting the phone down. 'That was a friend of mine. He owns and manages an adventure tour company. He's invited me to join a cruise for a week around Spitsbergen.' I see the look of disappointment on Annabel's face.

'When?'

'After you've gone. Next week.'

'I'd love to go there.'

'I didn't really think of it until the last couple of days in Bermuda when I contacted Ulf to see if there was any possibility, and he was away at the time. It's a last-minute thing.' I put my arm around her shoulder in commiseration. 'If I'd managed to get hold of Ulf earlier, we could have somehow changed our plans so you could join me. But we couldn't do everything.'

She concedes, 'And I've enjoyed everything we've done.' Annabel arranged a locum to cover her for just another week and she can't change her plans at this late juncture.

'It's about the only place in Norway I haven't been, and I've been dying to go there for ages,' I inform her while trying to appease my conscience for going somewhere so wonderful without her.

'I know.'

Sufficiently recovered to tackle dinner, I head off with Annabel to the hotel's massive dining hall. We are shown to a table for two. Most tables are joined together for parties of twenty or more. A well-dressed German couple sit at the table next to us but otherwise there's almost no one else in the restaurant. The Germans obviously know the waitress from visits here in previous years. They order a meal, à la carte. I whisper to Annabel, 'Look at those buffet tables. Even though the buffet dinner is more expensive it's a much better deal. We can just take our time and stuff ourselves on everything, including soup and dessert. We won't have to eat again for ages and anyway, we're going to be spending the next two days climbing over the Folgefonna Glacier. We're going to need as much energy as we can get,' I rationalise, wiping saliva from the corners of my mouth with a linen napkin.

We help ourselves to wild mushroom soup, which is so good I have to go for seconds despite the mountains of culinary delights loaded on the tables and just waiting to be demolished.

'We should see how long we can make this dinner last, then we'll have more room for all the food,' I tell her gleefully.

But then, from out of nowhere, some 200 guests invade the dining room, led by their guides.

'Where have they all come from?'

'Must be busloads of tourists.'

'Or an invasion.'

The feeding frenzy is something to behold. Doing exactly what I had hoped to take some hours doing myself, they attack the tables heaped with food. Suddenly it's impossible to get at the smoked salmon end of the table. Crowds of hungry guests desperately clutching plates in their hands, plan their assault on the exquisitely displayed cuisine. Elbows lash out aggressively as they push and shove their way to the front.

'They look like pigs with their heads down at the trough,' I observe pompously, annoyed that my own plans to gorge myself silly have been thwarted.

The dining room that had seemed so quiet and dignified a few minutes before is a seething mass of hungry stomachs asserting their right to the feast. They lay siege to invisible tables hidden behind tiers of legs and arms jostling hungry bellies into position.

'Did you see the Norwegian waitresses scatter when they arrived?' I ask. The waiters and waitresses stand on the periphery of the room, backs to the walls, out of harm's way. They were so attentive and diligent with us but have melted away helplessly before this onslaught. When the waitresses do walk into the melee, they have the wary, tentative looks of animal trainers stepping inside a cage with bad-tempered carnivores. In an attempt to appease the starving multitudes, waiters cautiously step out of the kitchen bearing more bowls of shrimps or, more hazardously, trays with mounds of smoked salmon. They step into the fray and are immediately swallowed up whole. Within seconds the silver platters are empty and the throngs dissipate from that end of the buffet table.

Some try to move clockwise around the table, others move counter-clockwise so that there is general chaos. Many eat food off their plates as they move around so that there should be more space left to pile on extra food, a trick I am normally wont to do. In a bewildering array of clothes, from semi-formal dress to T-shirts, shorts and sneakers, wave after wave of the diners come in for the attack.

A waitress tries to weave through the crowd to the German couple sitting next to us. Now I understand why they ordered à la carte.

'The waiters and waitresses should be wearing American football helmets, shoulder pads and mouth guards,' I whisper to Annabel.

A second pincer movement assails the hot food section presided over by three timorous cooks who deftly cut slices of lamb, pork and beef and slide them at arms' length onto plates thrust at them.

'The thing for us to do, and we have to do it quickly Annabel, is to eat the meal backwards. Fill our chest compartments first with dessert, then work our way to the cold buffet and then the hot meal.'

Annabel refuses to comply with my plan, so we wait. A pianist playing classical music has been ignored all evening. The first wave of tourists starts staggering out of the dining room, leaving a few openings at the cold buffet table. We wait for another tray of smoked salmon to arrive then quickly dart over and tentatively stab our forks at the slices before our hands get jabbed. Although I had every intention of stuffing myself silly, witnessing two to three hundred others do the same thing has given me a holier-than-thou attitude. By the time I go up for some hot lamb, there are six leg bones sitting under the heat lamps, but all the meat has been carved away. Fred Flintstone couldn't have done a better job. I wait a few minutes with several French farmer-types before a cook reappears with a fleshy leg.

It surprises me that Norway produces some of the best chefs in the world, and that these district hotels routinely produce gourmet meals that would stand comparison in the best restaurants in Paris, London or New York. Traditional Norwegian fare is far from epicurean. When Norway was a much poorer country, *lutefisk* on the coast, and *pinnekjøtt* in the valleys would be considered a feast. *Lutefisk* is dried cod soaked in lye-water for two to three days to soften the salted flesh. The cod is then soaked under running cold water for two days to rinse the lye out, and then the pieces are cut and boiled. It's an acquired taste. On the coast, *lutefisk* with a serving of stewed green or yellow peas and boiled potatoes is considered traditional Christmas fare.

Amongst farmers in the valleys, however, *pinnekjøtt*, or salted sheep ribs, is the preferred Christmas meal. Again, the dried and salted sheep ribs are soaked in water and then placed in a pan with pine needles to steam in an oven They are served with boiled potatoes and stewed turnip. Unbelievable for a foreigner who has not acquired a taste for either the *lutefisk* or the *pinnekjøtt*, these dishes are nowadays served as an expensive option in some of the best restaurants during Advent. *Lefse*, made of flour and cream and served with various toppings, is the traditional dessert as is *kransekake*, or almond-ring-cake, usually decked out with paper Norwegian flags attached to toothpicks. Meals like these make English fare look positively gastronomic by comparison, and yet consistently Norwegian cooks are justifiably rated amongst the best in the world.

The lobby, empty before dinner, is now filled with satiated guests washing their meals down with coffee.

I'm curious to see where all these tourists have come from. Outside in the parking lot we stroll around five huge buses with Norwegian, French, German, Italian and British license plates. If full, these buses alone must have carried an army of some 250 diners into the restaurant this evening.

In bed I pull out another of Mr Kirby's photocopied letters, and with the sliding glass doors open to the fresh air, read aloud. This letter I assume is written here in Ulvik.

> 2 July 1889 at Vik in Eidfjord
>
> We are here lodged out in a wooden house, and it is I think nothing but wood except the strong foundation, if foundation one properly calls it, which is not excavated at all. It is built like most of the houses in Norway. First of all there is laid a basement of big stones, and upon it a layer or two of logs, and then upon them the wooden house is built four square. Sometimes there are heavy square slabs upon the roof, sometimes wooden roofs, and often the roofs are of birch bark with earth upon it.

'Sounds like Harildstad,' Annabel comments.

> There is no darkness here. I have been looking at my watch every hour or so since 1 o'clock without the need of match or candle. Below us is the small

pier along which our steamer came. Such a beautiful water it is. So green that when I look out now I have to remind myself that it is not a green field. It is so motionless that I cannot persuade myself it is really the sea itself running up into this far, far away nook and that a little way off us, further down into the Hardanger, it is said to be 2000 feet deep. Across the water from me, it is yet so wide that a few storehouses on the opposite side, look quite small toys. Granite crags said to be 3,000 feet high rise almost perpendicularly from the sea. They are rifted and seamed by watercourses down which storms heavy torrents as they have evidently done for centuries, bringing rocks and debris with them. You would say, sitting here, looking out that this was a land locked lake, but I know that at the far corner is the sea way, and above the rocks on that side is a small glacier or ice field.'

'It's *exactly* the same view we have outside our window.' I turn to look at Annabel. 'Annabel?'

She's asleep.

I slip out from under the covers, wrap a towel around me and walk out to the balcony overlooking the scene so aptly described by R.L. Kirby.

Folgefonna Glacier

It's drizzling again, not heavily, just enough to spatter the smooth waters outside with tiny raindrops striking the surface.

By the old stone church we catch the bus that will take us to Odda. Nine kilometres out of Ulvik, the bus stops at Bruravik where a ferry meets it to transport it to the other side of the fjord. The ferry comes in to dock and the propellers churn the water, and with the deft precision of a surgeon the skipper coordinates the forward momentum with the reverse thrust so that the front of the boat barely touches the ramp. While the motorbikes, cars, buses and trucks are loaded on, I watch a fisherman on the dock cast his lure far out into the stirred up waters. He casts at least three times as far as I am able, and he makes it look easy.

It takes only minutes to cross the fjord and after docking at Brimnes on the other side, our bus continues along a narrow winding road precariously skirting the rocky edge where the mountain wall plunges immediately below into the fjord. The bus is empty and although we sit in the front seats offering a superb view, Annabel keeps falling asleep. Outside it is pouring with rain.

I watch with apprehension as cars, inevitably with foreign license plates, brake hard to avoid hitting the wide bus. In many places there's barely room for two large vehicles to pass each other. If there's a car with a trailer, or another bus or truck, one vehicle has to stop to let the other by, or reverse to a wider section. We wind around corners, often with sheer drops down into the fjord.

Tyssedal is proof of how tourism expanded during the time of the Kirbys' visit here at the end of the nineteenth century and the subsequent industrial development, based on cheap hydropower from nearby waterfalls. The industrial development has effectively destroyed the scenic aspects of the area and bleak factories now surround the old Tyssedal Hotel. A little further, at the end of the fjord, Odda is an awful example of how industrialisation destroyed both the community and its scenic qualities. Fortunately what happened in so much of the rest of Europe during the Industrial Revolution is a relatively isolated case in Norway. Øvre Årdal is another hydropower development, but being more recent, does not have quite the same oppressive old factory buildings that Odda has.

Odda is an odd mixture of architecture, of wooden buildings with slate roofs standing cheek to jowl with old factory structures. The present drizzle doesn't help dispel the dismal mood about the place and this feeling is exacerbated by the contrast of the centre to its spectacular setting. The Sørfjord is a fifty-kilometre arm, less than two kilometres wide at any point, of the Hardangerfjord. When the Kirbys were here in 1889, tourism in Norway from England and Germany was flourishing and Odda was one of the most visited places in the country. It's hard to believe now. From here to the Maurangerfjord on the other side of the Folgefonna Glacier is only some ten kilometres as the crow flies, but it was a spectacular trip popular with German and English visitors. Local guides took tourists up the path on one side, roped them up to walk over the glacier, or had a horse-drawn sled carry them over, to meet their steamer again waiting on the other side.

In 1908, the Tysso watercourse was harnessed by building a dam across the Ringedal Lake. A power station was constructed at Tyssedal with energy-consuming carbide and cyanamid factories sprouting up like weeds in Odda. With the damming and harnessing of what was Norway's longest free-fall waterfall, the natural attributes of the area were lost as factories were built to make use of the cheap local electrical power. The gloomy buildings stand testament to the industrialisation that hit pockets of Norway where there was hydropower to be harnessed, and unfortunately where there was always the most spectacular scenery. True, from a few hundred farmers scraping a meagre living from the soil, employment was created for several thousand industrial workers, but this area of unparalleled natural beauty was irreparably disfigured. Since Mr R.L. Kirby's visit, when this was one of the most fashionable tourist spots in Norway, Sørfjord has become one of the most polluted fjords in the world.

We head back to the bus station to meet Stephen, who will be our guide across the Folgefonna Glacier. Although he lives in Rosendal, not twenty-five kilometres over the glacier, it has taken him since half past seven this morning, or four hours, to get here, the bus having to cross the Hardangerfjord twice by ferry. A tunnel being built from Odda under the glacier to Mauranger will mean the same trip will take less than forty-five minutes.

On schedule, the bus arrives and Stephen gets off and gives me a bear hug, and I introduce him to Annabel. He hasn't changed over the five years since I saw him last. An Englishman, he fell in love with Norway after coming here from England to climb. He found summer jobs in hotels and kept returning until he eventually met Mian, his Norwegian wife, while giving a climbing course.

In Britain, young people might meet their prospective mates in a pub. In the United States they might get together in a gym. In Norway, a preferred way of encountering a prospective partner is in the mountains.

I had met Stephen within the first couple of months of arriving in Norway a decade ago. Together with a friend of his from Rosendal, Jostein Hatteberg, we had discussed different options for adventure tours in Norway. It wasn't until a year or so later that I mentioned to Stephen that his surname, Rowe, was the same as my mother's maiden name. Then we discovered both our Rowe families came from Rugby. Further investigation revealed our great-grandfathers had the same background, exactly – an illegitimate child of a Scottish nobleman, who had first moved to Ireland before settling in England.

We lost contact for some years and then recently found each other's new addresses again. He asks where Annabel and I met.

'In Bermuda about four years ago, or about a year after I'd moved there from here.' Annabel had already been working there for four years, and I had started writing full time. 'I was travelling about six months every year and we didn't really get together until a couple of years ago.' I divert to more practical matters. 'We waited to buy our groceries until you were here,' I inform him. 'To make sure we bought what you wanted.'

We have already left our packs unattended at the bus station for the last hour and a half. Stephen throws his pack with ours and we disappear into a nearby supermarket to load up on thick, top-quality steaks, garlic butter, chocolate, of course, and other goodies including bread and *pålegg*. The steaks alone cost the equivalent of US$40.

Annabel and Stephen go off to buy wine from the *Vinmonopolet*, the wine monopoly store, while I make some phone calls to Bergen, Oslo and Spitsbergen. By the time they come back, I've waited around for so long I was about to go out looking for them.

'They not only make you buy wine in a government-controlled store, but they put the store a couple of kilometres out of town to make it even more difficult to buy the stuff,' Annabel says. 'Did you speak to Ulf?'

I nod. 'It's been arranged. There's definitely an extra berth.'

'When?'

'Leaving next Saturday for a week on a Russian research boat that will attempt to circumnavigate Spitsbergen.' I feel bad for doing this additional trip without her but I also feel elated about having the chance to do it at all. It will mean I'll have to work faster getting all my belongings together from Kirsten's family farm outside Oslo.

The rain has stopped and mist hugs the mountains edging the fjord. We take a taxi out of Odda a short distance to where we start our walk up the steep, zigzag path towards the glacier. Every time we zig or zag by the stream tumbling off the mountain, cold air pulled down with the falling water blasts over us. If it feels this cold down here, where we are still below the tree line, I wonder what it will be like on the glacier itself.

The path is lined with juicy blueberries. I have to squat to pick them rather than simply bend over because if I lean over, with the heavy pack on my back, I run the risk of toppling down the hillside. Trailing Annabel and Stephen, I stop picking blueberries when I notice the extra workload on my quads from constantly squatting to get down to ground level; I need to save every bit of energy in my legs for the march over the glacier. When I catch up to them, Annabel bursts out laughing at my blueberry-stained teeth.

We cross over long, steep-sided snowdrifts that would be less dangerous if they weren't compacted into fields of ice. Crossing them is frightening. We kick steps into the ice so that our boots have some grip. If we lose our purchase on the tenuous ice-holds, we won't be able to stop our momentum and it's a long slide down to boulders at the bottom. At the second snowdrift Stephen unpacks ice axes so we have some way to stop our momentum into the rocks below should we slip.

In another section we have to scale steel reinforcing rods drilled into vertical rocks. A flimsy rope drapes across the rocks at head height, but hanging onto the rope with heavy packs dangling off our backs wouldn't do much good apart from prolonging the agony before letting go and plunging down. This is the first time Stephen has actually climbed along here in the summer. Usually he's on telemark skis in the spring or winter. As we ascend into the mist, it starts raining and visibility is reduced to several metres, just when we would most like to be able to see. It's seven in the evening now and Stephen is meticulous about taking his bearings as we reach the edge of the flat-domed glacier shaped like a giant egg on its side.

'It's difficult to see any landmarks; the rocks that would normally show through are still covered in snow, so we'll have to do this mostly by compass bearings,' he tells us. He has his map and compass in hand and sets course to bring us to the self-service hut at Holmaskjeri where we will take a break before continuing to Fonnabu, the main hut on the glacier. We follow a straight line in one direction, walking over snow until we reach a rock outcrop.

At this point we rope up and Stephen takes his bearings again, then heads at a right angle to the direction we were taking.

'Those are sinkholes you can see there,' Stephen says, indicating numerous small depressions in the snow. 'You don't want to step on those because we're on the glacier now and some of those holes are deep under that layer of snow.'

My feet are already soaking wet and now they are freezing as we cross the snow-covered glacier pockmarked with indentations hinting at yawning fissures below. Annabel is roped up after Stephen; I hold the rear position as we disappear into a world of white snow and mist. We continue walking like this, with no bearings, until we see the vague dark outline of rocks. This is the negative image of crossing a dark ocean and seeing the white outline of icebergs. As we approach I recognise the outline of a hut on the top of the rocks and the silhouette of someone standing outside the hut.

'You're like a hut-seeking missile,' I flatter Stephen as we untie the rope and climb the rocks, wondering who it is standing outside the hut waiting. It begins raining again.

The silhouette turns out to be a young woman who speaks Norwegian but from her accent I can tell she is a foreigner, probably German.

'What are you doing?' Stephen asks.

'Trying to decide whether I should go down or not.'

I wouldn't even contemplate it. It's starting to get dark, it's raining, she hasn't anyone to rope on to, there are slippery, steep stretches of ice to cross and those steel rods in the rock face to climb over. She obviously doesn't want to go on. 'Are you staying here?' she asks hopefully.

'We're resting here for a while then going on to Fonnabu hut. Are you here all by yourself?' Stephen asks.

'With my boyfriend, but he's gone to Fonnabu and then back to Sunndal.'

The hut is still relatively warm from their occupation. We strip off our wet clothes and Annabel and I put on dry ones and heat up some soup as the young German comes back in, trying to decide what to do. Within seconds of arriving, the hut looks like a laundry room. Stephen wonders around clad only in cotton underpants. Annabel and I place our woollen socks directly on the iron stove until they are sizzling like bacon rashers, adding their own aroma to the concoction of soup smells. As soon as we've finished our soup Stephen says it's time to move on. We tidy up after ourselves and reluctantly put on our wet clothes. The German is still undecided whether to go on or not. If we were staying here, she clearly would too but she doesn't want to stay alone. She has a compass but no map so she phones her boyfriend on her cellular phone and confirms the direction she should take. She's hoping to follow our tracks across the glacier to the rocks and then down across the snowfields. She's been up here before, but not under these conditions.

'If I ever meet her boyfriend, I'll give him hell for leaving her like that,' Stephen mutters as we part directions.

We head out over the glacier again, confident that our hut-seeking guide will get us over the top of the Folgefonna Glacier to Fonnabu without problem. We trudge one behind the other, roped together. I try to take photographs despite the poor light, but am pulled like a dog on a leash every time I pause to frame a picture. Most of the time we walk on slushy snow, but occasionally we come across deep, narrow cracks, a reminder that the glacier lurks underneath.

'The Folgefonna Glacier is 225 square kilometres, the third largest glacier on mainland Norway, and the route we're following is the same route tourists took a century ago,' Stephen informs us, slipping into his role as guide. 'Tourists in those days practically didn't have to put a foot on the ground; they'd be taken from Sunndal on horseback up the mountain, then transferred to a horse-drawn sled over the glacier, picked up by another pony and taken down the path into Odda.' It's hard to believe now. The considerable construction work that was done to build a wide track on both the Odda and Sunndal sides of the glacier was largely destroyed when they built the dams for hydropower.

Stephen is patient, going to great lengths to explain what he is doing. He takes compass headings regularly, and his manner is so self-effacing one has to wonder whether in fact he's lost, or doesn't know how to read a map. It's a deceptive mannerism. He's one of the top glacier guides in Norway and an instructor for DNT, teaching other instructors.

As the sun dips below a thick layer of clouds it reappears as a bright orange ball skidding horizontally over the vague horizon of the North Sea as we walk the last stretch to Fonnabu hut, barely visible on a ridge of rocks. We descend off the snow onto slippery blue ice and then reach the rocks and untie the ropes. Stephen congratulates us. 'You walked at a good pace.'

It has taken us one-and-a-half hours from Holmaskjerbu hut without the benefit of skis. As we descend we stop to admire a huge sculpture carved into the blue ice by the violent winds scooting around the edge of rock. Then we scramble up the glacier-smoothed bedrock to where Stephen tells us there are thousand-year-old rune markings. It's hard to imagine that a thousand years ago humans were up here carving their initials in this bedrock. But when Stephen shows us, is it obvious humans left these markings. 'They were just discovered last year and we don't know yet who made them or what they say.'

The last long Ice Age began approximately 100,000 years ago and lasted for almost 90,000 years when most of Scandinavia was under a massive sheet of ice. About 14,000 years ago when the ice sheet began to melt, the Norwegian coastline began to appear and the first humans, probably following the retreating reindeer herds, arrived in Norway from the south. The oldest Stone Age sites date back over 10,000 years.

At Fonnabu hut we clomp heavily into the outer room, take off our boots and jackets and walk in to looks of disappointment on the faces of the incumbent guests – a family of Norwegians play-ing cards at the table. It's half past ten and they would hardly have expected more hikers to arrive. They reluctantly make room for us and soon Stephen is wandering around semi-naked as Annabel and I change into dry clothes and hang our wet togs above the warm iron stove. Stephen keeps a pair of wool slippers permanently at the hut, taking great pleasure when he arrives in asking for them back from hikers who have taken advantage of finding a dry pair of indoor footwear.

While making dinner I glance through a photographic book on the area. There's a photo of the Tyssedal Hotel and the old communal hall 'Festivitne'. The photo has been cleverly framed so that the factories immediately in front of the hotel are excluded from the image.

Like other DNT self-service huts, this hut is supplied three or four times a year by helicopter. We carefully write down what we have taken from the supply of food, adding what we owe for the overnight accommodation. We talk for a while but don't want to keep the others awake so Annabel and I retreat to a cosy two-person hut just outside the main building. Inside the tiny stone hut we push our packs and belongings to the end of each of the narrow beds and spread out our sleeping bags.

'I'll read the remainder of Mr Kirby's unread letter from last night,' I announce. 'But try and stay awake, okay?'

'Okay.'

> We sailed nearly all day from Bergen by the Leiderhorn steamer, and had a most beautiful cruise 182 miles long up the Hardanger and down one of its arms, to Sørfjord, at the foot of which stands Odda, and we got comfortable quarters there at the Hardanger Hotel. There were a great many people there, and on Sunday you might have thought it an ordinary English service that we attended, there were so many English. Saturday we went up the hills to see the lake which feeds two of the many beautiful waterfalls that rush and roar and throw themselves down the crags on either side of this sublime and beautiful gorge.

I turn to see if Annabel is awake in the other narrow wooden shelf of a bed. She's lying on her back, eyes open – a good sign.

> On Sunday after lunch, we rowed over another lake and went to see a glacier down which the Folgefond is pushing its way, and that was a very grand sight, as also of the mountain farms, and the hay making, and the burnt up pastures and meadows, and the flowers and the magpies, and the group of cows looking over the edge of the precipice thousands of feet above us, and of the men who made a sail of a branch of a tree and skimmed away up the lake. And we shan't forget what a beautiful place this is, and the mountain mill, and the water driven grindstone and the spinning wheel, and the woman who went and cut a little bit of wool off the sheep's back whenever she was in want of some more to card and to weave and to dye to make up for the family clothing, nor must we forget the polite Norwegian peasant who when we asked him last night which of the two ways led us to the old church of this place, lifted his hat and replied, 'Like you this, like you that, either way that you like', meaning that both ways led there.

'Remember the old stone church?' I ask. 'We could walk from the Brakanes Hotel along the road by the water or the road through the centre just like he describes.' I turn to look at her.

'Annabel?'

Rosendal – the west coast

We sleep so soundly it's difficult to wake up. Early in the morning I stumble out of our diminutive hut for a pee. The weather is trying to clear and the heavy clouds are starting to thin.

Inside the main hut, the family of six is still asleep but Stephen is up making breakfast. He has to leave early to get back to Rosendal to prepare for a week-long course he's giving there that begins tomorrow. He still has to prepare the course equipment and meet the participants. He places his slippers in a conspicuous place before leaving.

Annabel and I take our time. All we can see is snow, ice and mountains ground smooth by glaciers. We set off under a clearing sky, following the trail of red 'T's' and staying on rocks, to Breidalikk hut, a tiny self-service hut for four originally built in the 1890s. From there we find several snow slopes we can slide down, holding our packs in our laps. I let Annabel go first each time, rationalising she has less to injure should one of us hit a hidden protuberance.

And then we are out of the snow with a view of a green valley that features the inevitable line of waterfalls pouring down vertical cliffs.

The sun comes out and it's so warm it gets hot as we descend a zigzag path a couple of metres wide, a remnant of the old tourist cart track between Mauranger and Odda. Before we duck into a birch forest with a floor of wild flowers, we have glimpses of the Maurangerfjord and spectacular views of the Bondhusbreen Glacier almost reaching down to Bondhus Lake. At the bottom of the flower-strewn path we come across a wider track. This is the old 'ice road' up to the glacier. In the nineteenth century, they used to carve ice out of the glacier in the summer, carry it down to the fjord, store it on sailing ships with sawdust as insulation, and transport it to England.

As we're walking along I realise we've walked a good stretch across Norway. Annabel and I have been together twenty-four hours a day for the last month. We've been cold, hungry and tired at times, and yet we never lost the sense of humour that exists between us. The past year, when my brother died and I broke my back six weeks later, was the worst time of my life and I became so dependent on Annabel emotionally and physically as we endured the trauma of my brother's untimely death and my own physical injuries. Sometimes there is a time for talking, and at other times there is a time for silence and peace. I don't have to explain to Annabel how I felt throughout this last year; it is good enough for us both to be out in this fresh air, surrounded by the beauty of Norway, physically exhausting ourselves every day and sleeping long hours. This trip has been a significant step in the process of healing and our own process of bonding, not because of my needs, but as equals.

Stephen's wife Mian has walked up to meet us on the path. Greeting us with her enigmatic, shy smile, she has thoughtfully brought a bottle of cold white wine to 'celebrate' our walk across Norway. At a gravel beach beside an inviting turquoise pool of water I strip down to my underwear and dive into the crystal-clear Bonde River. It looks more inviting than it really is and I'm out of the icy water again in seconds, but I've cooled down and it feels good to have the sweat of the last two days sluiced off me.

We talk as we walk down to her Volvo, catching up on each other's news.

Driving the short distance from Sunndal to Rosendal, Mian tells us, 'When they finish the Odda tunnel this year, we'll be able to drive all the way to England without using a ferry.'

I'd never thought about it, but although Sunndal and Rosendal are on the mainland, they might as well be on an island because the total extent of this road is barely sixty-five kilometres along this segment of the coastline. To the west the

road stops at a wall of vertical rock, short by only a few kilometres from connecting to the rest of the country. Road maps in
Norway are essential because there are so many convoluted
dead-end roads following the edges of fjords, connected by
ferry. There is no such thing as a straight line between A and B.
At one stage a tunnel was planned and approved connecting
Sunndal to the stretch of road on the other side of the rocky
wall. In anticipation of this, one of the major map publishers,
Cappelen, showed the about-to-be new connecting stretch of
road in their updated map, but unfortunately they had jumped
the gun. The tunnel wasn't built and the publishing company
had to erect signs at the ferry crossing twenty-two kilometres
from the dead end to warn people not to continue if they
expected to drive over the nonexistent linking section of road.
Before the signs were erected, so many visitors relying on the
newest version of the Cappelen map ended up unexpectedly at
the dead end and had to turn around and retrace their route.

Mian continues, 'And now that there's a bridge and tunnel
from Sweden to Denmark, and the Chunnel under the English
Channel between France and England, once they've built the tunnel to Odda, we'll be able to visit Stephen's family in England
and drive all the way.'

Rosendal, at the mouth to the Hardangerfjord, is the home of
Norway's only barony, built in the 1660s. While it would not be
much more than a manor house in France, it is nevertheless a
Norwegian barony complete with the country's only Renaissance
garden and a romantic park from the 1870s. The 'Baron' is long
since dead and without offspring, true to Norway's egalitarian traditions, the barony belongs to the people, or at least the
University of Oslo.

Stephen and Mian's house is just down the road. Their three
children play in the large garden amongst orchard trees. While the
two eldest boys have taken after their mother with their shocks of
blonde hair, Tuva, the youngest and my goddaughter, is dark-
haired, like Stephen. She comes running towards me and without
hesitation, throws herself into my open arms. I haven't seen her

since she was christened as an infant. 'Hi Andrew!' she exclaims as if I'd been her next-door neighbour all her life.

As are most Norwegians, Stephen is a do-it-yourself enthusiast. He has added portions onto the house and opened the attic. It amazes me how he, and for that matter so many Norwegians I have met, can put their hands to almost anything practical. Norwegians, probably because of their enforced isolation in many of the valleys and on the coastline, have developed a talent for being independent and this quality is reflected in their aptitude in building their own homes, putting on additions, restoring furniture, tending to a vegetable garden, making handicrafts, knitting, weaving, carving wood and just about any other handyman pursuit.

Mian shows us the guest room. We shower, stuff our filthy, sweaty clothes that haven't had a proper wash in over a month, into the washing machine, and sit in the bright sunlight on the back steps drinking tea, watching the kids play with a hose in their sandpit. It is so incredibly warm.

'We've been invited to a barbecue party tonight,' Mian informs us as we bask in the sun.

'So Stephen said. Where can we buy some wine?' I ask.

'You've forgotten,' Mian laughs. 'You can't buy alcohol, apart from beer, anywhere around here. You'd have to go to Bergen, and that's a day's drive away, or you could take the ferry to Stord, which is a bit closer.' Should have asked Stephen to carry more wine over from Odda. He could probably make a living bootlegging wine he carried over the glacier. 'If you were here longer you could always go to the post office and order the wine, but that takes about a week.'

There's no spontaneous drunkenness in Rosendal, or in many communities in Norway, especially along the west coast. If you want to tie one on, you have to plan it carefully and well in advance, or else have a stock of liquor on hand. No wonder they have so many illegal alcohol stills in basements; not only is it a lot cheaper but you don't have to spend a couple of days driving to and from the liquor stores, or planning ahead when you might want to have a drink or get drunk.

In Oslo on a late summer Friday or Saturday night, when I saw a drunk Norwegian passed out in the street, I'd wonder how he'd managed to save enough money to get obliterated like that when alcohol costs so much here. The answer of course is the home brew. You prime the pumps with high-octane alcohol brewed in the basement and then go out for the one beer that will topple you.

Most Norwegians wouldn't consider working in rural areas like Rosendal, as idyllic as Annabel and I might think it is on a glorious day like this. Mian works as an occupational therapist for the county and drives all around the local area, including the islands, to visit clients. Although Rosendal is hardly isolated in relative terms, like other rural Norwegian communities this county finds it difficult recruiting Norwegian doctors and other educated professionals who prefer to work in the cities. 'We offer nurses 50,000 kroner to come here,' Mian informs me, 'and give them cheap land and other benefits.' She relates how Rosendal has two German and two Danish doctors who couldn't find work in their home countries but jumped at the chance to live here in such a beautiful setting.

The extent of the social services offered to Norwegians has always astounded me. Stephen worked full time with two other county-employed social workers to assist a handicapped Nicaraguan child adopted by Norwegian parents. Three adults working full time to help a handicapped child must have cost the county millions of kroner per year and yet there would be no question of cutting those expenses.

Stephen won't be joining us at the party tonight. He has already gone back up to Fonnabu with the DNT members who have signed on for his course. When you are invited to a social occasion in Norway, certainly in Oslo but perhaps to a lesser extent in the countryside, you arrive at the party *on* time. It's a common occurrence in Norway for party-goers to end up sitting in their cars or go driving around the block until the time they are expected.

With three children in tow, we aren't quite so meticulous. Mian drives us down to a *rorbu*, a fisherman's cabin or boathouse with a dock and a ramp to pull up the small fishing boat that would traditionally be used to supplement the income from a small farm. On a tiny patch of flat grass, two paddles hold up a fishnet, providing an impromptu volleyball court. The sun shines brightly and the children play in the sea water, diving off the dock. Someone has hired a ski boat and the adults take it in turns to water-ski. Jostein arrives and gives me a big bear hug. He looks the quintessential Viking with his considerable size and flowing beard. A sheep farmer who sells his sheep directly to the customer via the Internet, a journalist and an adventure-tour operator, Jostein has now built several *rorbur* by the sea. He hands me a bottle of his home-brew beer.

'Still 10 per cent proof?' I ask.

'You don't measure beer by the percentage of alcohol,' he replies, thumping his chest. 'You measure it by the number of fights per bottle.' Jostein is the last person I can imagine getting into a fight, despite his size. Although he has only a couple of hundred metres to drive back to his house, he doesn't touch any of the beer because he's driving. In other parts of the world one might try to 'get away' with a drink or two and just hope that the cops can be avoided. Here there's a different implication to not drinking and driving. It isn't just a question of not getting caught by the police; there's a responsibility to the community and to the family. In my experience in Norway, I never encountered anyone who would drink and drive. It is socially unacceptable and there is zero tolerance for such behaviour. Driving with a blood alcohol level of more than 0.02 per cent will warrant loss of one's driver's licence and a jail sentence.

The setting, the clear sky, the warmth of the sun, the blonde children playing in the sea – it is the cliché Norwegian summer at its best. The hourglass reflection of the sun shining on the calm evening water reminds me of a Munch painting. But these long, sunny evenings are the exception to the rule, not the norm, which makes it all the more satisfying when it does happen.

Inger, a glamourous woman who speaks perfect English, sits next to me. When I ask how she perfected her English, she replies, 'Oh, I don't speak perfect English.'

'Well, your English is certainly as good as mine, so you didn't become so fluent taking language courses, I'm sure.'

'I spent some time in England when I was a young woman,' she replies cryptically.

I have to coax the story out of her. 'I escaped Norway with thirty Norwegian men during the German occupation of our country,' she continues. 'We were smuggled across the North Sea to Scotland where I served in the Norwegian navy.'

'You're that old?' I ask. She looks sixty.

She laughs. 'I'm eighty.' She recounts her epic escape with Norwegian nonchalance.

Many Norwegians, including King Haakon VII and his son Crown Prince Olav, fled to England during the occupation of their country rather than capitulate to the Germans. Despite German occupation, the King's continued freedom in Britain symbolised the freedom of the Norwegian people and their resolve never to give in. A much-loved monarch, he returned to Norway at the end of the war to a hero's welcome. Olav, who was the successive king, died the first winter I moved to Norway and I will always remember how the news announcer on television was so uncharacteristically emotional that he had almost been unable to enunciate the words: 'The King is dead.'

That same evening, now almost a decade ago, I walked to the palace on Karl Johan's Gate where crowds had gathered in silence, placing candles on the piles of snow that had accumulated during the previous days' snowstorm. There were tens of thousands of candles lit that night with emotional messages written like prayers on cards or bits of paper. Even when Princess Diana died seven years later, the spontaneous outpouring of grief was no more intense than that of the Norwegians for their dead monarch. Although I had been in the country for only a month, the Norwegians' depth of love and affection for their king was moving to witness.

Mian and Stephen's children stand around with purple lips, hands clasped together against their bodies, shivering, but they don't want to stop playing in the water. In my apartment in

Bergen, on the mountainside above the town, there was a *barnepark* or 'children's park' across the road. Not a kindergarten with classrooms, the *barnepark* was a daycare playground with a basic open shelter where children were left to play under the supervision of adults. I would sit inside, working at my computer, and watch the children play outside in rain, sleet and snow, through winter, fall and spring. These tiny little bundles with pink cheeks, wrapped up in padded waterproof clothing, wearing gumboots, played happily in the kind of weather that might be deemed dangerous anywhere else. It's no wonder they're so hardy, swimming in this sea water with temperatures that would have me succumbing to hypothermia in seconds.

A guitar and a piano accordion are played while others sing. The tradition of folk songs, music and dance is as strong here as in Ireland. As a Canadian coming from the 'New World', I envy this strong sense of identity Norwegians have that is more profound than just knowing the words to the national anthem. The Norwegian sense of tradition runs broad and deep and is something that I've always admired.

Soon after the sun dips below the horizon it becomes cold, and we take our leave, stopping in the centre of Rosendal to pick up Stephen's bicycle on the way home. I'm amazed it's been standing there all week, unlocked.

'Weren't you worried someone would steal it?' I ask. I can't imagine many places in the world where you could do that.

'Maybe when the tunnel opens to Odda, then we'll have to be careful, but not yet,' Mian replies confidently.

We put the bike in the back of the Volvo and once we get home the kids are so tired they head immediately to bed.

Annabel undresses in our room. 'What was it one of the adults said this evening when he surfaced after diving off the dock into the cold water? It sounded like an expletive and it started with an "f".'

'I can't say it.' I've lived in Norway enough that I can't repeat the two words to her.

'You can't say it, even in Norwegian?'

'Nope. It's too shocking in Norwegian.'

'Is it the same as the English "f" word?'

'Nope. It's worse.'

'Well then, can you tell me what it translates to?'

'It doesn't have the same meaning in the English translation.'

'Try it on me, in English.'

'Okay, you asked for it.' I pause, then spit out: 'Naughty devil!'

'*Naughty devil*? That's it?'

'Yep.'

We spend the sunny morning walking up to the barony, what the children call the 'castle', then come back home to pick raspberries, blackberries, gooseberries and cherries from the garden. Learning from my previous experience, I don't stuff myself full of these fresh fruits although I can't stop myself from sampling a good portion of what I put into a bucket. Later we drive Annabel to Sunde where she'll catch the ferry to Leirvik, switch to the fast catamaran to Bergen airport, and then catch her flight to London to attend a medical conference, before returning to Bermuda.

'I'm going to miss you. And the sound of waterfalls,' Annabel adds quickly, giving me a hug and whispering in my ear before boarding the ferry.

'And I'm going to miss you too,' I whisper back into her ear.

With Tuva grasping my hand, we wave goodbye to Annabel as she stands at the back of the ferry, until we can no longer see her.

'She's nice,' Mian says as we get into their old Volvo. 'I like her.'

'She's easy to be with,' I reply. She's easy to be with, and so much more. I can't ever recollect being so much at peace with another person, as I am with Annabel. So much of my life I seem to have been struggling upstream, against the current. Often, with careers and even my move to Norway, I've felt like a fish out of water. So often in the past I've gone for long walks on my own.

It's been good to share this trip with Annabel. It was worth waiting this long to get this far and to share my life with the right person. I'm not at all sure that creativity stems only from the struggle and pain of life rather than happiness and contentment. If I'm wrong, then who can honestly say they would rather be creative and suffer all that angst? I stop to look over the roof of the car and wave one last time, but even with my long eyesight I can't make out her lone figure any longer. I feel as if I've lost part of myself.

We drive back to Rosendal, sit down for dinner, and when the three children have finished they shake their mother's hand and thank her for the food, then rush off to watch Saturday children's television from six to seven in the evening. Tuva suddenly remembers its *snop* night and runs back to her mother asking for their Saturday night *godteri*, or treat – a mug full of assorted chocolates and sweets. Mian and I clear the table then sit down with the kids and watch NRK, the Norwegian Broadcasting Company, the only television company with national coverage.

Prior to 1993, Norwegian television didn't have commercials. Even now NRK, like the BBC in Britain, has no commercials. There's a quaint, naive, even innocent style to NRK broadcasts without any of the razzmatazz of US television stations. Both NRK radio and television play important roles in unifying the social fabric of a country where so many live on isolated islands, valleys and fjords. In the winter, the television announcer sits at a table with a simple backdrop and a candle burning to announce the shows that will be seen that day. The weather readers are so non-charismatic, presenting the weather forecasts in a monotone and barely moving their hands or lips, that they have become an institution, even amongst Norwegians. Watching NRK, I imagine, is to go back to American television the way it was in the 1950s. But to me, watching NRK television is a poignant reminder of how simple, pure and untainted Norway can seem to an outsider.

The kids sit on the sofa, mesmerised by Norwegian children's shows that date back to the previous generation. Mian would have sat watching the same television shows at exactly the same time in the evening, with the same tradition of Saturday night children's television 'treats'.

Mian tells me in a whisper how her young son Bjørn had gone over to the next-door neighbour's house earlier that day and knocked on the front door. The mother opened the door and, seeing Bjørn there, asked if he had come to play with her daughter, Sarah.

'No,' Bjørn replied formally, 'I want to tell you that I love Sarah.'

There's something almost surreal about the Norwegian way of life; sometimes it seems to come out of a child's book of fairy tales, reflecting a perfect, innocent world. Of course, it isn't a perfect, innocent world. Recently I saw a BBC documentary comparing the case of the two British boys convicted of killing another child, and a Norwegian child who had killed one of his classmates. What was so dramatic in the comparison between the two murders was how the Norwegians immediately worked to rehabilitate the child murderer. While it was carefully explained to him the significance of what he had done, he went back to school immediately with the rest of his classmates, under careful supervision. Even the murdered child's mother had no sense of revenge, despite her grief, and fully supported the process of making sure her daughter's 'murderer' would not suffer more than was necessary. There was a genuine sense of sorrow from everyone. The senior police officer in charge could barely hold back his tears when he was interviewed, not only for the dead girl but also for the future of the boy who was responsible for her death. It was as if the two children were from the same family and while there was sorrow on the one hand, there was also a sense of responsibility to make sure the boy did not become excluded from society. In Britain, there was almost a tribal lust for revenge and retribution, of adults hurling stones at the police cars carrying the two young boys to court.

In my room I sort through my notebooks and business cards collected from the trip. Where else do business cards have the *home* address and phone number included with the business address and phone number? It's another measure of how ingenuous Norway is compared to the rest of the world. In fact, I could find the address of any Norwegian living in Norway by contacting *Folkeregisteret*, the public register directory. The home phone numbers on the business cards reflect the accessibility of everyone. Even the people at the top of government organisations or businesses are easily reached, often answering their own phones without relying on a personal assistant.

Opening my notebook while lying in bed, I see Annabel has scrawled in typically barely legible doctor's writing under my last entry, a few words of endearment and then the admonition: 'BE SAFE. I'll miss you heaps.'

Underneath she's drawn two hearts.

Jostein and a friend of his, Øystein, pick me up to walk with them up Bjørndalen Valley to Jostein's *seter* where his 108 sheep graze during the summer. I've a backpack full of food and drinks for our overnight trip. We walk up the valley past the barony and then reach a vertical waterfall. I had thought, from Jostein's description, that this walk to the *seter* was just a short stroll. Soon we are struggling up a slippery path, crossing a rickety suspension footbridge over the cascading falls, and then climbing what is almost a vertical wall of rock. Iron rods stick out of the rock with ropes attached to facilitate the climb, but it's a dangerous section of path. The drop down to the rocks below is made even more daunting by drizzle, rendering the footing even slipperier. But my doubts at undertaking this walk dissipate immediately when we climb to the top of the falls. It's as if we've entered a Shangri-la, a pass into a beautiful valley with a lake, sprawling waterfalls, nestled amidst a bowl surrounded by mountains.

We skirt one lake, ascending alongside a second lake into yet another hidden valley. If the previous lake, valley, surrounding waterfalls and mountains were stunning, they are nothing compared to this scenery. With mist blowing behind us over the lip at the top of the first waterfalls and drifting across the lake, this landscape is as remarkable as anything Annabel and I have seen together on our trip, and yet this anonymous corner of Norway is known only to the locals.

Jostein's *seter* is a rustic stone hut so well camouflaged with moss-covered boulders and turf roof, you'd assume it was an abandoned, centuries-old ruin. But the interior has been totally renovated; the walls are pinewood with custom-made bunk beds, shelves and wooden floor. The inside could be the interior of a modern house. We dump our packs and continue up the valley to count Jostein's sheep and to drop off two salt licks. There is no path here and I accompany Øystein, a trout and salmon biologist working for the university in Bergen, up the stream while Jostein climbs along the edges of the steep-sided valley.

Øystein sniffs the air. 'Can you smell the trout?' he asks.

I study him, trying to figure out if he's pulling my leg or not. 'Are you joking?'

'No, I can smell trout in streams. Not where there is a lot of pollution, but in an area like this, if there are trout in the streams, then I can smell them.' He doesn't seem to be joking.

I can't smell the trout but I do find lots of cloudberries – yellow berries the size of a raspberry and similar in shape. Unfortunately the cloudberries aren't ripe.

The mist and clouds break up and blue sky reappears. Jostein stops occasionally to stare up at the mountains through his binoculars, counting his sheep. Some are perched on the succulent grass emerging on the edges of the melting snow. They are so high it doesn't look as if they could climb down. In fact, every fall when they are driven back down to his farm for the winter, Jostein and Stephen have to rescue some of his sheep stranded on rock ledges.

After Jostein lays down the two heavy blocks of salt he has carried up in his backpack, we return down the valley to his *seter*. There's plenty of evidence of trout in the lake as they rise to feed, breaking the glassy surface of the water. 'Do you have a fishing rod here?' I ask Jostein.

He shakes his head.

'None of us brought a fishing rod when we have a *private* lake *full* of trout? We can't do *anything* about it?' I suppose I could try tickling them.

Instead of frying up freshly caught trout, Øystein cooks sausages on a kerosene stove. He says to me, 'I've been to the Rockies in Canada. It's so beautiful there.'

'But look what you've got here! Look at this view!'

'But it's not a wilderness area like Canada has.'

'Look, we've *walked* for a couple of hours from your homes on the sea and here we are in a hut beside a lake, surrounded by waterfalls and mountains. If we go up the valley, we climb onto the Folgefonna Glacier. If we go down, we come to the entrance to a fjord. Meanwhile, here we are, sitting by this lake, sleeping in a wonderfully comfortable hut tonight. We've got all the wilderness experience we can cope with close to your homes. You can take the train to Finse and be in Arctic conditions in just a few hours. You can walk from here to the end of the valley up over the glacier and stay in another hut. Then you could continue onto the Hardangervidda Plateau and walk hundreds, even thousands of kilometres of trails, with a hut of some kind, at the most, eight hours apart. It's like a wilderness playground in your backyard.'

Jostein says nodding, 'But our wealth can be a curse.'

'Why?' I agree with him, but I'm interested to hear what he has to say.

'Because we have the resources to dam this river and lake and make it yet another hydropower project. In the north of the country the price of hydropower is going down because they can't sell it all and here they want to destroy this beautiful area to create more hydropower than we need. Folgefonna should be a national park,' Jostein says emphatically, 'And we need all the help we can get to stop Kvinnherad Energi from damming that waterfall and destroying this paradise.'

❄

Øystein has promised to take me to see a salmon farm. He says that fish farming will eventually replace the oil industry as Norway's major export, which is hard to imagine. I go with him and Jostein to Sunndal where we look at the tanks holding the young salmon. Both salmon and trout are anadromous, meaning that spawning and the first phase of growth take place in freshwater. There are some 250,000 young smelt in each freshwater tank the size of a large suburban swimming pool, fed from the adjacent stream. In a workroom we watch two workers operate the machines that automatically inject the young fish with antibiotics. Then we drive to a dock where we board a boat to take us out to a fish farm anchored beside a sheet of bedrock that rises some hundreds of metres vertically above, and probably descends below the surface just as far. The steel girders forming the sides of the salmon cages are the size of the legs of a small oil rig. Even if fisheries are already the second biggest export industry in Norway, it is difficult to fathom how fish farming could ever supersede oil as the country's top revenue earner until one sees the size of the fish farms first-hand.

In an isolated area like this, fish farms provide an economic base for small communities, helping maintain a dispersed population in coastal Norway. Salmon is by far the most important farmed fish, followed by trout.

There are some twenty cages covered in netting to prevent the salmon from jumping out. The salmon spend one to two years in these sea cages. Every few minutes, the automatic feeder spits out a handful of feed in each holding pen and there's a flurry as the fish compete for the food. On most of these rigs, if submerged video cameras monitor uneaten food reaching the bottom of the net the automatic feeder is slowed down. The problems presented when food containing antibiotics blanketed the seabed have been minimised in the late nineties, if not eliminated, by injecting the fish directly with antibiotics rather than including it in the feed. But now, Øystein admits, the biggest problem is from fish escaping and mixing with the wild salmon and reducing the genetic stock of the wild salmon. The other significant problem, he tells me, is that these salmon farms are breeding stations for sea lice which are passed on to wild salmon.

The size of the individual salmon in the holding pens is enormous; they look the size of tuna, some five kilos and more. Fish farms such as this produce 400 times as much farmed salmon as the 1000 tons of wild salmon caught annually. This fish farm alone produces 600 tons of salmon annually.

'One hundred and twenty million salmon young are released every year into holding pens, compared to two and a half million sheep wandering around our mountainsides,' Øystein informs me, putting the fish farming versus traditional livestock farming in perspective.

Øystein is working on a university project that's aimed at trying to restore the habitat of rivers that were previously frequented by salmon or sea trout. He takes me to the river he is studying. In one of his traps he removes two sea trout and shows me where sea lice have eaten away the dorsal fins. This river, once an important salmon fishing run, is being rehabilitated to encourage the trout to migrate up its course again. Fascinated as I am with his research, we spend so much time on the fish farm I barely have time to say goodbye to Mian and Tuva and the boys before racing with Øystein to catch my ferry to Leirvik and then to Bergen.

I board the ferry at Sunde in the nick of time, and stand on the deck watching the scenery as we cross over to Leirvik. This is the same ferry my Swiss clients took on their ten-day cycle tours around the district of Hordaland. I led the first couple of trips, then found two guides to continue leading them. The very first tour I did, it rained every single day for ten days. The trip could have been a disaster but it wasn't because each evening we had accommodation somewhere beside the sea where we could go out in the long, light evenings and fish. Every night we caught more fish than we could eat. It was so easy sometimes we just had to put a hook in the water and jerk it up to foul-hook a fish through the tail or body.

On the second trip we had absolutely glorious weather but each night when we fished, we couldn't catch a sausage. The clients were disappointed because I'd built up the fishing scenario and I had told them we'd be catching masses of fish every night. On our last day we were cycling from Sunndal across Tysnes Island back to Bergen. The tour included a lunch break at Lysøen, Ole Bull's summer island, outside Bergen. Cycling past a supermarket, I stopped and ran quickly inside. I bought a whole frozen salmon and hid it in my saddlebags. When the small boat taxi took us across the water to Lys Island, unseen by my clients, I attached my fishing line and hook to the mouth of the still semi-frozen salmon and dropped it surreptitiously into the water. Halfway across I jerked the line and yelled, 'I've caught a fish!' Everyone crowded around me as I pulled in the heavy line. The frozen salmon didn't put up much of a struggle as I heaved it onto the deck with a solid thud. One of the Swiss clients, a fishing enthusiast, picked it up. 'It's frozen!'

'It's the cold water,' I replied, having been uncovered as a cheat.

The car ferry approaches Leirvik on the island of Stord where several tugs tow a massive oil rig out of the harbour. Since the first exploratory drilling was made in 1966 there have been a series of discoveries of oil reserves on the Norwegian section of the continental shelf. Within thirty years Norway has become the world's second largest oil exporter – it makes up a whopping 30 per cent of Norway's exports. From one of the poorest countries in Europe earlier in the century, Norway has become one of the wealthiest in the world. With a population of only four and a half million, the revenue from oil, at almost two billion dollars in 1998, has led to a massive surplus in the government budget. An 'oil fund' has been established, with investments in foreign stock and securities to safeguard financing of the welfare state for future generations.

The ferry has radioed to the catamaran in Leirvik that there is one passenger coming their way. I disembark the car ferry and as soon as I board the cat we skirt to the western coast of the island of Stord. My ten-day bicycle tours went via Stord, on a ferry to Bømlo, the island to the west. Now there is a huge new bridge linking these two islands. I loved these bike tours; I loved the landscape of these islands and skerries – the sea-lashed rocks, the windswept fir trees bent to the shape of the prevailing winds, the purple heather, the tiny fishing villages tucked into protected harbours. Probably more than the rest of Norway, more than the mountains and fjords, it's the islands off the coastline that had the greatest appeal for me. And it was on these islands that I found a breed of Norwegians different from the rest. These are the Vikings – outgoing, friendly, hospitable and even extroverted. It was hard for me sometimes to equate Norwegians on the west coast, from Stavanger to Kirkenes, with the rest of the Norwegians; they seemed so different in character.

It starts raining, but that doesn't diminish the experience cruising amongst these skerries. I sit back in the comfortable seat, the speed and motion of the vessel through the calm, protected waters not dissimilar to the sensation of being in a low-flying jet aircraft. I often wonder if I had moved to an island community like Bømlo, whether I'd still be in Norway now. The darkness of the winter would be just as depressing, and the rainy weather throughout the year would have added to those feelings of melancholy, but there was something about these islands, Bømlo in particular, that rang consonant with me.

We weave amongst the rocky islands and their clusters of brightly painted wooden houses with slate roofs set amidst pockets of green pasture, bordered by pines. We skim around several fish farms, their horizontal oil rig-like structures tethered to the rocks. Several times we stop in small harbours, the occasional passenger embarking or disembarking. Now the shrill cry of seagulls has replaced the ubiquitous sound of waterfalls.

The rain stops. I look ahead. Against a backdrop of black clouds, soft light bathes Fløyen and Ulriken, the mountains around Bergen.

Norwegians, at least those in Bergen, don't jaywalk. They patiently wait for the little green man to indicate when they can cross. When I look both ways at a pedestrian crossing, and can see there are no cars for hundreds of metres in either direction, I cross. But here in Bergen, no one else follows. Not only do they not follow me, they stare at me as if I've done something unlawful, which I have. As if by jaywalking I am proving myself to be the kind of character that would rob a post office with a gun.

I kept a tiny apartment in Bergen and there were times it rained so much I honestly thought there couldn't be enough air outside to breathe. Such a wall of water would fall, sometimes for days, that it didn't seem possible you could survive walking around without a scuba tank attached to your back. And yet when it was clear weather, there was nothing like Bergen. On a fine summer night I'd take my sleeping bag and climb up to the rocks above my apartment and sleep out. In the winter under a clear blue sky after a heavy snowfall, Bergen was a magical place with the kids tobogganing down icy paths as slippery and convoluted as bobsled runs.

Generally though, winter was dismal here. At least in the winter Oslo had the snow, but Bergen just tended to be wet – the snow on the ground never lasting more than a couple of days. The walk into Bergen from my apartment perched on the hillside was fraught with danger in the winter as I descended the zigzagging pathway. Often the dark path was covered in a slick layer of black ice, which was deadly to step on. Iron handrails were worn smooth over the decades from the gloved hands that glided over their surface for stability. There were many older people who wore clip-on *pigg* on their shoes or boots. *Pigg* are like miniature crampons or spikes attached to shoe soles, and even onto the bottom of walking sticks. It wasn't such a far-fetched idea to be clamping on crampons before walking back up the hill to my apartment in the middle of winter with a pack full of fragile groceries.

Although the winters in Bergen are darker than Oslo, spring comes earlier here, because it is on the coast. The first flowers appear in February and I vividly remember the sound of birds singing frenetically in the early spring. The translucent green leaves would come out on the trees and there'd be a happy reawakening of the senses, a feeling of rebirth, and life seemed so bright and full of optimism with the whole glorious summer ahead.

In the wintertime, I'm most likely to hear from my Norwegian friends. The evenings are long and depressing, and there's plenty of time to think, to ruminate and to send letters to sunny, far-off corners of the world, as if sending out a lifeline to a place that isn't so dark will somehow illuminate their world. It's hardly surprising Norwegians read books, newspapers, and magazines to such a degree. In the summer though, the letters evaporate as the days become longer and the willingness to sit at a desk at home or at the office diminishes. On a warm summer afternoon, you'd be lucky to find any Norwegians still sitting in their offices, especially on a Friday. The greatest asset for self-employed Norwegians is the mobile phone. On a fine day they can be out boating, hiking, drinking a beer outside, fielding office calls forwarded to their cell phones where they might carry off the charade that they're still at work.

The last two years I was in Norway, I worked as a consultant on both the Norwegian and Swedish governments' foreign aid programs. The work conveniently took me out of Norway during the winter months to warmer climes in Africa. Frequent trips to Tanzania, Namibia and Botswana were welcome diversions from the gloom of Norwegian winters. But I also enjoyed the camaraderie of working with colleagues. Norwegians often have partial jobs, being employed 50 per cent or 70 per cent or percentages thereof. I worked as a consultant on the Norwegian foreign-aid program over a two-year period at 50 per cent, which allowed me to legitimately run my summer adventure programs as well as take on freelance consulting jobs with the Swedish government on their aid programs in Africa. Working in a Norwegian environment I was surprised at how lengthy the decision-making process was because everyone was involved in the process of deciding what to do. I also detected this sense of cooperation in the *spisepause,* or eating break usually held late morning, when everyone in the office sat down at the conference table and shared lunch of bread and *pålegg*. Once a week, someone would stand up at the table and summarise the week's events, decisions, functions and other matters of interest. It helped to instil a feeling of family into the workplace.

Loaded with my backpack, I look at my watch, check the traffic both ways and, despite the red light, scurry along faster. I don't want to miss the train to Oslo. The first year in Norway, I missed many a train and flight because of the curious way Norwegians say what time it is for half past the hour. Half past three will be *'halv fire'* or half four, which to me means half *past* four, not half past three. Anything between a quarter past the hour and a quarter to the hour is even more complicated. A simple 'twenty to five' becomes a tongue-twisting 'ten past half five'. A straightforward 'twenty after five' would be a mathematical computation of 'ten to half six'.

The likelihood of missing this train is diminished by the fact that it leaves at five to eleven, simple and clear in either Norwegian or English.

I've taken the Bergen to Oslo train some forty times and yet I can never sit there and read or fall asleep. Each segment of the trip is different, but equally spectacular. Every time I do the journey, I see something special. The colour and even the shape of the landscape changes with the seasons. The two Japanese people sitting opposite me have reserved and paid for four seats so that the two of them can move from one side of the train carriage to the other, whichever side the scenery is. But instead of playing musical seats across the aisles to maximise their investment of four booked seats, they both promptly fall asleep. I push my seat all the way back and with the sun shining brightly through the window on my face, half close my eyes, half take in the scenery. We skirt fjords with perpendicular walls of bedrock and I see porpoises breaking through the surface of the water perfectly mirroring the mountains and waterfalls on the other side.

We trundle by an old wooden fishing boat tied up outside a *rorbu* where children wave at the train passing by and then, showing off, jump into the fjord. Further along, two impish, blonde-haired children pull faces at the passengers as the train goes by while a third waves the Norwegian flag. Every tiny patch of cultivable land is farmed. Farms dot even the higher edges of the mountains. Derelict huts have flowers and trees growing out of their turf roofs. On the upper reaches of the railway we pass through snowsheds with windows cut into them and the view changes to the flickering frames of an old-fashioned film.

The sense of nostalgia instigated by the train trip is heightened by the fact that I have to go to Kirsten's family farm outside Oslo and sort through all my belongings in preparation for the shippers. The process of sorting through these boxes will be an emotional tug, but it is one I feel I am able to face now. Instead of a sad process of disassembling a past life, it's a harbinger of the future. Most of the belongings, furniture and trunks full of mementos from my travels are still in the original packaging from when they were shipped from my house in Ottawa. Because our home in Oslo wasn't as large as my home in Ottawa, much of the stuff has been stored in the family's barn where it's remained for almost ten years.

I spend the best part of the day sneezing in the dusty barn, sorting through some sixty rotting cardboard boxes that seem to be relics from a previous life twice removed. Most are clearly marked and still intact, but one cardboard box has had water leaking on it and the cardboard has fallen apart so much I have to repack the contents into another box. There is an accumulation of odds and ends, obviously packed at the last minute in Ottawa. Of all the sixty boxes, only one has to be repacked and yet this one box has a letter, still wrapped in a pink ribbon, with Kirsten's clear writing. When we moved from Canada to Norway, Kirsten flew here six weeks before me to secure a job before I came over. I had driven her to the airport and when I returned I had found the letter on the kitchen table.

Although she is in Denmark on holiday, it's as if she's there with me as I untie the pink ribbon and read under the glare of a naked light bulb in the dusty old chicken barn the smudged words.

The letter is a poignant reminder of Kirsten's arrival in Canada with Bonso, our life together there, how she became homesick for Norway and how those dreams of a new adventure in Norway came off the rails. It's a reminder of how difficult I found it to fit into Norwegian society, how the gloominess of the winters depressed me, how the rain and darkness finally deflated my ambition to live here. Despite Kirsten's considerable efforts, I slowly realised I couldn't make my home in Norway.

Friends would say, 'Well, you're from Canada, you're used to the cold, it shouldn't be so different in Norway.'

It was very different. I don't mind the cold. In Ottawa, my favourite season was the winter. It was a cold, dry winter there. I loved cross-country skiing in the Gatineau Hills or skating on the Rideau Canal. Winter in Norway is absolutely magical after a heavy snowfall. But the big difference between Ottawa and Oslo, or Bergen, is the light, or lack of it, in the middle of winter. Norwegians are used to it. I wasn't. Ottawa, although it is further north than Toronto, is further south than Venice in Italy. Conversely Bergen and Oslo are as far north as Canada's Hudson's Bay, north of Churchill, and at the same latitude as Whitehorse in the Yukon or Anchorage in Alaska. In Oslo and Bergen in midwinter, the anaemic sun barely skips over the horizon. At nine in the morning it's still pitch-dark and it gets dark again soon after three. I felt like a plant slowly wilting due to lack of sunlight. It wasn't depression so much as a general lack of energy, of life. During my last years in Norway I felt a pathological fear as the first heavy grey clouds drifted in during the fall and I knew winter would settle in.

Spitsbergen

The SAS flight for Tromsø and Spitsbergen leaves late at night. I take the new, fast train to Gardermoen. Within minutes of leaving Oslo, bathed in soft, late evening light, the train enters a tunnel and hurtles through it for a good ten minutes before emerging into rolling farming countryside surrounded by pine forest. This is all a new experience for me. Since I left Norway, the airport at Fornebu – a peninsula in the Oslofjord – has closed and Gardermoen – the new airport in the middle of the pine forests north of Oslo – has opened. This fast train to a large, new international airport is a reflection of the rapid changes taking place in Norway. I had always found it appropriately quaint arriving in Norway at the old Fornebu airport; its terminal resembled a high-school cafeteria rather than the country's main international airport terminal.

The fast airport train – an example of the kind that will run on most of Norway's railway lines in the near future – stops directly under the new terminal building. I take an elevator up into a cavernous space that is the departure hall. Walls of glass open to the outside, revealing wispy clouds catching the setting sun's rays. In a spectacular display of golden light, the forested slopes around the airport are sharply silhouetted against the cobalt blue evening sky. While waiting to board my flight, the heavens turn from cobalt blue to a rich golden colour and then deep red. But then the sunset lingers, a brilliant display filling the walls of glass under the curved wooden beams arching under the high-roofed terminal. The effect is stunning. It's not often an airport terminal can look aesthetically pleasing, but Gardermoen does, at least at half past ten on a clear, midsummer night.

When the aircraft takes off, we head directly north, straight into the sun. By the time we start our descent into the rain clouds at Tromsø at midnight, the sky is already a paler blue. When we take off again at quarter to two in the morning, continuing directly north, another day has started and the sun is already high in the sky. Looking at the in-flight magazine's map in the back pages, I see Spitsbergen lies directly between the northern tip of Norway and the North Pole. The permanent solid white representing the pack ice that is the North Pole almost reaches the northern edge of Spitsbergen. If it weren't for the warming influence of the Gulf Stream, the pack ice would undoubtedly have much of Spitsbergen locked permanently in its frozen embrace. From Spitsbergen's northern tip, it's a few hundred kilometres walk over ice to the North Pole.

Visitors to Norway are often surprised that the Arctic Circle cuts through Norway. In fact, the Arctic Circle almost cuts Norway in two thirds. I've been up the coastline as far as North Cape at the northern tip of Norway. Spitsbergen is so far north it doesn't have much else to compare with at that latitude: the northern tip of Greenland and some obscure islands belonging to Russia. Spitsbergen itself is the largest island, but only one of several in the archipelago, and is the internationally recognised name for the archipelago, although Norwegians call the islands Svalbard.

I try to get some sleep on the plane but it's impossible. I'm too excited about the next ten days in Spitsbergen. At three in the morning we descend into low-hanging clouds until the brown craggy cliffs outside Longyearbyen appear through the mist just before we land. Shafts of coal mines, the elevated sifting station and the pylons of the mine's cable-car system loom out of the mist.

In the tiny, one-room arrival and departure lounge there's a loud bong of an electronic bell as an announcement is made in Norwegian and English that 'permission is required from the Governor of Svalbard to go to areas outside of the settlement of Longyearbyen itself'. At the information counter I pick up a postcard with two polar bears eating what looks suspiciously like a bloody human carcass. With a sense of relief, I read on the back of the card, written in Norwegian, English and Russian, 'The photo shows polar bears eating a seal'. But there is also written the following warning:

TAKE THE POLAR BEAR DANGER SERIOUSLY!

The polar bear has been protected from hunting since 1973. It is also illegal to chase, entice, feed or disturb polar bears unnecessarily.

Close encounters with polar bears can be lethal.

Be well prepared before moving into the field.

Always be alert and keep to open areas.

Be correctly armed at all times.

It is prohibited to carry loaded weapons in the settlements.

Since the 1600s people have been hunting and fishing on the Spitsbergen archipelago. The fact that it did not belong to any particular state was not a problem; there were not many people interested in being here and therefore few conflicts. Although in the early 1900s mining activities created pressure to obtain sole mining rights, it wasn't until after World War I that the Spitsbergen Treaty of 1920 was signed, giving Norway and the Governor of Spitsbergen absolute and unlimited sovereignty over the entire archipelago. Curiously, while Spitsbergen is deemed to be under the jurisdiction of the Kingdom of Norway, Norway is obliged to grant equal rights to citizens and companies from all the countries that are party to the treaty. They are allowed to enter and live, fish and hunt, mine and acquire property here on an equal footing to the citizens of Norway. The parties to the original treaty are an eclectic mix and include such disparate nations as Afghanistan, the Dominican Republic, Japan and South Africa. Someone from the Dominican Republic or Afghanistan, or any of these signatory countries, could legally come to Spitsbergen, find a job or acquire mineral rights. Of course, they'd have to get a visa into mainland Norway first, because the only commercial flights to Spitsbergen or Svalbard these days are from Tromsø.

Taking the bus into Longyearbyen, I'd imagined it would be snow-covered. It isn't. It looks like an instant community, with mostly new buildings and even new blacktop bitumen on the few roads. The buildings, I notice, are built on stilts above the permafrost, as is the hot-water supply for heating the buildings and sewerage pipes. The buildings are all connected by this visible spider's web of pipes constructed a metre off the muddy earth. As per the request posted on the front entrance, I remove my shoes, put them in a neat line with scores of others, and in stockinged feet check in to the SAS Radisson Hotel after taking careful note of the sign from the reception desk: 'To all our Guests: The risk of polar bears in the Restaurant isn't very big so can you please hang your weapons in the weapons cabinet (rifle, gun, revolver).'

In contrast to the superficial plushness of the hotel and the new buildings that seem to make up the community, I get the feeling that Spitsbergen is still like the Wild West, except everyone speaks Norwegian instead of American and it's seventy degrees or so further north.

While waiting at the front desk I open a copy of *Svalbard Posten*. This issue headlines why a Polish researcher shot three polar bears in self-defence after they tried to break into his hut.

In the same issue is a piece on an American couple who were returned to Svalbard – already I find myself referring to Spitsbergen as Svalbard – on board the retired Hurtigruten coastal steamer *Nordstjernen* when they became a security risk after they became dissatisfied with their cabin on board. Police took them away in handcuffs although it's not clear what kind of security risk they were. I've been on the *Nordstjernen*, one of the oldest boats still in service on the famous coastal steamer service between Bergen and Kirkenes, which is amongst the best boat trips any-where in the world. But for Americans expecting to be on a cruise ship, the old *Nordstjernen* would have been a rude awakening.

Despite the unearthly hour I feel wide awake. This is the furthest north I have ever been, or am ever likely to go. There are no trees here, not even bushes. In the distance, far over the silvery flat fjord, snow-covered mountains and glaciers lurk beneath overcast clouds. The midnight sun lasts from 19 April to 23 August in Longyearbyen. Of course, the flip side is that the perpetual night endures from 26 October to 16 February. I stare out at the windswept wilderness shrouded in mist before drawing the heavy curtains tight against the strange light.

Midday and I've managed to sleep in but I've missed breakfast. I open the curtains. It's still misty. There's no difference in the light from four this morning to now. I walk past scores of snow-mobiles mothballed for the summer, and head down the main pedestrian walkway, finding myself behind a woman carrying a rifle slung over her shoulder.

'Um, excuse me, but is it really necessary to carry a rifle here?' I ask, without a hint of superciliousness. I'm paranoid enough to think I shouldn't even be walking a couple of hundred metres from the hotel to the post office in case there's a polar bear hid-ing behind the corner of a building waiting to gobble me up. I notice she has duct tape over the barrel opening to stop the rain getting in.

'No, I've just walked a couple of kilometres from out of town.'

'Where'd you get your rifle?'

'From the bicycle rental shop.'

'You just walk into the bicycle rental shop and they rent you a rifle with your bike?' I ask. 'Just to go a couple of kilometres?'

She points at the hillside, towards a line of rocky balustrades looming out of the mist like the ramparts of a giant fortress. I wouldn't be surprised to see gargantuan gargoyles appear out of the tops of the gothic parapets. 'A couple of years ago a woman was killed by a polar bear right up there. That's "just a couple of kilometres".'

'Did they show you how to use the rifle?'

'No.'

'Have you used one before?'

'No.'

Hope the polar bears know she's armed. 'How much was it?'

'A hundred kroner for the rifle per day and ten kroner per bullet, but you get your money back on the bullets if you haven't used them.'

The rifle looks like a World War II Mauser that may or may not work, no matter how proficient the shooter is. She'd probably have more effect throwing bullets at a polar bear than putting them down the chamber and pulling the trigger. 'And you don't need a licence?'

'Just need to be older than twenty-one.'

What do kids do when they want to go out to play and aren't twenty-one, I wonder?

Without a rifle to defend myself, I sidestep into the supermarket, bypassing a sign asking me to leave my weapons with the cashier on the way in. At least I don't have to remove my shoes. I buy two expensive New Zealand apples and try to visualise someone picking them in New Zealand, literally half a world away.

Remembering to buy a bottle of whiskey to take with me on the Russian research vessel as a possible present to the crew, I enter the section of the store selling alcohol and select a bottle of whiskey, then take it to the cashier.

'Can I see your air ticket?' the cashier asks.

'Air ticket?' What is this, a duty-free?

Resigned, she repeats to me what she obviously has to repeat countless times a day. 'Unless you live here and have a ration card, you have to have your airline ticket to buy alcohol.'

'What happens if I came by boat?'

'You can't buy liquor.'

None of it makes any sense. With an airline ticket I am allowed to buy two litres of liquor, one case of twenty-four beers, one litre of fortified 18 per cent proof wine, or an unlimited amount of regular wine.

Alcohol has far less tax on it here than on the mainland, making Spitsbergen in effect a duty-free environment. Visitors are allowed to take back with them two bottles of liquor. Residents are permitted so many bottles per month and, in a strange throwback to when Longyearbyen was a company town, have a ration card to keep track of how much of their allotment they have consumed. Because the managers of the coal-mining company had 'refined' tastes and consumed only wine, wine wasn't, and still isn't, rationed and still doesn't have a voucher system although it is of course alcoholic. I can buy as much wine as I want and get totally pissed without restriction, but unfortunately, with my more plebeian tastes, I am limited to how much beer or hard liquor I can purchase.

Tourism to Spitsbergen is only a relatively recent phenomenon. Until the 1980s there were no hotels, just the campsite and Funken, where the coal miners stayed. Visitors had to bring with them everything they needed, including tents and food. Longyearbyen was, in effect, a coal-mining town. The building called Lompen used to be the coal miners' showers and changing room but has been recently converted into exclusive shops catering to tourists. New buildings, colourful imitations of Norwegian mainland architecture, are replete with the steep roofs not needed in this arid climate. The buildings' mountings on stilts are cleverly disguised behind wooden-slat skirts. I assume they are designed this way to allay bouts of homesickness amongst the inhabitants, mostly mainlanders. Most buildings have been constructed in the last decade and it's the employers – the coal-mining companies, the state and the Sysselmann's (governor's) office, hospital, university and the adventure travel companies – that own most of these quaint houses.

I walk around to Huset, a pink building that serves as the community hall, theatre, dance hall and, once a week, the cinema. In the

pub-like atmosphere of the restaurant I order seal with fried potatoes. The alternative is a combination plate of arctic char, seal,
smoked salmon, smoked reindeer heart and tongue, fish eggs, scal-
lops and shrimps. Both the seal and the reindeer have been government inspected on mainland Norway, so the fact that there are seal
and reindeer within gunshot is entirely beyond the point. The seal
meat is purple in colour and bleeds profusely into the gravy.

Feeling slightly queasy after eating the meal, I continue walking back towards the centre of Longyearbyen, past the cemetery
where two wild reindeer feed, quite unconcerned by my presence.
I stop to look at them and can easily see by their short legs that
these smaller reindeer are a subspecies endemic to Spitsbergen,
more closely related to the Canadian caribou than the wild reindeer of Norway. Given they were hunted almost to extinction, it's
hard to believe they are so tame and trusting towards humans. I
keep nervously looking over my shoulder to make sure I'm not
the latest addition to Longyearbyen's polar bear attack folklore.
Ubiquitous road signs warning about polar bears don't ease the
paranoia. A car goes by and I resist the temptation to hitchhike. I
notice the vehicles here have black license plates, normally used
on construction sites on the mainland. While there are only sixty
kilometres of roads on Spitsbergen, there are 1500 snowmobiles,
or an average of one per person.

Shoeless, but within the safe confines of the sumptuous SAS
Radisson Hotel, I head into The Pub. Sitting at the bar, I notice
that several of the bottles of alcohol on the shelves have names,
presumably the owners', written on the labels. Beside common-
place Norwegian names like Lars and Tore there is one bottle
marked 'Jesus Christ'. I ask the bartender why.

'If someone has enough money to buy a whole bottle and
wants to keep it here under the name of Jesus Christ, or anyone
else for that matter, that's fine by me,' the bartender replies in
impeccable English.

It's a motley group of Norwegians collected here, a bit reminiscent of the *Star Wars* pub scene where the intergalactic
denizens come to meet. In my few encounters with those who live

here, it seems they are often escaping something on the mainland despite their claims that they have come here for the nature. They are friendly enough though, and soon I'm talking to an off-duty guide who joins me at the bar.

She relates how an American woman on her trip to Pyramiden, a Russian mining town, was disappointed about the midnight sun.

'She was thinking the midnight sun would be more like a mid-night sun,' she says.

'But it *is* a midnight sun,' I reply.

'No, she meant like a sun in the middle of the night.'

'But then it wouldn't be night.'

'I know, but she couldn't understand that. She wanted to see the midnight sun sort of like the full moon in the middle of the night, I guess. She said she was disappointed it wasn't like that and she'd been misled.' Like everyone else I've met, my new friend has left behind a long-term relationship and already she loves it here, the sense of family, community, the fact that every-one seems to know everyone else.

For those who live in Spitsbergen, particularly Longyearbyen, tourism is becoming big business and the lives of those who have been here for fifteen or more years have changed substantially. Now there is fresh milk, brought in on the daily flights from Tromsø. Also stuffed into the commercial airliners are huge quan-tities of meat and alcohol, flying to Spitsbergen in the cargo bay. Passengers from the Norwegian mainland fly to Longyearbyen, load up on cheap, tax-free alcohol and meat (frozen legs of New Zealand lamb are piled high in the supermarket and souvenir shops), and fly back to the mainland. To save all the extra con-sumption of aviation fuel, the authorities should short-circuit the whole unnecessary exercise of flying this stuff in and out and allow people to buy these goods in a little 'Svalbard' enclave in Tromsø on their way back, rather than ferrying it to and fro.

The Svalbarders in the murky pub are a friendly and gregarious crowd, but at one in the morning I take my leave, stepping out of the completely blacked-out 'Puben' into broad daylight. With the sun shining brightly, I'm suddenly awake and it's difficult to persuade myself to go to bed. A few tourists like myself wander around Longyearbyen aimlessly, probably waiting for their four o'clock flight out. Too cold to wander around for long, I head back to my room and draw the heavy curtains shut and try to pretend there's a midnight sun just like the American woman wanted.

As a measure of how times have changed here – fifteen years ago there were no tourist facilities besides a camp site – the SAS Radisson Hotel serves the best breakfast I've had anywhere in Norway, and that is saying a lot. Baked beans, bacon, sausages, fried mushrooms, tomatoes, seal meat, fried potatoes, porridge, pancakes, toast, cereals, waffles, and the usual fish market's worth of pickled herring, butcher's shop of sliced meats and dairy's allotment of cheeses.

The morning is spent on a tour in one of the closed coal mines, in the company of an ex-miner guide and several Germans. The Germans are vacationing sailors whose boat hit a drifting Siberian log, damaging the keel so badly they had to abandon the crippled craft. After sleeping most of the afternoon I have dinner with Ulf Prytz. I met Ulf within a month of arriving in Norway ten years ago, soon after he had started up a new adventure company, Svalbard Polar Travel. In the ten years since I met him he has successfully operated SPOT and the SAS Radisson Hotel.

'Thanks for booking me on this trip. I'm looking forward to it,' I tell him. As his guest, I owe him a small fortune for including me.

'Have you got a good camera?'

'Nikon.'

'And a good lens?'

'An excellent lens.'

'What focal length?'

'Twenty millimetres.'

'Twenty millimetres?' he repeats, astounded. A wide-angle lens is hardly the lens for photographing wildlife, especially walruses and polar bears.

I shrug. 'I dropped my other camera with the 35 to 135 millimetre lens and it's not focusing properly.'

We catch up on each other's news. I admire Ulf's drive and competence. He has the piercing, driven eyes and personality of a polar explorer. His bushy eyebrows and beard enhance this adventurer image. In addition to these tours around Spitsbergen, he plans to begin ship-based cruises into the Antarctic, thereby operating at both poles as the season allows. He enlightens me with his plans for the future. What he has already achieved with Svalbard Polar Travel in these ten years seems astounding.

'Do people think you are an overachiever?' I ask.

'No,' he replies. 'Do they think you are?' he asks back, not batting an eyelid over his deep-set blue eyes, before adding, 'Normally I'm quiet, shy and private. When the two of us get together I get excited. I still dream of doing adventurous things. I'm always thinking of new projects, but I've had to learn that I can make mistakes, and to listen to others.' He's been listening a lot because, from all accounts, he's doing very well.

Behind Ulf the mist and cloud lift and for the first time I see the tops of the mountains on the other side of the fjord. The evening sun shines through the tall pane-glass windows into the dining room. While we talk, the sunset seems to take ages to set, and then I remember: of course, it's not going to 'set' at all. It'll sink at an angle towards the horizon and slowly rotate around us before it rises higher in the sky again.

It isn't an auspicious start when the *Victor Buynitskiy* pulls out of the quay at five in the afternoon under dark clouds and a bitterly cold wind. We pass glacier after glacier; some are almost exclusively blue ice, their tongues reaching down to the sea, others are massive white valleys, as if they were dense clouds locked in between mountains ranges rather than glaciers.

I wander around the 55-metre long Russian research vessel that is chartered by Svalbard Polar Travel for the summer season. According to the ship's information brochure, it belongs to the USSR State Committee for Hydrometeorology and Control of Natural Environment.

Soon after we are underway we have an information meeting in the dining lounge. Two guides are on board and we will pick up a third guide at Kapp Linne. Jens, originally Danish but Norwegian or Svalbardean for all intents and purposes, wears a tatty T-shirt that can't hide his rippling muscles. His hair is unwashed and uncombed, and he sports several days' beard growth but that's okay because, in a way, that's what we expect. Ann-Jorid wears long woollen underwear under loose Norrøna Gore-Tex overalls, her blonde hair casually pulled back behind her head. She too, despite the loose-fitting garb, can't disguise the firmness of her body. The fact that neither of them can be bothered dressing up only enhances their attractiveness. Their smiles and the twinkle in their eyes reflect their unselfconscious confidence.

We take it in turn to introduce ourselves. We are as diverse a foreign crew as the Norwegian clientele at The Pub last night was. There's Nigel, a nuclear physicist from England with a dome as polished as Friar Tuck's and a single dark hair growing mysteriously out of the tip of his nose. Next to him is Ulla, a retired Swedish doctor. Berit is a quiet single Norwegian woman in a Norwegian sweater who, oddly enough, speaks almost no English. Geri and Pia are wealthy Swiss Germans. Yosuke is a giggling Japanese woman married to Philip, an English investment advisor living in Japan. Andy, their twelve-year-old son, is so goggle-eyed at being on this trip his eyeballs look as if they might fall out. Bengt and Berit are a quiet Swedish couple. Beate and Hans-Peter are from Germany. Stefania is an Italian physical education teacher with a body to match her chosen career, and an equally good-looking and fit husband Sergio who, together with my room-mate Guilio, look as if they could be models for Ralph Lauren casual wear. By contrast, Alma and Flora, Italian sisters, look as if they are widows – dressed in black with matching mournful faces. I wonder whether they boarded the right vessel. Grey-faced Giovanni must be eighty and looks like a mafioso boss, peering out the bottom of thick, soda bottle spectacles, sporting a perpetual five o'clock shadow and with a husky, godfather-like voice. His much younger wife lets the don do the talking – usually loudly in Italian and accompanied by wild gesticulations when addressing the rest of us. These hand signals are punctuated frequently with an Italian 'Eh?', and are accompanied by a dropped jaw and a shrugging of shoulders. Rumour has it that Giovanni is here to escape hitmen back in Sicily. There's a good case to argue they already got him; he's as pallid as someone who'd died a week ago. Maybe that's why the Italian sisters are dressed in black, they're expecting an impromptu funeral. Then there's Knut, another quiet Norwegian wearing a Norwegian sweater. And finally, the oddest of us all, are Hans and Andreas – two Dutchmen wearing grubby jeans, worn workboots with steel toecaps, and dirty plastic anoraks. When I first saw them I thought they were the Russian crew, or else stowaways.

Jens welcomes us on board, in Norwegian and English. Ann-Jorid does the same in Italian and then the Russian captain, Uri, and the first officer, Alexander, are introduced. The two Russian stewardesses, with bleached white hair and several centimetres of black roots, nod self-consciously. The stocky stewardess fits the stereotypical image of a Russian woman, while the other is more elegant, with her hair combed back and pulled up over her head much like a clipped poodle's tail, and a skirt so tight it looks like it would explode rather than rip if she bent over. They both have red lipstick carefully outlining their lips, and generous dollops of eye shadow. The captain takes his leave after the introductions to take command of the ship, and the first officer gives us our safety instructions. As part of the safety presentation, the first mate, Vladimir, dons a survival suit that makes him look more like an astronaut than a shipwreck survivor. 'In this,' on cue Vladimir waves his arms as if signalling the Mir Space Station, 'you survive two, maybe three, days in water if ship hits iceberg and sinks.' Sobering thought.

And then we are left to our own devices, to explore the ship, hang out on the bridge, or savour the fresh air on the bow.

Long before we get there, we smell the Russian coal-mining settlement at Barentsburg. A smudge from a tall smokestack stains the atmosphere all the way to the glacier tongue at the end of the fjord. It's hard to imagine now, surrounded by glaciers and ice, but Spitsbergen's rich deposits of coal were formed at the equator millions of years ago and were subsequently pushed north by continental drift. What was once a shallow, sea-water plain has turned to sedimentary bedrock that has subsequently risen up and folded over. Volcanoes existed on Spitsbergen around the time it passed the same latitude as France, when it was still covered in thick forest and dinosaurs roamed about. Presumably it is those ancient forests that they are digging out now as coal.

Our boat docks alongside derelict buildings grimy with soot. Equally grubby apartment buildings, in brick and stone and concrete rather than wood, loom out of the landscape. Whereas colourful Longyearbyen, despite its origins as a coal-mining settlement, gave the impression of being spotlessly clean, Barentsburg seems a grubby leftover from the Industrial Revolution. Patches of snow left from the winter are grey streaks. Not only the whole town, but the whole area seems to be covered in a layer of soot.

This was the main Soviet foothold on the militarily strategic archipelago during the Cold War, and the disproportionate resources they put into this uneconomical mining settlement are still evident. Longyearbyen looks like a colourful collection of fishermen's *rorbur* compared to these substantial building blocks reminiscent of mainland Russia. Whether I photographed Barentsburg in black and white, or in colour, it wouldn't make much difference, both sets of prints would look much the same: shades of grey. Only 200 women and 900 men, mostly Ukrainian, now live here under two-year contracts. Despite the dismal feel to the place, they regularly sign up to extend their contracts, the conditions here being better than back home.

Anya, our Ukrainian guide, meets us on the sooty dock. Her ghostly pale skin is so smooth it is almost translucent. She wears fashionable platform running shoes and a leather jacket with fur lining the edge of the pulled-up hood so she resembles Julie Christie as the romantic heroine in that epic film *Dr Zhivago*. Anya's thin lips are rendered fuller and more curvaceous with a generous application of lipstick. She starts almost all her sentences with 'Dear guests' and tells us she was raised here as a child and has come back as an adult; this is her second two-year contract. She smiles constantly and despite discoloured teeth, she is remarkably beautiful, with high cheekbones and finely chiselled features.

Patriotically she accounts for how wonderful Barentsburg is, while ignoring the sullen stare of several Russians trying to hawk Russian souvenirs. We bypass the hawkers while ascending a series of steep wooden staircases. Judging by the potted flowers on the window ledges, the buildings seem to be inhabited despite many broken windows. Climbing the stairs, Giovanni the Mafia boss doesn't look as if he's going to survive our first excursion ashore. He is breathing so heavily I am sure he's about to have a heart attack. His young wife helps him up but she's not much fitter. We pass more brooding Russians selling souvenirs: military fur hats with the Communist Party badge, hunting knives and Russian babushka dolls. I feel sorry for these people; they watch rich tourists disembark from a redundant Soviet research vessel taking photos of them like so many animals in cages at a zoo. An occasional Russian or Ukrainian, inevitably wearing a black leather jacket, walks by, eyes averted. Anya, despite her smiles, seems embarrassed by the presence of the souvenir sellers and her compatriots. It's hardly surprising. Although she talks positively about Barentsburg and Russia, the remains of the Soviet empire are crumbling before us.

Barentsburg no longer exports coal to the Russian Federation. The mines are so inefficient and understaffed now that much of the coal produced here is consumed here. With no resources, the considerable infrastructure is slowly disintegrating.

We pass by a log building. 'Dear guests,' Anya relates, 'this is one of the original buildings in all of Spitsbergen, made by the Pomars from Russia who were the first people to hunt and trap here many centuries ago.' I notice she uses the name Spitsbergen rather than Svalbard. 'This hut is from the sixteenth or seventeenth century and it is very nice to sit here on a summer evening and to look at the view. It is also quite interesting because the Pomars lived in northern Russia from the tenth century and came here long ago, before anyone else.'

I go inside the log hut. Scattered everywhere are empty vodka bottles.

Anya leads us to the Barentsburg greenhouse heated by the hot water pumped around the town. The greenhouse is stuffed full of thriving vegetables. 'Dear guests, welcome to our greenhouse. This greenhouse is the furthest north greenhouse. Isn't so bad. Here we grow tomatoes, cucumbers…'

Across the way is the barn. 'Dear guests, here we have our barn with five cows, one bull and four calves. As for their names…' She gives us their names. 'Here we produce forty litres of milk for our children. Isn't so bad.'

She proudly points out the huge, relatively new consulate building, where the Russian flag flutters; the canteen; a factory where thirty women produce textiles; the sports hall and gymnasium; the swimming pool filled with heated sea water; the cultural centre with 30,000 books; and a movie hall with 400 seats. It must have cost a fortune to build this infrastructure in a place as inhospitable and isolated as Spitsbergen. As if highlighting its current decrepitude, an antique Soviet fire truck drives slowly and noisily by, its muffler falling off and dragging on the ground.

I walk alongside Anya, trying to get an insight behind her projected image of goodwill ambassador for Russia. 'Where do you live?' I ask.

She points out a nondescript apartment building. 'It is just one room plus a small bedroom.'

'No kitchen?'

'No, we must eat in the canteen.'

'You have a good job.'

'Yes.' She smiles genuinely. 'I like my job very much but I want to learn Norwegian.'

'Maybe then you could work in Longyearbyen.'

'Yes.'

'How much are you paid to be the official guide?'

'The equivalent of US$80 a month.'

Uri, the captain of our boat, is paid the equivalent of twenty US dollars a day, when the boat is being used.

Anya digresses from my questions. 'Written in stone on the hillside is "Mir, mir". It means "Peace, Peace".'

Those willing to pay the entrance fee to visit the Barentsburg museum follow Anya. The others, most of the group, visit the 'hotel' to look at more souvenirs.

'Come in, come in,' Anya welcomes. The few of us who have elected to follow Anya take our shoes off and put on cheap plastic slippers. Anya takes off her cool pumps and puts on a pair of dirty pink sandals decorated with colourful rubber flowers and picks up a long lecture stick to point out items of interest as we move from room to room. A stuffed musk ox looks more like a tatty hairy boar. The musk oxen were imported from Greenland, and while the reindeer were hunted indiscriminately the musk oxen thrived, but they couldn't compete successfully for scarce food once the reindeer numbers started to recover. The stuffed polar bear looks entirely lifeless, as if a steamroller had squashed the life out of it. A five-kilo polar bear heart in a jar of formaldehyde fascinates me as much as the polar bear penis bone I had seen at the tiny museum in Longyearbyen. Anya leads us around the museum. Outside the window I hear the muffler-less fire truck passing by again.

Twenty years ago there were twice as many Russians and Ukrainians in Spitsbergen as there were Norwegians, and Barentsburg was both a testament to the might and influence of Soviet communism and the madness of the Cold War. The grimness and griminess of life in the semi-ghost town is a depressing, although realistic, start to this voyage around these islands.

Anya stands on the dock and smiles. She waves until the closest souvenir seller has cast off our lines. No one bought anything from him although we had taken plenty of photos of him without asking and without even talking to him.

The ship leaves Barentsburg at midnight. The weather has changed again and the perfectly calm sea lends an ethereal quality to the scene. The seamless monochromatic blue of the ocean and sky is slashed to the west by a strip of luminescent light glowing on the horizon. Fulmars, related to the albatross, glide over the still water. They remind me of ghosts with their pale grey colour and their large sorrowful eyes. Puffins fly busily overhead with more purpose, little fish dangling out of their colourful beaks.

The night assumes a dreamlike reality as sleep deprivation and the constant twenty-four hour daylight confuses my body clock. We stop at Kapp Linne to pick up a third guide, Gustav. It's four in the morning when I finally leave the bridge of the ship for my cabin. When I am woken by one of the two Russian stewardesses knocking on the door at seven-thirty, I've only had three hours sleep. I look outside the window at icebergs surrounding the boat as we cruise into the Kongsfjord to Ny Ålesund, previously a Norwegian coal-mining settlement and now an international research centre on all things arctic.

Walking around Ny Ålesund, our guides carrying guns for security against polar bears, one of the immaculately dressed Italians has a fit when an arctic tern drops a long streak of bird do down the back of his stylish jacket. From the fuss he makes you'd think he'd been mauled by a polar bear, or shot by the guide, not dumped on by a measly bird. The Italian stops to remove the bird poop while we continue to a bust of Roald Amundsen. Jens reminds us how this great arctic explorer became the first to sail the North-west Passage in 1906. He also beat Robert F. Scott to the South Pole by a matter of weeks in 1911. After unsuccessfully trying to drift across the North Pole with the pack ice in the *Maud* he became the first to fly over the pole, in the airship *Norge*. Jens' talk is interrupted occasionally by the deep rumble of a sky-scraper-sized piece of glacier breaking off Kronebreen Glacier into the fjord.

It must be something genetic, inherited from the Vikings who'd go *berserk* and migrate south to warmer climes to do a bit of pillaging during the dark winter, because Norway has produced more than its fair share of seafaring explorers. After skiing across Greenland's icecap in 1888, Fridtjof Nansen tried to reach the North Pole in the *Fram* in 1893, drifting with the pack ice from the Siberian coast. Thor Heyerdahl and his *Kon-Tiki* captured world attention with his successive bids to prove ancient cultures had migrated far from home, drifting across oceans on reed rafts. A more recent throwback to the Vikings is Ragnar Thorseth who rowed to the Shetland Islands when he was twenty, and then in the early 1980s sailed a replica of a Viking *knarr* along the his-toric route of northern exploration from Norway to the Faeroes, Iceland and Greenland. To celebrate the Vikings 'discovery' of North America, he again set out in a replica of a Viking warship to Newfoundland and the Eastern seaboard. Seems incredible the Vikings 'discovered' America half a millennium before the more flamboyant Portuguese and Spanish, but couldn't be bothered talking to the local North American Indians and, probably being homesick, set off for home again.

Far less adventurous than these intrepid explorers, everyone in our group makes a beeline for the souvenir shop cum post office, which is as well equipped with T-shirts, polar teddy bears made in China and Norwegian sweaters as any souvenir shop in Bergen or Oslo. I send a postcard to Annabel from this 'northernmost community'. I wish she were here.

After Ny Ålesund we head further north. The sea is so calm there is no sense of movement on board apart from the vibration of the ship's engines. Dinner could as easily be breakfast given my complete discombobulation. I stand on the deck for hours and watch the sea, which is as still as bath water. The view is mostly gunmetal blue ocean indistinguishable from the overcast sky, but on the horizon to the north-west a thin wedge of orange light glows, and to the south-east a line of snow-clad Spitsbergen mountains basks luminescent and golden in the subtle evening light.

Once again the ghostly fulmars escort us, approaching from the stern, gliding alongside, riding the invisible current of air created over the stillness of the ocean by the passing of the hull. The fulmar is so totally comfortable living out at sea that it can sleep on the ocean and drink sea water by processing it through its beak and removing the salt. It comes to shore only because it can't lay eggs on water.

We pass icebergs, the portions underwater a brilliant Caribbean turquoise. Occasionally we pass an ice floe with a seal flopped out on top. The ringed seals look normal enough but the bearded seals, weighing 300 kilos each, have disproportionately tiny heads sticking out of fat bodies, like a human head protruding from an overstuffed sleeping bag.

We pass Danskøya Island where the Swedish balloonist Andree and two others set off in 1897 to fly over the North Pole. They crashed on pack ice and walked to White Island where their bodies, diaries and unexposed camera film were found. The preserved film, when it was developed thirty-three years later, provided a poignant if macabre insight into their last days.

At midnight we cross the eightieth parallel and approach a small iceberg with several walruses sprawled on it. Although walrus skin is too tough for the polar bears' teeth, it was not protection enough against bullets. Hunted primarily for their ivory tusks, their hides were also harvested to make industrial belts during the Industrial Revolution. The walrus was slaughtered in such numbers that, by the time they were protected in 1962, only around 100 were left.

Donning every bit of warm clothing I have, including two Gore-Tex jackets and a life-vest, I watch the deck hands lower two Zodiacs over the side of the *Victor Buynitskiy*. Remarkably, Giovanni the Mafia boss manages to descend the gangplank, manhandled down by two burly shipmates, Vladimir and Vasilijev. Wearing a padded snow outfit borrowed from one of the Russian crew, Giovanni looks like a plump, dead dwarf.

Stepping into the Zodiac I have this feeling of being on the point of panicking, akin to claustrophobia. If we fall out of this relatively insecure inflated rubber boat into the freezing water, we'll be like rats falling into a vat of acid; our chances of survival would be about as slim. We sit balanced precariously on the bouncing rubber sides of the Zodiacs, holding tightly onto life-lines while Vladimir and Vasilijev steer the outboard engines. Peering through my twenty-millimetre lens, the walruses are barely recognisable blobs of brown on white ice, floating on a deep blue. As we approach the ice floe, the smell becomes as pungent as a zoo.

Peering through my wide-angle lens again, I see the vague pin-prick of one of the walruses slipping underwater. It resurfaces, surging out of the water in a threat display. Click. It disappears again and then reappears in my lens somewhat closer, now easily recognisable as a walrus heaving itself up out of the water in a convincing threat display, its long ivory tusks quite apparent, even through the optic distortion. Kneeling on the bottom of the boat, elbows resting on the side of the rubber Zodiac, I take another photo as it lurches out of the icy water; this time I can see the individual hairs of its moustache. Click. Leaning over the rubber sides, I follow the walrus moving underwater and take yet another photo just as its head breaks the surface, looking ridiculously as if it has two cigarettes sticking carelessly out of its mouth. I'm thrown backwards as the walrus lunges out of the water and plants its tusks firmly on the rubber gunwales where my face had been just an instant before. Despite its considerable mass, the thick rubber fends off the attack and there are enough of us in the large Zodiac to counterbalance the walrus' weight.

Not wanting to push our luck, we motor over the perfectly still water to another, unoccupied ice floe. It seems ridiculous motoring about in an inflatable boat at midnight in the middle of the perfectly calm ocean, out of sight of land, in waters so cold it would kill you in minutes if we developed a leak and sank. The whole experience seems surreal. I would have thought this inhospitable part of the world would have been a dangerous place, but aside from territorial walruses and freezing waters, we're as relaxed as if we were larking about on Round Pond in Hyde Park.

To celebrate having crossed the eightieth parallel, we bail out of the two rubber dinghies and climb onto the ice floe. Several bottles of champagne are popped and the bubbly contents distributed to each of us in clear plastic glasses. With empty stomachs, and after the giddy excitement of the walrus attack, we are soon giggling, then laughing at our strange predicament. Here we are, standing on an ice floe in daylight, at midnight, about as close to the North Pole as any of us are ever likely to get, on water as smooth as a backyard swimming pool, our closest neighbours a bunch of belligerent male walruses on the adjacent floe.

Slightly inebriated, we are safely on board the *Victor Buynitskiy* again. The others retreat to their cabins, but I remain on deck and watch the subtle play of light on the calm ocean. At three in the morning my diligence is rewarded by our first sighting of a polar bear, walking on a large pack of ice floes. The Russian officer on the bridge makes an announcement over the intercom and everyone comes stumbling sleepily onto deck. The polar bear in the meantime flops on his back and ignores us. The ship manoeuvres around the ice to get a closer look and we see yet another polar bear, beside a dead seal, diligently pawing ice over the remains of the carcass like a dog burying its bone. Seagulls wait patiently within a couple of metres but when they approach too closely, the polar bear lunges at them. It is so fat it doesn't seem at all dangerous, rather resembling an overstuffed teddy bear with buttocks so rotund they look laughable, at least from the safety of the boat.

The others head back to bed when we continue northwards but I stay on the bridge as we coast through this extraordinary combination of landscape and seascape in infinite shades of white and blue. Depending on the quarter of horizon observed, it is impossible to discern where sky meets sea; they bond seamlessly into a cold blue backdrop somewhere in the vast distance.

The pack ice, which often extends this far south from the pole, has retreated temporarily and for the first time this season our boat manages to squeeze around the north side of Spitsbergen. It is bewildering how calm this sea is, as if the pack ice must weigh the water down, suppressing whatever surge there might otherwise be. Since we left Ny Ålesund there hasn't been a ripple, except for the symmetrical lines of waves forming a 'V' in our wake. The fulmars carve sweeping streaks where a wing tip creases the surface of sea. There's such a profusion of birds it's like a giant open playground; the fulmars, guillemots, auks and puffins darting above us, creating a traffic jam of anxious parents bringing home beaks or gullets full of tiny fish for their fledglings clinging to perpendicular rock faces. The fulmars seem to glide alongside the boat for no other reason than the joy of flight. Their constant companionship is spooky, as if they had some other-worldly connection to us, like the ghosts of sailors lost at sea. In this midnight light and with the tired state of my mind, anything seems possible.

Watching this weird panorama as we cruise slowly, I take to staying up all night on the bridge and going to bed after breakfast. This schedule, while allowing the most time exposed to the mysterious twilight, doesn't provide for maximum sleep. I am woken mid-morning to board the Zodiacs for another excursion to a wall of glacier ice adjacent to cathedral-like rocks rising a couple of hundred metres vertically.

Giving up waiting for the glacier to calve spectacularly into the sea, we approach the bird cliffs. Unlike the fulmars, the guillemots are not terribly good flyers but their short wings enable them to swim well, almost like penguins to which they are distantly related. There are so many of them they darken the sky overhead like locusts. The noise of the birds can be likened to the buzzing of bees, and the smell of guano is overwhelming. Vladimir brings the Zodiac within a metre of the rock wall and the nesting brown-and-white guillemots, so close that there are complaints we are too near the birds for those with telephoto camera lenses. Vladimir lets Andy steer the outboard engine further out. The boy's eyes boggle wider as he points ahead. 'There's a polar bear.'

We assume he has made a boyish error, mistaking a patch of guano or snow for a polar bear. It's hardly likely we'll see a polar bear climbing up nature's equivalent of a Gothic cathedral. But we look in the direction he points and sure enough there's a polar bear climbing the vertical rocks with the dexterity of a trained circus animal.

The rock-climbing polar bear is thin and obviously desperate for food. His cream-coloured fur is green from rubbing against the moss covering the rocks. The birds seem to sense the bear's limitations despite his apparent nimbleness and don't move away from him until he is just a tantalising paw's swipe away. As he feels his way around the rock ledges looking for fledglings I take numerous photos, his mountaineering antics filling the viewfinder even with the twenty-millimetre lens.

Collectively we must take thousands of photos of this rock-climbing polar bear before the ship continues slowly around the northern tip of Spitsbergen. While everyone seems ecstatic about what we are seeing on the trip, the two Italian spinsters in black walk around deck looking vaguely disgruntled with life. The German couple, who had seemed rather dry and serious the first couple of days, walk around with smiles on their faces, the holiday no doubt having worked wonders. My Italian roommate spends much of his time in our cabin reading or sleeping. The Swedish and Norwegian passengers are so quiet it's hard to know whether they are on board or not. By contrast, the two Dutchmen are excited about everything they see. They consume copious amounts of wine at dinner every night, and in the bar afterwards splash out drinks into other people's wine glasses as if they were on an expenses-paid trip, which they patently are not. We try to guess what they do for a living. They claim they are bodyguards for our guide Ann-Jorid, who, they say, is actually Princess Märtha Louise in disguise.

Andy's father Philip asks, 'Sorry, but what do you really do?' He has been in Japan long enough that he bows slightly when he says 'sorry'.

'I'm a dreamer,' Hans replies, speaking English the same way he speaks Dutch – with a guttural hoick that tends to spray phlegm all over us.

We head out for an evening excursion walking around Franz Island, which is littered with enormous whalebones. Here Andy makes his first bonfire, before we continue heading south between the two largest islands, Spitsbergen and Nordaustlandet. The others go to bed, except Hans and Andreas who dance and shout on the bow before they finally run out of energy and head below. Alone on the bridge with Vladimir, the first mate, and Alexander, the first officer, we pass an endless variety of ice floes, many of which could be pieces of modern sculpture.

In the early hours of the morning we spot a polar bear lying on a floe directly in front of the ship. With a vivid splotch of blood around its head, it appears to be dead. Alexander glides the *Victor Buynitskiy* in slowly, engines at idle. The hissing of hydraulics and the electromagnetic whirling of the radar on the bridge are the only sounds as our forward momentum carries us towards the ice floe where the polar bear is sprawled on his side. We lose momentum just as the ship drifts up alongside the floe. The first officer announces on the loudspeakers that another polar bear is outside but the broadcast wakes the bear. He lifts his head, peers at us over his shoulder and, astonished at this apparition, plunges over the side into the calm-as-a-millpond sea. By the time the other passengers come up on deck, he is just a head and a floating rump, swimming away. Although we are several kilometres away from Nordaustlandet, which is mostly an inaccessible glacial wall hundreds of kilometres long, the polar bear has apparently no compunction about jumping into the frigid ocean.

I had never realised that the polar bear is so totally at home on and in the water that it is in fact termed a marine animal. The polar bear's hair is hollow and each hair acts like a miniature greenhouse, providing warmth as well as flotation. The most visible thing about this bear paddling around in the water is not its head, but its rump, floating quite a bit higher than the head. Jens informs us that polar bears are capable of swimming hundreds of kilometres, floating south with the ice and then swimming back to shore. They remain on the ice floes where they earn their living sneaking up on unsuspecting seals and return to land only to migrate northwards to catch the next floe heading south.

For hours we skirt the southern side of Nordaustlandet, the whole of the foreshore a wall of unbroken glacier ice. Chunks of icebergs look like so much floating marble. Some are opaque, others are translucent blue like gigantic shards of broken thick armour-plated glass. Depending on whether they are opaque or translucent, they are as stunning as sculptured glass or gigantic diamonds.

Exhausted by staying up all night, I sleep after breakfast and am woken up at ten by another polar bear sighting. I look out the window and see we have stopped amidst some pack ice so I drag myself out of my berth and climb on deck. Not only have we found yet another polar bear, but this one has discovered us and seems intent on boarding the *Victor Buynitskiy*. Yosuke waves, cooing at the polar bear. Her son is at the back of the boat where the deck is much lower. The bear climbs onto a hump of ice at the edge of the ice floe and standing on its rear legs, reaches up to the railing. Suddenly Yosuke's coos are replaced with shrieked warnings, 'Andy! Andy!'

Jens moves everyone away from the stern of the boat. If the polar bear had boarded our ship, it would have been carnage with only one staircase leading to the upper deck and a bottleneck of tourists encumbered with telephoto lenses trying unsuccessfully to escape. The engines of the boat are engaged and the thrust of the propellers pushes us out of harm's way, then we stop so that we can get more photos.

But the polar bear doesn't give up. He skirts around the channel of water cut through the loose pack ice by the ship and approaches the stern from the other side. He advances so close that my wide-angle lens is once again put to practical use and I take dozens of photos of a curious polar bear, metres away. The wide-angle lens captures not only the polar bear, but also the deep blue of the sea, the pack ice and the glacier walls in the background.

As we head north again along the eastern side of Nordaustland, I try to catch up on more sleep. Six more polar bear sightings are reported, none of them as close as the last one but they are frequent enough that I no longer bother to strip when I go back to bed, electing instead to flop down on the bunk with all my clothes on.

At Ice Point, a tiny outcrop of rock set amidst hundreds of kilometres of glacier, the Zodiacs are lowered into the water again and we make a quick excursion to shore under the armed escort of Jens and Ann-Jorid. We have hardly begun walking on this narrow strip of rock, the only bedrock to surface under the Austebreen Glacier, when Jens' radio crackles with a warning from Gustav that a polar bear is heading in our direction, swimming between floes. We abandon our walk and jump into the safety of our Zodiac. Zipping out of danger to our mother ship, we observe the polar bear making his way rapidly towards where it was expecting to have lunch.

Some of these bears show no concern for us, others seem somewhat scared, and yet others seem quite determined to get as close to us as possible, for whatever reason. It's odd that some of them seem so scared of us, as they've been protected from hunting since 1973. They are intelligent and curious animals, and often hungry, which is why they can be so aggressive.

We head directly south now and for the first time encounter heavy seas.

Meals have taken a pattern. The Swedes and Norwegians always sit together and are always on time. The young Italian couple is always late and consistently appear with looks of satisfaction on their faces when they walk in. My Italian roommate is also always late, fortunately not so sexually satisfied, but like the young Italian couple, always immaculately dressed in a different outfit every day. All the Italians stick together at a table, except the spinster sisters dressed in black. It's as if they have the plague, no one wants to sit next to them, least of all the other Italians. Their pasty faces are made grimmer by the white sun block they slather on in copious quantities. They sit blinking silently, as if slightly stunned that they are here.

Nigel's trousers are far too short, barely reaching the top of his white ankle socks. When he crosses his legs he reveals an expanse of hairless white leg. I shouldn't be so critical. I've been wearing the same clothes pulled out of my backpack for six weeks now. Jens with his perpetual bed-head and bedroom eyes, Ann-Jorid with her sexy woollen long johns and Gore-Tex overalls, and Gustav the perennial diplomat, all play the dutiful guides as they even-handedly rotate tables amongst us. That leaves the rest of us playing musical chairs at meals. Hans and Andreas the Dutchmen are the life and soul of the group, finally admitting they aren't bodyguards for Ann-Jorid. Andreas is a plumber. Hans is a professional bird-watcher paid by his government – this could only happen in the Netherlands – to study birds.

Yosuke asks Jens if the icebergs drift seasonally backwards and forwards from the Arctic to the Antarctic every year, then covers her face with her hands when she realises from the stunned expressions on everyone's faces that she's said something foolish. Her husband bows and says 'Sorry' on her behalf.

Exhausted by lack of sleep, I take refuge in my cabin and pass out.

Half Moon Island is a bottleneck for bears migrating with the ice floes and a favourite spot for Pomars, whalers and trappers, who have been using the island for centuries. The polar bear traps were wooden boxes resembling miniature coffins mounted on a stand, containing bait and a small hole through which the barrel of a gun poked at about the height of a polar bear's head. Tugging on the meat tied with string and connected to the trigger of the rifle, the polar bear in effect shot itself. There are several trapper huts here and the remains of their grisly business are still in evidence. Polar bear bones still litter the ground around the huts and the traps. The snouts of the old skulls are inevitably cut off, sent complete with the teeth and hide to be mounted as a polar bear skin rug.

Interestingly the ground around the bones is always covered in a thick layer of moss, the barren soil obviously having absorbed the rich nutrients from the blood and bones. Jens relates how one trapper alone shot 150 polar bears here in a year.

The beach is scattered with sculptured chunks of transparent ice. Walking across the island we stumble upon a polar bear sleeping on a snowdrift. When it hears us, it quickly lopes pigeon-toed away but not before Gustav has pulled out his revolver; he has already shot a polar bear, with the same revolver, in self-defence. Ann-Jorid has a rifle and an enormous flare-gun. With her blonde hair pulled back in ponytails she looks a bit like an arctic version of Annie Oakley. Jens' pistol is discreetly hidden under his jacket. We walk to the melted indentation in the snow where the polar bear had been lying. Its paw prints are enormous.

We make a second landing where a small boarded-up hunter's hut has been broken into by a hungry polar bear. Despite the shuttered windows, the bear's claw marks on the outside wall reveal where it had pulled off the heavy wooden shutters and then climbed up and through the smashed windows. The inside of the hut is bedlam – overturned tables and supplies indicate where the hungry bear foraged for anything edible. The bear's teeth have perforated several tins of food. Wouldn't have wanted to be in here at the time . . .

Avoiding the others, I walk along the shore to savour the solitude of this place, imagining what it must be like to be a trapper living here alone for months. I hear a voice. It is Ann-Jorid, rifle slung over her shoulder, yelling at me. 'Bye-bye Andrew,' she shouts. 'See you in the next life.'

I find an arctic fox skull, perfectly preserved. Despite my temptation to keep it, I put it back.

On our last day the weather is windy but warm and the sky clears. From the bridge last night I saw Hans and Andreas on the bow of the boat, dancing and shouting, drunk as skunks and just as happy. This trip has taken a substantial chunk of their savings but they love every minute of it. At least until now. At breakfast Andreas admits to us that Hans is so badly hungover he can't participate on our last shore excursion. It's hardly surprising.

Sadly, there is a rumour of a Russian nuclear-powered submarine that has sunk in the Barents Sea, not so far from here. The *Victor Buynitskiy*'s crew are from Murmansk, the place where the submarine was based. They put a brave front on it but our hearts go out to these Russians who have to endure yet another tragic episode in their history.

The boat anchors off the mouth of the Van Miljenfjorden. We board the Zodiacs and land on the tip of Akseløya Island where there is a substantial trapper's cabin. The scuttlebutt here is that the trapper who owns this hut spends half the year here and half the year in a mental hospital in Tromsø. It is easy to understand. For six months Spitsbergen must seem like a paradise of sorts, especially on a clear, sunny day like this. And in the winter it must seem like an icy hell. Jens leaves him an offering of chocolate and fresh fruit at the entrance to the hut, but the reclusive trapper doesn't come out.

We walk the relatively green Akseløya Island for several kilometres, spotting a few reindeer. Unlike the reindeer in and around Longyearbyen, these ones are skittish – it's no wonder, they are still hunted during the season – and take off at the first sight of us. When Andy finds out how far we have walked, he exclaims,

'That's further than from my home to school in Tokyo. I'd never walk that far.' This trip has been the voyage of a lifetime for him. He's had the run of the ship: Vladimir lets him drive the Zodiacs, the crew-members have shown him the engine room, the communications room, the bridge. Like all of us, he's sad this trip is about to end. At six in the morning tomorrow we arrive back at Longyearbyen to catch our flights out.

From Akseløya Island the ship continues around the coast to Kapp Linne where we anchor offshore and crew and passengers alike go ashore for a barbecue. We stand around in our shorts and T-shirts, basking in the clear evening sky and warm temperature. It's hard to believe it's evening and late August and we're north of seventy-eight degrees latitude.

Gustav is the manager of the hotel converted from Telenor's communications buildings. He has constructed a pub out the back, a short distance from the main buildings so that there's no need to keep the noise down, even though there is no one else here. The doors and windows to the pub are thrown open, admitting the sharp orange midnight light. We take off our shoes, the bar is opened, Russian music plays on the ghetto blaster and soon copious quantities of liquor are consumed. Vladimir, Vasilijev and another young Russian crew-member we've hardly seen until now strip to the waist and perform Russian Cossack dances, leaping acrobatically and defying the laws of gravity as they throw out their feet while bending their knees and slapping their heels. As the evening wears on, Ann-Jorid, ashore for the first time without her rifle slung over her shoulder or flare-gun tucked into her waist belt, has increasing difficulties fending off the amorous overtures of the testosterone-laden Russian men.

Certificates testifying to the fact that we have crossed the eightieth parallel are handed out to each of us amidst cheers. Finally there are cries of 'Gustav, Gustav', and he is hoisted into the air and thrown around with abandon. The two nuns return to the boat to pray for us sinners, and Giovanni the Mafia boss has retired too, no doubt plotting his next evasive move with his young wife.

I slip out and walk to the end of Kapp Linne. It's past midnight and the sun slides low towards the horizon. Next week, on 23 August, for the first time this summer the sun will dip briefly below the horizon and within another couple of months the sun will disappear permanently for the next four months. It's hard to imagine now, with this midnight sun casting its warm, benign light over the landscape, that in such a short time this same scene will be totally devoid of the sun's direct rays. I take rolls of film of the fulmars as they glide past Kapp Linne like a long line of fighter jets, flying along the cliffs just for the joy of it. The light is perfect.

At two in the morning Gustav shuts off the music, closes the bar, and we reluctantly head back to the Zodiacs. Clearly emotional as we part ways on the concrete dock, he's been the ever-talented ambassador, keeping the Russian crew happy with kilos of chocolate deposited on the bridge, sensitively working out with Jens and Ann-Jorid where we should go, when, and how. He's also the consummate Svalbarder and after fourteen years here, I can't imagine Gustav living anywhere else.

We fish out of the sea a young Russian crew-member who insists he wants to swim back to the boat. Wearing only underpants his pale skin is as red as a boiled lobster. The boat is more than a kilometre offshore; he'd never have made it. At least his hormones have cooled down as he sits at the back of the Zodiac shivering uncontrollably.

The ship pulls anchor and we continue at half-speed into Isfjorden towards Longyearbyen. Although it is two in the morning I stand outside on the deck watching the antics of Hans and Andreas as they shout and scream and dance and laugh on the bow, ecstatic to be here. But even they head below deck at four in the morning.

The fjord's surface is perfectly calm, as if it were heavy viscous oil rather than sea water. The light is intense as the sun slides over the tops of the mountains of Oscar II Land. A three-quarter moon hovers over the peaks as the sun skims around the pole. I'll never forget the light on this trip, from the monochromatic blues of overcast skies the first few days to this brilliant sharp light under a cloudless cobalt blue. I didn't know what to imagine before coming here, but in every way this week has exceeded my wildest expectations. We counted twenty-three polar bears in total, and despite having only a twenty-millimetre lens with me, I have wonderful close-up photographs of walruses and polar bears, fulmars and flowers. The Russian crew couldn't have been more accommodating, and the self-effacing and relaxed way in which Gustav, Jens and Ann-Jorid worked as a team was faultless. Even the passengers were a wonderful, complex mixture and for someone like myself, thoroughly jaded with group tours, I can't imagine anything I'd have changed on this excursion.

Apart from the fact that it is all coming to an end.

Farewells

Several hours after disembarking from a Russian research vessel in Longyearbyen, I meet Kirsten outside the front entrance to the Royal Christiania Hotel in downtown Oslo. It's a sunny summer day. We walk up Karl Johan's Gate where street cafés spill over with people enjoying the Saturday afternoon sun. A group of Chileans dressed in traditional costume play their haunting flute music. A Russian man stands on his own, formally dressed, singing operatic songs. A gold statue proves not to be gold at all, and not even a statue, but a man covered in spray paint. When money is placed in a hat, he bows like a mechanical mannequin. Norwegian girls with pierced bellybuttons and low-slung pants walk hand-in-hand with dark immigrant boys. I read somewhere that after Japan, Norway is the most racially homogenous nation in the world; but this is changing too.

We cross in front of City Hall – a huge pedestrian plaza with Vigeland statues and flower beds. The only traffic is electric streetcars, a definite improvement over the convoluted highway that snaked through this strip of prime real estate only a few years ago. Now the same highway passes through a tunnel underneath the city; the one tunnel I will never complain about. We walk by the waterfront where I hear several dark-skinned people of different races speaking broken Norwegian together, their lingua franca in this world so far removed from their own native one. Men approach to sell us roses. Three police officers skate past on Rollerblades as we continue on to Aker Brygge where we share a bowl of shrimps on one of the floating barges tied in front of the boardwalk. It's good to see Kirsten again. When Annabel and I had come through earlier in the summer Kirsten had been away on a business trip. We talk about old times, about new times. We've moved on, both of us, in the last few years, but the friendship and respect remain.

Sailboats and yachts are tied to moorings in the marina. Long-snouted powerboats cruise by. A couple of weeks ago there had been an international speedboat contest and the Oslofjord resounded to the noise of these cigar-shaped boats roaring around the water. The race was organised and partially sponsored by Kjell Inge Røkke, a fisherman who made his fortune in the fishing business in the United States and has now returned home. To me it seems out of character with the Norwegian way of thinking for Norway to host a powerboat race as environmentally unfriendly as this one, when it's a country that's forward-thinking enough to be on the verge of outlawing jet skis, not just on lakes, but also on the sea. But money talks, even in Norway it seems. There is a more conspicuous display of wealth now compared to ten years ago.

Norwegian heroes in the past have been the arctic explorers – self-effacing adventurers in the tradition of Askeladden, depicted in the fairy tales collected by Asbjørnsen and Moe, and brought to life by the painters Erik Werenskiold and Theodor Kittelsen. But in the last few years, the modern Norwegian folk hero seems more likely to be a wealthy businessperson, like Kjell Inge Røkke, or one of the many soccer players commanding lucrative salaries playing football in England, or a sponsored cross-country ski champion gracing cereal boxes. Even so, there are still a number of prominent Norwegians that fit the more traditional mould. Jostein Gårder, author of the unexpected best-seller *Sophie's World*, gives a portion of his earnings to an international environmental award. And unassuming Johann Olav Koss – the Olympic speed skating gold medalist who won four gold medals in Lillehammer; a three-time world champion who broke eleven world records and donated his Olympic skates to be auctioned for charity – is chairman of Olympic Aid, a member of the Sport Humanitarian Group and a medical doctor.

Kirsten drives me to the 100-year-old home we shared in Sandvika, overlooking the Oslofjord. It's strange being an outsider in the same house Kirsten and I lived in. Some of the furniture and decorations are different, but otherwise it is identical. I stand at the window where I sat at my computer writing my first book during two winters. I might not have ever started writing if I hadn't had to endure the Norwegian winters. So many thoughts went through my head then, so much angst as I tried to adapt to living in Norway. I used to watch each and every plane land and take off from Fornebu airport – across the water, behind the islands – as if they were a crucial link to the outside world. Now Fornebu is closed and the silence is noticeable. So much has changed.

I look at the corner where Bonso's basket used to be. It is odd being here without him. The last time I came to Norway for a short visit I had arrived unannounced and walked into the back garden. Bonso saw me and ran at me barking, but as soon as he smelt me he started jumping around happily and then searched for a stick or ball for me to throw. In the winter I'd throw snowballs and he'd try to catch them in mid-flight. I'd be the quarterback and, like an American linebacker, he'd run past me at full speed; I'd coordinate my throw so that he could jump up and snap the snowball as it arced over him. As long as my passes were good and his timing perfect, he'd do this happily for hours until he was so tired he'd barely be able to stand up. Once he was so exhausted I had to carry him home.

Seeing me study his basket, Kirsten fetches Bonso's urn from her bedroom and shakes the contents. 'Sometimes I think I can hear him bark,' she says, eyes glistening. He was her devoted friend for fifteen years. He died just a week before I arrived this summer.

Before dinner I visit our neighbours and landlord. Herr Oma seemed like my best friend in many ways. He was so patient with my broken Norwegian. Coming from the west coast of Norway, I suppose he was always an outsider in Oslo too. He is surprised by how good my Norwegian is. It amazes me how esoteric Norwegian words pop into my head even as I am talking. I recall

all those long, frustrating evenings taking courses with other immigrants, trying to learn the language, and ironically how, after finally mastering it, I no longer have use for it.

Marta-Louise and Lars, whom Kirsten and I met twelve years ago in Kathmandu, arrive for dinner with their four children, including my godson Endre. Annabel and I had spent some days with them earlier in the summer at their family *seter*. They are quintessential Norwegians, demonstrating equality in everything they do, from sharing the housework to taking turns to have time off from their professional roles as doctors to look after the children. Over the years, Lars has almost become like a brother to me. Critical as I can be of others, there was rarely a Norwegian I met, and got to know, that I did not like. Norwegian men in many respects seemed to epitomise the ideal man: sensitive, liberated and earthy.

Kirsten has handmade the children an impressive tent, which she has filled with toys and books. The four children play inside the tent on this warm, sunny evening no longer punctuated by the roar of jets taking off or landing. I recollect flying back from a consulting trip to Namibia and getting out of the taxi, standing at the front door fiddling with the lock, and hearing the clip-clop of hooves. I turned around to see an adult and juvenile elk, what I still think of as moose, in the driveway staring at me.

I stand on the lawn now with its spectacular view over the fjord and islands and recall how on summer days and evenings like this I would be frantic to be out in the mountains, or on the water, maximising the good weather. In the winter, Bonso ran unleashed beside me when I went skating on the fjord for an hour or two at midday. My constant companion, he'd sit at my feet as I wrote and I'd tuck my toes under his body for warmth. Although he was originally Kirsten's dog, he adopted me readily and would follow me everywhere, even when I got up to make a cup of tea or to walk to another room.

Across the stretch of water is Kalvøya, an island connected to the mainland by a suspended footbridge, where I walked Bonso at least twice a day, all year round. The evening light illuminates the scene: the sailboats, the converted fishing boats tugging gently at their moorings, the islands, the exposed pine trees with their windswept branches, the children playing on the curve of beach. But there is a chill in the air too, and a reminder that the short summer will not last much longer. Tomorrow I take the train back to Bergen and the ferry back to Newcastle.

Lars drives me into the centre of town. Kirsten has given me a present. Alone in my hotel room I unwrap the gift paper and inside is a CD – Secret Garden. I open the plastic container and there, wrapped in a ribbon, is a tuft of Bonso's hair.

Sitting alone on a bench at the Zachariasbryggen in Bergen; it's my last evening in Norway before taking the ferry back to England, a train to London, a plane to Bermuda, and Annabel. Already it is the end of August. The summer has flown by, as every Norwegian summer did. The sun slides down towards the horizon lighting up the peaks of Fløyen and Ulriken in its warm benevolence. The soft light heightens the colours, the greenness of the pine trees, the browns and reds and yellows of the old timber Hanseatic warehouses huddled along the waterfront. Sailboats and motorboats are double-parked along the quay, their owners self-consciously sipping beers in the cockpits. Patrons sit outside the pubs and restaurants and there's the excited chatter of conversation, punctuated by the performances of buskers. Gleaming motorbikes, helmets hanging from the handlebars, line the sidewalk along the empty Fisketorget fish market. A fast catamaran from Stavanger spins on its own circumference, its jet engines roaring briefly as it manoeuvres slowly into position along a jetty. I look up the hillside to the tiny apartment I kept here in Bergen, and recollect how on magical summer evenings like this I would sleep out. There was, and is, nowhere I would rather have been than Norway during these gloriously long summer days.

The mountainside is bathed in the sunlight even as purple

clouds appear menacingly behind Fløyen and Ulriken. A brilliant double rainbow arcs over the mountains on either side of Bergen and lingers for the longest time, the sunset's last rays finding a gap on the horizon, illuminating the clouds gathering above in a blaze of colour.

And then the sun dips behind the outer islands and sinks into the North Sea. It suddenly becomes cooler, and the buskers pack their bags, the motorcyclists mount their machines and head home, the Norwegians basking in the last vestiges of warm light disappear with the sun. Without the sunlight, the hillsides around Bergen turn a dull brown. Without the warm glow on the colourful wooden warehouse buildings, there is no sense of energy.

This time of year the heavy clouds would gather, the days would become shorter, and I knew the darkness was coming.

In the end, it was all about the light.

LONELY PLANET JOURNEYS

JOURNEYS is a unique collection of travel writing – published by the company that understands travel better than anyone else.

It is a series for anyone who has ever experienced – or dreamed of – the magical moment when they encountered a strange culture or saw a place for the first time. They are tales to read while you're planning a trip, while you're on the road or while you're in an armchair, in front of a fire.

These outstanding titles explore our planet through the eyes of a diverse group of international writers. JOURNEYS books catch the spirit of a place, illuminate a culture, recount an adventure, or introduce a fascinating way of life. They always entertain, and always enrich the experience of travel.

'Lively, intelligent and varied . . . an important contribution to travel literature' – *Age (Melbourne)*

KIWI TRACKS
A New Zealand Journey
Andrew Stevenson

From being caught in a snowstorm on an exposed mountain track to spending time in a Maori settlement to the dubious gastronomic delights of packet soups, Andrew Stevenson captures the highs and lows of hiking in New Zealand's famed wilderness areas, and provides an illuminating and gently humorous view of his fellow backpackers.

'evidence that walking can be exciting, dangerous and, dare I say it, sexy' – *The Great Outdoors*